no darling it's called...

B<small>A</small>D ORGANISATION

ISBN: 978-1-5-272-5597-5

Shoestring Book Company

info@shoestringbooks.co.uk

www.wendybakerinteriors.co.uk

mob. 07778 769904

A very dear girl friend of mine phoned one day saying, 'Darling would you like to join me for lunch today at the Ivy?' I replied, 'no darling, I can't today.' She snapped back 'why not darling?' And I simply said, 'It's called working for a living, darling!' She replied 'No darling. It's called BAD ORGANISATION!'

She put the phone down.

She was right in a way as her life was so well organised but mine, I'm afraid, is sometimes rather chaotic, thus the title of the book...

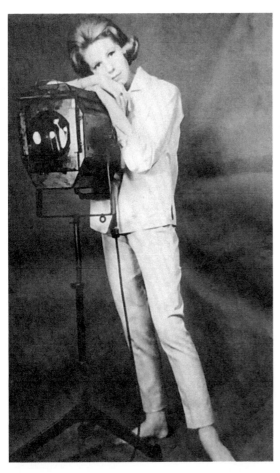

...so this is my story

INTRODUCTION

Thinking back over my life while sitting here in my studio in the Cotswolds is very therapeutic, but I wonder if you will enjoy reading about my very complicated, but full life. You may not have heard of me or maybe you are not into memoirs. So with that in mind, I have decided to write each chapter with a beginning, middle and an end. That way, it gives you, the reader, a chance to swap to another part of my life, should you get bored!

There are a few 'asides' at the end of some of the chapters, which I hope you will find amusing; they may also clarify some of my chattering.

I've lived quite a long time, really, through some truly exciting decades. Too exciting and important to just allow the memories to fade away; so stick with me, and I will tell you about my unusual life so far. Chaotic it may have been, sad, at times, but every so often some of the messes I found myself in have ended up being very, very, funny, and that is what life is all about! Cry a little and laugh a lot.

Perhaps if you take a look at the list of contents at this stage, you will be tempted to carry on reading. I hope so.

My mother, my father and me.

Contents

Contents

Contents

Contents

no darling it's called...

BAD ORGANISATION

Chapter 1 part 1

Born on Paddington Station - platform 6 maybe

Obviously, I was born somewhere, but as one is not born with a label around one's toe, you have to rely on your birth certificate. Well, that says, 'Wendy Ann born in Paddington London'. It seems my mother wasn't sure whereabouts and said it was close to Paddington station. So that's all I know. As far as I am concerned, I was born Wendy Ann on Paddington station. I added platform 6 as it could be true. I will never know!

my Uncle William and my mother

Looking at the few pictures I had of my mother when she was young, you could tell she was great fun. Her hair was a platinum blonde, she was tall with long, long legs and had a big smile. Later, I was told she used to go to the car racing at Brooklands and cause quite a stir. She went out with a saxophone player in Ambrose's band. As I was growing up, she never told me much about herself; people didn't in those days. All I knew was that she was brought up by her grandmother, who was very Victorian and strict...and she had squeaky boots!

Paddington platform 6

My mother seemed to have no parents, and I always thought she was an orphan. None of this was true. Years later when we went online, I discovered she had a brother called William, who had had Polio and lost the use of his arm. The only job he could get was as a sweeper in Kew Gardens. Just recently, I met Uncle William's daughter, my cousin, and she told me the family story as she knew it. Apparently, my grandfather, so my mother was not an orphan after all, had seen her walking over Kew Bridge pushing a pram, with me in it, smoking a cigarette. He went up to her and slapped her face. The cigarette fell to the ground. My mother just looked at him for a few moments and then, without a word, pushed the pram with me in it over the bridge and no one ever saw her or me again.

I understand now that on the day she walked away, she started a new life with my wonderful father and me. Well, the wonderful father bit didn't work, but who knows what happened there, again I was given the wrong information. My belief then was that I had a mummy and a daddy, and we were a little family living in Kew, and the Germans dropped bombs on us every night. I thought, or did I make it up, that my father was in the Navy and he was very brave. I promoted him to an Admiral because I thought he was the most wonderful man in the world. We didn't see him very often as he was always on missions somewhere in the world. Tripoli, I think. When a telegram came one day and my mother read it, I knew at once something terrible had happened. My hero was dead...no, actually, my hero had run off with a Wren and was last seen on Kew Bridge station 'canoodling' with her on a bench on platform 1.

When my mother told me that my hero had been killed in action, I believed her.

I couldn't think what to do, so I ran out of the house to be with my friend Mercedes. I didn't get there as there was a huge blast, and I fell to the ground. I was not crying. Only when they picked me up and took me back home did I cry. I had lots of shrapnel in my knees, the scars are still there today, and it hurt. So now mummy and I were alone with nothing. I didn't know the true story, so I mourned daddy and prayed every night that he would come home...but I was five when he left. I had made raspberry jelly for his tea, but he never came back!

AN ASIDE

That blast was a delayed bomb that went off as I ran down the road. There were three houses at the end of the road, and they were destroyed and everyone in them was killed. My lovely babysitter Mr Candle was among the dead, so I added him to my prayers.

I went down Courtlands Avenue just a few days ago. They have built a little brick building at the end of the road now to replace the rows of houses. There is no sign of what happened that dreadful night, but I was there and will never forget it!

Chapter 1 part 2

Surviving in London during World War 2 - bravery at Dunkirk

Mummy and I managed as best as we could. The siren seemed to go just when we were eating or going to bed. I was so nervous, I couldn't eat or sleep but nor could my mother. Also, as we had very little money, I remember thinking that both mummy and I looked a bit skinny. At night we had a mattress under the stairs with all my dolls and Big Bear as well as Little Bear. Mummy had a picture of daddy and me when we were a family and 5 Woodbines, but no matches! That was our safe world through the night. When the siren started, mummy used to nip out to the kitchen to put the kettle on before the 'doodle bugs' flew over us. I will never know why she needed tea then, but as they flew over, she always made a sort of slurping' noise as the tea was hot. Years later, when I went to my first tea party, I copied her 'slurp' until someone told me it was not correct!

As mummy had her tea, I would automatically wet my knickers! It was a Pavlovian response to the fear. We were afraid, but we understood each other. It was our way of standing up for our country. It's what we did together, a sort of comfort, I suppose, looking back on it now.

Even at that young age, I understood that if the 'doodle bug' stopped over your home, you were safe as they then drifted on for a while and dropped the explosives further on down the road. Everyone in our street was so kind; there was always someone to help one way or another. The people who had been bombed were wrapped in blankets and given a cup of tea, and then everyone would pull at the rubble looking for a person or a cat or a dog. It was great fun, I thought, but people were crying, so I had to have a sad face, my mother said. We lived in Courtlands Avenue in Kew in a tiny garden flat. Unfortunately, there was a German lady living upstairs, and someone said that she was under house arrest. Now I know why she stomped up and down in heavy army boots the whole time there was an air raid on. It was very upsetting, but I suppose she was doing her best for the war effort and for her country Germany.

I was sent to kindergarten at Kew College and I loved it. We sang 'Onward Christian Soldiers' every day at the top of our voices. It was our way of telling the Germans we were not afraid. I was allowed to draw and spent the whole time trying to make everything bright by squeezing paint all over me and my best friend Mercedes. Wonderful self-expression it would be called now, and it seemed to make me forget the awful bombs and the crying that was everywhere. We all had to file down into the air raid shelter when the siren went, and the teacher collected her books and we would go underground. Wonderful. We sang loudly and made teapots and saucepans out of candle wax. What fun we had I wasn't frightened until we came up into the daylight. Then I would start to shake, with relief I think, and my best friend Mercedes would be sick, but nobody minded. It was the war.

Mummy got a job at somewhere called Harrods and was very pleased, I think.

So, every morning we would get dressed, and I would be taken to school, and mummy would go by bus to Knightsbridge. When she was walking away, she always turned and blew me a kiss. I think even then I understood that we might not see each other again.

At weekends, we went out to lunch at the local café. It's a bookshop now, but in the war it served mugs of tea, lemonade and Welsh Rarebit, no butter but melted cheese. And when we walked down the Kew Road, we would sing 'Run rabbit run rabbit run run run'...oh those silly but important girlie memories...no wonder we won the war!!!

AN ASIDE

My father had been a writer, so I was told. When I was old enough, I would go to the library in Richmond every Saturday and read all of my father's books one by one. I knew if he was still alive, we would have had so much in common. We seemed to have had the same sense of humour. As I read his stories, I began to pretend he was reading them to me. It made him seem closer somehow. Months later, I mentioned to my mother that I had been reading my father's books. She looked surprised and said, 'What do you mean? Your father worked on the Furnishing Weekly in Fleet Street!'. The books I had read and enjoyed so much were the works of another Peter Leslie Lewis...

When I finally went into publishing, I wrote six books with no words. Just sketches. They sold in the millions around the world and because there were no words, there was no language barrier! I think I was frightened of expressing myself. Now I've written my first book with words. Let's hope people like it and understand my struggle with getting myself understood.

Chapter 1 part 3

A Man Called Arthur and a brother called Michael

We stayed in our tiny flat in Kew after my father had been 'killed' in the war.

I don't remember much as I was in 'little girl's deep mourning for my father' as little girls do. One Sunday, my mother and I were doing some gardening. We had only six irises, but they had been planted by my father, so I decided to care for them as part of my duty to his memory. Then I saw a large man coming up the road. I remember him exactly. He had a Trilby hat, a big overcoat and the biggest nose I had ever seen. He smiled at me, and when he saw my mother, he spread his arms to greet her. I remember watching and pretending to dig, but somehow I felt uneasy and wanted to run and cuddle my mother. I had a funny feeling that I had been forgotten.

I can remember thinking that something bad was going to happen. My instincts were correct. The man had come to tea, but I stayed in the garden. I heard a lot of laughing. Something I had never really heard before, as we rarely laughed during the earlier part of the war. It seemed then that my mother was having fun; in fact, I was told later that she had known the man for years, long before his wife died during childbirth and before I was born. So, they had many memories to share. When my mother called me in from the garden to introduce us, I felt that I disliked him immediately. Perhaps I was jealous as he made her happy and I felt excluded, which had never happened before.

I suppose it must have been a few weeks later that our lives changed totally. There had been lots of phone calls and more giggles between my mother and this man who was called Arthur Cowen. I knew something was wrong from the whispers and looks that passed between them. I felt completely alone. Shortly after that, I received the first shock in my life, never to be forgotten and remembered clearly even though I was only 5 and a bit years old. My mother told me to sit down as she and Mr Cowen had something to tell me. Taking a deep breath, she said 'Nice Mr Cowen has asked me to marry him, and he has offered to adopt you. So, you will have a new Daddy and a little brother called Michael!'. Who knows what I felt. I only know I had tears running down my face but that was it. I didn't understand what was happening. I have never got over what seemed to me at the time that my mother had given me away to the man with the big nose. I grew to hate his nose throughout my life.

My mother and stepfather at the Trocadero

Everything moved very quickly after that. I was sent to stay with some friends on Kew Green, and apparently my mother and Arthur Cowen got married at Caxton Hall with a wedding breakfast at the Trocadero in Piccadilly. I heard from one of my 'aunties' that he was very rich, but that afternoon they spent in Court in Hammersmith where he was declared bankrupt! My poor mother was always one of the unluckiest people alive.

A few days later, my adoption papers came through, and I was now called Wendy Ann Cowen instead of plain Wendy Ann. Well, I suppose he was pleased with himself; it was a neat package. One new wife to look after his son Michael and a little girl with a father complex. Phew! Neither he nor my mother knew what was to come.

We moved out of our little flat in Kew. I remember asking Mercedes to water the irises. We moved to another flat over a butcher's shop in Teddington. It was not only cold and smelly, but it had two resident rats. We had moved in just before the Germans decided to bomb Bushey Park; 'there were 'things' hidden there,' so Charlie, the butcher downstairs said.

As well as a new home and a new father, I had a little brother called Michael John Cowen. He had been put into an orphanage when his mother died. When he was brought home, he was in a terrible state, having been in the same nightie for several days. But as he was being washed and scrubbed up, I had a feeling that this little guy was going to be my friend not my enemy. He never stopped smiling, and my life seemed better just for him being there.

Bombs fell every night, and I was so nervous that I slept with my dressing gown on and my slippers in my hand. When the siren sounded, we all squeezed under the kitchen table as in those awful days it was most probably the safest place to shelter if you didn't have a basement or an Anderson shelter.

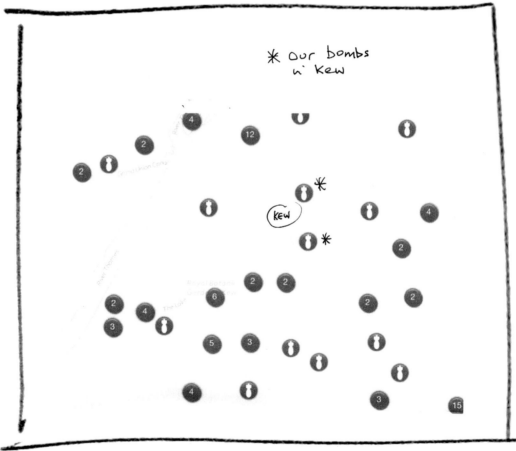

Total number of bombs dropped from 7th October 1941 to 6th June 1943 in Richmond upon Thames: 1,005

whole area bombed...

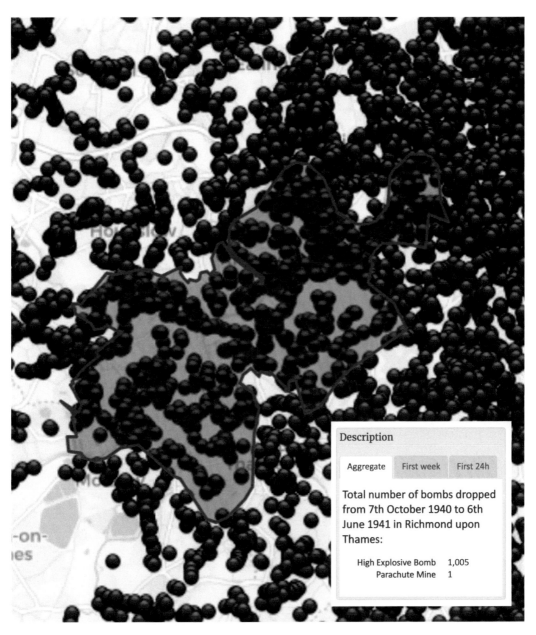

Description

Aggregate	First week	First 24h

Total number of bombs dropped from 7th October 1940 to 6th June 1941 in Richmond upon Thames:

High Explosive Bomb	1,005
Parachute Mine	1

blue area is Richmond and Kew

Chapter 1 part 4

762 Christchurch Road - B&B for Pilots and Vaudeville Artists

Christchurch Road . the Tucker family... the picture was taken in-between the bombing

1944

1. Uncle Cyril Uncle Leslie's father and inventor of the Douglas motorcycle

2. Thelma ... Uncle Leslie's mother

3. Peter ... Barbara's husband - and my first crush

4. Ray ... Uncle Leslie's brother ...he took me rowing and put his hand up my skirt and said smile and wave!

5. Elsie ... my mother - often wore funny hats

6. Olive Perring ... never spoke to anyone and lived over the garage. She came with the house we think!

7. Myra ... Auntie Vi's sister - we all laughed at her but she was everyone's agony aunt.

9. Leslie ... Bernice's husband - a really wonderful person

9. Bernice ... the youngest of Auntie Vi's 3 girls and a real drama queen

10. Sybil ... came to rent a room and stayed as a friend for a year and then ran off with her toy boy

11. Auntie Vi ... the leader of the pack

12. Wendy ... me in my first proper long dress

13. Mrs Creesy ... my babysitter who lived in the flat downstairs

14. Beryl ... the big bridesmaid - she taught me to skate

15. Arthur ... my stepfather

16. Barbara ... Not seen in the picture as she is standing behind my mother in the tall hat!

My mother and I first went to stay at 762 Christchurch Road, Boscombe in 1944 as paying guests to escape the bombings in London. The plan was for my stepfather and stepbrother to follow later. The house was large and Victorian, rather imposing, with a coach house at the back for the chauffeur and three garages (needless to say, no chauffeurs or cars when we moved in). I was told that my real father, the writer, had met someone at a pub in Fleet Street after putting the paper to bed and they knew someone who had let the old house to the Tucker family. They, in turn, made it into a B & B for 'artists' who performed at the Hippodrome in Boscombe.

Everyone had to find a way to survive in those days, and having a B&B may not have been 'right and proper' for the middle classes in 1939, but in 1943 it was quite acceptable as we were at war and everyone had adopted the 'anything goes' approach...the spirit was there wherever you looked. We would survive however we could. This was World War 2 and we were British!

The landlady, Violet Tucker (Auntie Vi), was a real beauty in her day; she sang on stage and played the mandolin in a Brighton theatre. She married a very respectable dentist, who drank rather a lot. When they fell on hard times, the marriage broke up and Auntie Vi left for a better life in Bournemouth. Rumour had it that she had a lover called Cecil who was very rich and always secretly looked after her...who knows? She left with her three daughters, Joan, Barbara and Bernice. All three daughters were beautiful in their own way; they were so alive. Laughter, well giggles, could always be heard whenever they were around, never a dull moment, and the girls never missed a trick. There was no money, but each one of them found ways to look attractive. Elsie, my mother, was roughly the same age as the three girls, so she fitted in beautifully and after a short time, the neighbours called them Auntie Vi's four girls.

For my mother to find happiness was like a miracle. She had had a rough time in London trying to dodge the bombs, looking after me on her own as well as working to pay for our little flat in Kew. She always told people that my father had been killed in the war in Tripoli, and nobody knew her secret, well my secret too, but I didn't know the truth then. When I was older, my mother told me that my father had offered to pay 30/- or £1.50 for my upkeep which she refused. Good. I'm sure I must have been worth more than that! The trouble in those days was that you never knew if you would see your family again. Saying goodbye in the morning could really be 'goodbye.' If you weren't killed in an air raid, there was always the temptation to run off with someone and have an affair as you had to live for today as tomorrow might never come...good manners and bad morals seemed to be the motto for the day!

Although I was very young, I remember the day we went to live in Boscombe very clearly. Certain memories stick, and this was one of them. We arrived, just the two of us, at Pokesdown station with our two bags and an address written on the back of our ration book: '762 Christchurch Road'.

We looked around for someone to help us, but there were no porters as they had been called up to serve in the forces. Seeing a group of young girls by the entrance we asked them, 'Are you the Tucker family?'. They were, and, immediately, our bags were taken from us, and we set off down the road in a convoy, all talking at the same time. It was the most adventurous thing I had ever done, and my mother had a great look of relief on her face.

We were going to be alright, I thought to myself.

When we arrived at the house, we pushed open the big green door. As we climbed up the wide staircase with mahogany balustrades, a wonderful smell of freshly baked bread wafted through the house, a smell never to be forgotten to this day. As I write this, I am transported back to that time.

The bags were dumped in the hall, and we were shunted into the kitchen. The kitchen was the hub of the house. Everything happened in this room; here we would meet every day for breakfast and for high tea. There was a long table down the centre of the room with an oil cloth on it. The room was heated by a black stove which was never turned off, even at the toughest time. It was the 'strength of this house', Auntie Vi used to say, adding that 'you can't think over your problems if you are cold'. So, hungry we were, also broke and sad but never cold!

It didn't take long to understand Auntie Vi ruled the roost. She was short with thin lips. 'Beware of short people with thin lips,' my mother would say, but she was wrong in this case. Auntie Vi clucked not only over her three daughters, but also over her guests, calling them visitors, which immediately promoted them to friends.

We were shown to our room, a large double-bedded room with a slatted wooden 'put you up' on the floor. The room was known as 'Barbara's room' as it was hers before she married Uncle Peter. After that, they moved upstairs to the little flat in the eaves. Auntie Myra, Auntie Vi's sister, used to live there before but now lived downstairs next to the lavatory, which she frequented for many hours a day. There was only one light on the ceiling, which had singe marks on it, but there was a wonderful gas fire with a shilling meter beside it. It turned out to be the centre of attraction in our lives. For when it was on with its flames licking away, it meant we had a little money, and everything was going to be good again.

Not that the shilling lasted very long, but it left us with hope of another shilling, and, in those days, my mother and I lived one day at a time. The main thing was that we felt welcome and very, very safe. We would be fine if my stepfather sent the weekly postal order for £1, which we picked up from the Post Office. But sometimes it didn't arrive and we were in trouble. That was the time that the brushes came out. The brushes were silver and pink mother of pearl. I don't think they were worth much, but it was all we had of any value, and I was in charge of taking them to the local pawn shop. I hated doing it, but I knew I was good at getting money for them.

I had a set patter, and I acted the whole part beautifully. I would put the brushes on the counter and peer over the top of them with my big dewy eyes. Then I'd say, 'Sir I wonder if you could help us out? We have no money and I need to buy food for my sick mother'. Well, it always worked, and I came out with a ten shilling note. For a few minutes I was a star, and everyone clapped and patted the top of my head!

The bathroom across the corridor was special to me as we were given our own tall enamel jug to collect water in from the bath tap to wash in the china basin in our room. The immersion heater went on at 7 am sharp and went off at 8am, so if you missed it you had to wash in cold water. In winter, the ice would form on the insides of the windows and my mother commented that 'it crept into your bones!'. There was, of course, no central heating. One special feature of the bathroom was that there was sandblasted glass on the window, which was great as if you spat on your finger, you could write rude words on the window and they would disappear. It was very liberating, a good way to let off steam. BLAST was my best swear word. I learnt that one from Auntie Vi and soon found it was her favourite too, along with the occasional DAMN. On Sundays a fire would be lit with coke in Grandma's room at the front of the house, and we would all take it in turns to stand there with our skirts lifted so that the heat would burn the back of our legs and heat up our knickers... glorious! The best part for me was the songs we sang with our skirts in the air. The one I remember was 'Deep in the Heart of Texas'; at the end of each verse, you had to let your skirt drop and clap.

Auntie G & Bernice in front room

We settled in very quickly, and one by one the family were introduced to us.

There was a story attached to each person, and Auntie Barbara and Auntie Bernice told us all the gossip about each one. Really, there was a bit of rivalry between the two youngest daughters as they were both pretty, and they tried to outdo each other in everything. Auntie Bernice was rather spoilt, I heard my mother say one day. She did seem to scream a lot, and there was always a drama when she was around. One evening Bernice was getting ready to go out with an American officer and was trying on her new silk stockings when a loud hysterical scream came from the bathroom. The door was flung open, and she ran up and down the corridor screaming, 'Mouse! Mouse!'.

Apparently, the mouse had been nesting in the linen cupboard, and when it was disturbed, it ran up her full taffeta skirt! It took Auntie Vi about an hour to calm her down. When she calmed down, she shouted at her sister, 'Where the hell is Blackie? (the black cat) 'His job is to catch mice, not sit around sleeping'. So, as usual, they had another argument, nothing new. Another time, Auntie Vi's friend Stella came to tea, and her dog wouldn't stop barking. Auntie Bernice

Me in jodhpurs

picked it up, it was a tiny Pomeranian, and threw it over the balcony. I didn't like her much after that, but she made up for things later as she took me riding every Sunday. I loved horses, and later I decided I would become a horse. I did pretend to be one at my next school, but having missed a lot of lessons due to 'grazing', I was told by the Head Mistress that perhaps this was not the right school for me; it was a school for young ladies, not horses. Politely, I was asked to leave. Anyway, I was relieved as I was pretty fed up with neighing all the time, and I had also decided to be a Prima Donna like Margot Fonteyn instead.

Auntie Barbara was the prettiest of the three girls. She was deeply in love with Gordon who was a pilot billeted at Marston aerodrome nearby. They always looked unhappy, they never said anything but just gazed into each other's eyes. It looked pretty boring to me. There is a funny picture of them when they swapped over their clothes. My mother and Barbara became great friends and when they were older, they went on trips to Spain. They never stopped giggling even when they were really old. It was wonderful to have her in our lives, except she loved squeezing my blackheads, and bribed me with little bits of her chocolate ration to allow her to squeeze! Well, unfortunately, one day she had a telegram from the War Office. Gordon's plane had been shot down on its way back from a dangerous sortie. He was awarded a posthumous medal for bravery, but that doesn't help when the love of your life dies, I suppose. Poor Barbara never said very much. I had a funny feeling that they had known that it was only a matter of time before he was shot down.

Because 762 Christchurch Road was close to Hurn airport, it was popular with the pilots and was always filled with them saying hello and goodbye. They always came with gifts for everyone, some extra butter, sugar, always tinned ham from the Canadian pilots and chewing gum and silk stockings from the Americans. When they arrived with all their kit, it would be dumped on the kitchen table and each contribution was greeted by us with an 'ooooh or an ahhhh'. The big kettle was always on the hob, so tea was made or coffee if one of them had managed to smuggle some coffee from the NAFFI. It seemed like

Barbara with her first love Gordon

Auntie Barbara

Christmas Eve to me, and the excitement lasted until I fell asleep at night. I would fall asleep hearing laughter from the kitchen, then perhaps a song and more laughter. I told my mother one day that I could never remember all their names and she said, 'Just call them all Uncle Johnnie'. So I did. If they were flying at the crack of dawn the next day, I would be allowed to stay up for a while whilst one of the Uncle Johnnies popped me up on his knee and told me a bedtime story. I loved it, and they seemed happy too. Many we never saw again. There was a lot of crying and a lot of rushing up and down the corridors.

1944 Marsden pilots

The map that charts Hitler's route into

Britain

By Richard Savill

HITLER'S detailed plans to conquer Britain have been discovered in a rare Nazi briefing book which reveals how and where German troops hoped to land on the south coast.

The book pinpoints the coastal towns in the path of the Nazi ground assault, which was only avoided because RAF fighter pilots managed to win air supremacy in the Battle of Britain in 1940.

It also reveals that postcards of landmarks including Brighton Pier, and Land's End, were given to Nazi troops to identify their targets in preparation for their attack.

The original copy of the book *Militärgeographische Angaben über England Sudkuste* for Operation Sealion detailed every attack point and weakness along every mile of the south coast, locating quicksand, shingle, steep terrain and railways.

It included large colour maps of the coast, from Land's End to Foreness Point in Kent.

On Sept 17, 1940, Hitler was forced to postpone Operation Sealion because of the Luftwaffe's failure to gain air supremacy over England.

The 446-page dossier, which is being sold by a German collector, is expected to fetch £500 when it is auctioned in Ludlow, Shropshire, later this month.

Brookes, from Mullock's Auctioneers, said: "The book on Operation Sealion gives a fascinating insight into what life could have been like if the Germans had invaded.

"It is a chilling reminder of what could have happened 70 years ago, virtually to the day, had not 'The Few' won the decisive Battle of Britain.

"It really was the blueprint for the Nazi invasion."

Historical records show that Hitler planned to invade with six divisions moving through Kent via Folkestone and Ramsgate.

Another unit would invade Sussex and Hampshire through Brighton and the Isle of Wight, while a third group would attempt to take Dorset via Lyme Bay.

Editorial Comment Page 27

A 446-page book, above, detailing Hitler's plan to take the south coast includes a map marking invasion points, left, and postcards of coastal landmarks and towns, such as Penzance, right, for Nazi troops to learn to identify

The map charts Hitler's route to Britain

Then new pilots would arrive, and they needed to have tea and so it went on.

Mummy said it was our war effort to support the brave young pilots, and some of them were very young; I think they missed their mothers too!

Having so many people in and out of the house took everyone's mind off the constant bombing at night. They left us alone during the day and that was good; washing could be hung on the line and shopping bought. I would go with my mother to help hold the basket to Edgerton's, the local grocers in Christchurch Road. Mr Edgerton would greet everyone by name. It took a long time to get to the counter, and even then, we couldn't buy much with the coupons in the ration books. Naturally, everyone grumbled, and poor Mr. Edgerton looked very upset, but it wasn't his fault. With powdered eggs, sausage meat and little packets of butter for the week, our basket was never very full. We would go to Thunders, the paper shop and sweet shop, and I could choose my 2 ounces of sweets. I always chose wine gums as you could suck them for ages and could take them out and continue sucking the next day too. There were ways of making things work, and, generally, people seemed content in a funny sort of way!

Almost next to Edgerton's was the competition, a grocer called Sainsbury's. There were white tiles on the wall and big mounds of butter on the marble counters. The shop assistant would take a piece off the big pat and with two wooden spades would pat the butter into small two-ounce squares and wrap it up into greaseproof paper. Not that any of us went in there; we were loyal to old Mr. Edgerton, and it was all very new at the time. Well, that little Sainsbury's survived the war, but poor Mr. Edgerton was killed in an air-raid.

At night, I would go to bed knowing that we would have to get up in the middle of the night to go down to the coal cellar. Consequently, we rarely got much sleep as we didn't dare go into a deep sleep for fear of not getting to the shelter in time. This also was the time I started to blink non-stop and then to stutter more and more each day. Some people laughed at me, which made it worse, and I would blush bright red as well. It seemed to me then that grown-ups wanted so much from me, and I didn't have a lot to give. My mother decided that as well as elocution lessons, I should start tap-dancing, all the rage at that time. Imagine my horror when she came back from the shops with a roll-up tap dancing floor. My life was miserable from then onwards. I knew I should have been only too pleased to show off my dance talents to everyone, but even then I knew I had little talent for dancing or, in fact, anything else, and I was far far too shy to recite poems aloud. But my mother was so proud of me. So, when she rolled out the dance floor, I tapped away with a bright red face, and when she pulled a chair out for me to stand on, so I could be seen when reciting a poem, I did my bit for her. But it was my biggest nightmare - worse than the bombs. I can still see the faces of the family, some sniggering and some just downright bored. I knew I was a disaster, but I couldn't let my mother down. I was so unhappy I would hide in the loo, so nobody could find me. That's if Auntie Myra was not already in there smoking her Woodbines!

Thinking back, I feel that it was then that I started to retreat into my own private world. I rarely spoke and kept all my thoughts to myself.

Now, in order to make ends meet, Auntie put an advert into The Stage publication offering B&B for the artists performing at the Hippodrome up the road. That's when the fun started. Word soon got around that 762 was not only inexpensive but fun. We had drummers, jugglers, fire eaters and my favourite artist called Rubye, who had worked at the London Palladium in her own show. Her son was a famous film star called Bonar Colleano, and he gave me his autograph. Naturally, I fell in love with Auntie Rubye and asked all my friends to call me Rubye. I knew then and there that I was going to go on the stage. My

friend Anne from the ice cream shop over the road was in love with Betty Grable, so that's what I called her. We spent days and days dressing up and would swan around the house, both retreating into a make-believe world. Even when the siren went, we would float down to the coal cellar in our dresses... it took our minds off the awful situation.

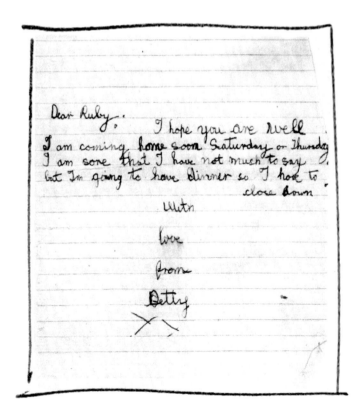

One night was different though. The siren went. Everyone called out to Auntie Bernice to come to the cellar, but she said 'No!'. Auntie Vi was crying, so, finally, Bernice came down followed by my school friend Jennifer who was staying the night with us. The Air Raid Warden came in last, shining his torch into the cellar to check we were all OK. At that very moment, there was a huge blast from a bomb that had landed nearby. The warden fell into the cellar and underneath him was Jennifer. She fell into my arms and I cuddled her. She was dead. Somehow Ernie, the warden, survived. That bomb had missed its target which was the Barracks in the Landsdowne, but the second bomb didn't miss; it dropped directly on the Barracks and exploded killing all 178 men as they sat down to dinner. The Daily Echo called it one of the worst air raids in the South of England. Nobody talked about it. It was too sad. I didn't really understand at the time that with one blast so much could happen, my great friend was dead, and all those brave soldiers were dead. It was too much for me to understand, but today I remember it clearly.

Auntie Rubye at the Palladium. I pretended I was her and all my friends had to call me Rubye

Life went on at 762 as before, but there was no singing, and nobody said very much about that awful night. Things cheered up a bit when Rubye Colleano came back to do her show at the Hippodrome. This time she came with a three piece band, so there was a lot of noise in the house, which helped cheer things up. The drummer and the trumpet player shared a room, and Rubye had Grandma's front room with the fire. I found it all very exciting, and as I think Auntie Rubye could see my look of admiration every time I passed her on the stairs, she asked my mother if I would like to come to rehearsals with her.

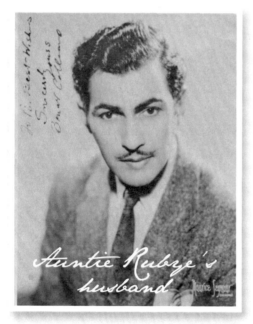

Auntie Rubye's husband

What a treat! There was no way I could sleep that night. At about 12 o'clock, we all walked down Christchurch Road; the drummer, the trumpet player Auntie Rubye and me!

Just sitting in the wings was amazing. They sat me up on a high stool and told me not to make any noise. I was star struck. I think my mouth was open as it got very dry, and I even stopped blinking, which was wonderful. The drummer bashed away at his drums, and Auntie Rubye kicked her legs higher and higher in the air. She was so beautiful, I clapped by mistake at one point. Then there was a break and the drummer came over to me and asked if I would like to have a go on the drums whilst everyone was having a cup of tea. That was it. I remember thinking there was no doubt I wanted to be a drummer when I grew up. I seemed to be very good at it, or at least I thought I was. I closed my eyes and just smashed away at the three drums and the cymbals. I will never ever forget that moment in my young life.

If I hear drums now, I go into a trance and relive that experience, always to be remembered.

After Rubye and the band left the house, it seemed so quiet, except for the sound of the falling bombs. We still had the coming and going of the pilots, but that was not fun like the vaudeville days. Auntie Vi was always worried about the gas bill, and every time the gas man turned up at the door, she would tell me to go to the door and say everyone was out and then close the door. Of course, even I knew he would not keep falling for that, but I went along with it.

Auntie Barbara confided in me one day that the gasman had a soft spot for her mother. I was not sure what she meant by that, but if it worked, I was willing to play my part.

One day, Auntie Vi declared that we all had a big problem; there was no money! So, she decided to put an advertisement in the Daily Echo for a lodger. I went up the road with mummy to get some carpet dye and a small tin of bright blue paint. I was given the job of dyeing the floorboards dark blue to match the carpet as the floorboards were showing. Auntie Barbara painted the chair and table bright blue, and mummy and Auntie Vi cut up an old dressing gown of Grandma's to make some short curtains. There was a candlewick bedspread on the bed, and we found a picture of flowers to put over the bed. It looked wonderful. The next day someone came to see the room and decided to take it. He paid one week in advance in cash and you could see the joy on everyone's face.

His name was Mr Chad; the poor man never fitted in with the silly antics in the house. Like me he had a stutter and was very skinny and bald, so all the girls, and me, made fun of him. The day he arrived, he was shown to his room and given a key for the front door. Thinking that all our worries were behind us, we put the kettle on. But before the tea was made, there was a screech from Mr Chad's room. When he opened the door, we saw a very blue person! He had sat on the chair and taken his shoes off. He had a blue bottom from the newly painted chair and navy blue feet from the newly painted carpet. He did look funny, but once he was cleaned up, even he thought it was quite funny.

I took his supper to him every evening. Auntie Vi had found a side plate, not a dinner plate, and put half a slice of ham, a tomato and some potato salad. Not very filling, so I expected he would get thinner by the day. Pudding was junket, ugh! When the siren went, he was very nice and made sure he was the last man to go to the cellar. We all noticed that nice gesture and tried not to tease him too much. Auntie Vi found him quite a gentleman, which was very important in those days. I suppose it's rather silly telling you about this unimportant event, but little silly things like this made our lives easier. Although we laughed easily, we also cried easily. However, inside we were all terrified of the dreadful war that was going on all around us. Perhaps, it was indeed the British 'stiff upper lip' that we became famous for that kept us going. Who knows?

Auntie Barbara and Auntie Bernice were in the Land Army, and they worked very hard on the land. Auntie Vi and my mother kept the house clean and did the shopping. One evening, Auntie Barbara said she had a date with a man called Peter. She looked happy at last, and we kept our fingers crossed. Weeks later, her new man came to ask Auntie Vi if he could marry her daughter. How wonderful. Another party, I thought!

Uncle Peter was Auntie Barbara's new husband. Their marriage didn't last long as they lived upstairs in the top floor flat and Auntie Vi interfered continuously. I expect she meant well, but the marriage wasn't strong enough to fight Auntie Vi and the war, so he left and I cried. When I was older, I decided that I loved him and went to his garage in town to tell him of my love. I was only 14, and although I was sure it was real love, he looked shocked and told me to go home and do my homework.

The next excitement was when Auntie Bernice and her nice young man declared that they loved each other and again we were to have a party. This time it was a big white wedding. Auntie Bernice always got her own way, and although it was in 1944, and we were still at war, she wanted a white wedding dress. It couldn't have happened but for the help of our wonderful airmen. They 'found' a parachute for the dress, and Auntie Barbara had an old Singer sewing machine. With lots of arguments she managed to complete a spectacular dress. I helped with the jellies and the paper chains.

Auntie Barbara's new husband

I proposed to him when I was 14 years old

The Canadians managed to get flour and raisins, and everyone gave up half of their butter rations so that Auntie Vi could make the wedding cake.

Poor Auntie Myra was still working for Woodbine cigarettes, so she couldn't help much. Nevertheless, she helped in the kitchen and put £5 in the wedding kitty, which was a great help, so I heard from the others.

The thing about Auntie Myra is that I think she was lonely and didn't seem to fit in anywhere. She was very plain, but she had a heart of gold, everyone said. Also, she had this very annoying habit I have already mentioned to go into the lavatory every morning at 7 am and stay there for an hour smoking and reading the newspaper. Then again the same in the evening. The main problem here was that there was only one lavatory in the house, and when she did come out the smoke was so thick the window had to be opened in order to breathe.

The wedding was wonderful, I was a bridesmaid and it was my first long dress. The family were all there. The music was loud and I had so much to eat I thought I would pop.

Wendy, Auntie Bernice and Beryl

Everything went smoothly except for one problem, the queue outside the lavatory. I knew how long it could last and as I was only third in the queue and I knew had to do something drastic. Uncle Leslie was in front of me in the queue and he turned and took my hand and led me to the bathroom. 'This is going to be our secret forever', he said. 'If I use that end of the bath by the taps and you use the other end, we need not see each other, and no one will ever know!' All I could think of saying was, 'I wonder what my mother would say!'. But we did it and we both kept the secret. Nobody ever knew except Uncle Leslie and me.

We did talk about it, actually, many years later, and we laughed at the memory. But at the time, it had been such a serious business and very daring for those days. The oldest Tucker daughter was called Joan. She had married young to a farmer called John. 'John-with-the-long-face,' I always called him. One day they asked if I would like to come and help on the farm as the bombs were not so bad in the countryside.

So, I was bundled off with clean socks, knickers, my Liberty bodice and a pair of shorts Auntie Barbara had made me. I enjoyed my stay and helped with the cows and swept the yard. One day, they asked me to go up the ladder on the plum tree with a basket to collect as many plums as I could without falling off the ladder. They didn't tell me not to eat the plums. I did eat a lot of them and will never do that again as that night my tummy rumbled, and I was not a happy bunny. They thought it was funny and John-with-the-long-face said, 'Serves you right'. Auntie Joan never said much to me. Apparently, she did needlepoint, and she had made some of the prayer mats in Salisbury Cathedral, which are still in use now. That's all I know about her!

Auntie Vi's brother was called Ewart, and he was married to Binnie. They were a gentle couple, and I liked to visit them. They lived near the seaside, and they had a little bungalow with an enormous garden filled with fruit. Raspberries, gooseberries and strawberries. I loved going there because I filled my basket with the fruit, and we had picnics in the field. Uncle Ewart had a little boat, and he told me about the time he went with his three friends to save our soldiers at Dunkirk. We were all very proud of them. They saved 15 soldiers. Uncle Ewart said he was very frightened, but he was so brave. He was given a medal after the war.

Dear Uncle Ewart. He didn't say much, but he always had a bit of a twinkle in his eye. I remember one evening, many years later, I asked the whole Tucker family out to dinner, somewhere rather smart. Everyone looked uncomfortable, and I realised they were out of their comfort zone. I noticed Uncle Ewart had not eaten his grilled chops and asked whether they were alright. 'Wonderful,' he said. A few minutes later I noticed the chops had disappeared! Only when I had paid the bill did I notice the big gravy stain on Uncle Ewart's jacket pocket, I realised he had not wanted to leave them, so he put the whole meal in his pocket!

We stayed friends with the whole family forever it seemed. We went away and then came back - it was our base. I know they loved us as much as we loved them. My stepfather used to come down sometimes and flash white five pounds notes around, so he was always very welcome. Auntie Vi flirted with him, so he flashed even more notes her way! Later on, my stepbrother came to live there. He had his own bedroom - 'the balcony room', a tiny room overlooking Christchurch Road and Rodney Scott the funeral director. He continued to rock himself to sleep as he had always done, and one night he went straight through the wall. I thought it was really funny, but Auntie Vi went into a real theatrical flap. Well, it blew over quickly as there was always another drama ready to happen. This is how wonderful my adopted family were and how lucky we were to find a family like them to take us in from the storm.

AN ASIDE

Auntie Joan was the first of Auntie Vi's daughters to die, and her bad-tempered husband, John, died a few years later. With nobody to bully there was no point in living, I suppose.

Auntie Myra was next to die, poor Auntie Myra. She was such a generous person, but people didn't really understand her. She died of cancer through her terrible chain smoking habit.

Several years later, Auntie Bernice was the next to die. She had throat cancer and had a pipe inserted into her throat. When she was dying, I took Auntie Barbara, who was in a care home, to the hospital in a wheelchair to say goodbye to her sister. Looking at them was the saddest thing I have ever seen. They had argued a few months before, and as I left them alone to say their 'goodbyes', they just held hands without a word. So sad.

My mother died shortly after that, and I have never cried for her. I go to her grave every so often and talk to her, but I can't cry.

Next to go was Auntie Barbara. She had had to go into a home as there was nobody to look after her, which is so sad as she was such a lovely person. But when it comes to caring for someone, it generally comes down to family, and she had no family left. She was pretty happy in the home in Bournemouth, I think. She fell one day, and I rushed down to see her. I said, 'Poor darling! You were OK when I saw you a couple of weeks ago,' and she came back quickly saying, 'You have not been here for nine weeks!'. The fall had brought her memory back, bless her. Anyway, the next call I got was to say she was fading, so I drove down the A338 on one wheel. They had put her in a little room to die and she died ten minutes before I arrived. She was still clutching her hankie and I noticed her fingernails were so long that they had grown into her palm. I felt dreadful. The thought that she had died with nobody at her side upset me so much that I cried all the way back as I felt I had let her down.

Then things got worse. I had made arrangements with the funeral director Rodney Scott over the road from 762 to take care of the cremation. All the family had always wanted to have him arrange their funerals, but they never had the money, so I paid for Auntie Barbara's. I felt good that one of the Tucker family went out in style. I didn't go down for the cremation as I was in Paris at the time, but when I came back, I got a message from Rodney Scott saying Auntie Barbara was in a special Urn and awaiting collection. Again, I drove down that A338 with a heavy heart. Halfway there my mobile went. Mr Scott sounded very upset. He said as he knew how important Auntie Barbara was to me he felt he had to tell me the truth: somehow the urns had got mixed up and Auntie Barbara's ashes had been sprinkled in the Rose garden and the ones left belonged to someone's Uncle Jimmy. I think I said sprinkle his there too and I was on my way. I stopped at a florist and bought all the red roses they had and went to the cliff where Auntie Barbara and I had often said we would do a 'Thelma and Louise'. The cliff was at the end of Woodlands Walk. It was always a special place for me too as I vowed when I was little that one day, I would be a writer like my father. Well, it has taken 60 years but hey - I'm doing it!

Anyway, I climbed over the fence to get to the cliff edge and shouted, 'Goodbye Auntie Babs'. I was about to throw the roses over the edge when a big wind blew all the petals off the red roses. So, I actually threw a bunch of stems over. At that point, I saw the funny side of it all and laughed and then cried. When I turned around to get back over the fence, I realised I was on lower ground and I couldn't get back, so I had to wave to passersby to help me. It was no use explaining and as I was laughing so much, I think they thought I was just mad!

Last to die was my lovely Uncle Leslie. What a dear man. He was very gentle and kind and always had a twinkle in his eyes. His father invented the famous Douglas motorbike, and Leslie worked in his garage for years on his own invention, an electric bicycle. I tried to get interest in it from various companies, but nobody seemed interested. Regardless of that, he went on and on trying to perfect it. He had the naughtiest smile in the world, and there were many parties when he was around. I kept my eye on him as much as I could from a distance. One night he called me and said he was tired and was going to have his supper in bed.

We said 'Goodnight' and that was the last time I spoke to him. I received a call in the morning from Chris, his son, to say that his dad had choked on his cornflakes in bed and died. And so that was the end of the family who lived at 762 Christchurch Road!

AN ASIDE UPDATE!

In 2016 my brother and I went down to Boscombe to see 762 and to walk down Woodlands Walk where, as children, we would play houses in the branches of the trees and bushes. When we parked the car, we saw a demolition sign. The house was to be knocked down to build flats. It was a terrible shock as we both felt our 762 would be there forever! I called the Daily Echo to see if they could send a photographer to take pictures before the image was lost but they were busy, so I took rather bad pictures. I think, in a way, it was a good ending for us as we had arrived the day before it was turned to dust, and we had time to remember and say our goodbyes.

…OH, I FORGOT. In the Summer, during the war, there was not much to laugh about except we were lucky enough to live by the seaside. At weekends, we would all march down the zig-zag path at the end of Woodlands Walk. It was magical. The golden sand and the shimmering sea … what wonderment. There was a small blight; the Government had concerns that the Germans might decide to land their boat along the beach, so they took all the scaffolding they could find, and it zigged and zagged from Bournemouth to Christchurch. That didn't stop us kids; we climbed to the top and jumped into the water, screaming. Oh, such screams, I can hear them now!

I had an elasticated floral bathing costume. My pride and joy and the envy of all my friends…Let's see if I have a picture…

I have found a picture of me in the bathing costume, note the pose!

Chapter 1 part 5

Boarding school for young ladies

Finally, World War 2 was over, and my stepfather was back. Somewhere there is a picture of a blue Austin 7 with me as a little girl sitting alone on the backseat. My stepfather had bought the car with some money he had made on some 'funny' deal. He was a true 'wheeler dealer', and I think, perhaps, it was he that made me into one later in life. He would approach owners of bombed out houses or pieces of land and agree a price to buy; then he would go to the pub and sell it before buying it. A clever idea. Soon we had enough money to buy the Austin 7. He persuaded us that we should go to the Mall to celebrate VE day. Well, we did, but we ran out of petrol on the way, so my parents went in search of a petrol station, my stepfather optimistic as ever, my mother mumbling under her breath. They left me safely in a locked car. I was terrified as people were shouting and jumping up and down with happiness - I too would have been happy if I hadn't been so scared.

Life changed after that, and we were all of a sudden rich. I was taken to Baker Street where my mother bought me a whole new wardrobe of clothes from Daniel Neals. Dresses with lots of smocking and a pink organza one for parties. Mummy had a new fur coat, 'Skunk'. It didn't smell and she loved it and wore it all year round, even in the summer! Then whilst my stepfather built us a house in Chorley Wood, which he called Windy Nook, we moved into the Dorchester hotel in Park Lane. I spent most of my time in the kitchens with the chefs and got to love and understand good food early in my life. When the house was nearly ready, we had what now I know is called a 'cash flow' problem. So, one evening there were raised voices and some shouting, which was not unusual between my mother and stepfather. Then I saw that my mother had been crying. Michael and I were told to put on all our clothes: for me, three pairs of knickers, three liberty bodices, four frocks and my coat. It was so funny as we all looked so fat! Then we climbed down the backfire escape clutching our dolls and soldiers! Later on in my life, I found that we had no money left as my stepfather was a gambler and had lost everything on a horse called 'Lost Horizon'. Now when I go to the Dorchester for a drink or tea, I expect someone to put their hand on my shoulder and say, 'Come this way!'

We survived by staying a few weeks in a dirty hotel room in Kings Cross, which in those days was the pits. But we all survived. Then the house was finished, and with the help of two really nice Italian POWs who were not paid anything, just fed, the house was ready to move into. The house was quite ugly as the money had run out, but my mother thought she was a Queen in a new palace, so we all went along with it. The garden was enormous, and we had inherited some chickens and a duck, which I called Alexandra. I loved Alexandra to bits and told her all my secrets.

Happiness didn't last long since it was decided that all nice little girls went to boarding school, so that's what happened. We had done a 'good deal' on a block of flats, so we had money again. I had a school trunk with WAC on the side and a new school uniform, red and white check with a grey blazer and a Panama hat with a check ribbon. I was told I would be happy there. I was not.

Being a new girl and still having a stutter, I struggled to fit in. Who wants a friend with a stutter? That's when I started to think for myself and worked out that if I were more daring than other girls, I would acquire a following. So, when we were told not to walk along the top of a high wall around the school, I walked it. Yes, I was terrified, but all the girls started to dare me to do other things, and I did them. My plan worked and soon I was very popular. Every night in my pink dormitory you could hear sobs coming from under the sheets, but it was never mentioned; it was just part of being away from your family. In the day time everything was alright again. At last I found something I was good at, gymnastics. I suppose it helped being in love for the first time. I had a crush on the Gym teacher. She was always smiling and had big breasts. She made me believe I was good at everything, which was all I needed to boost my confidence. With her encouragement, I won all the school gymnastic prizes, three cups and a brooch saying GYMNASTICS, which I still have today. I stopped my stuttering and felt on top of the world, my own world for the first time in my almost grown up life. The headmistress was amazed at my transformation, and I was made a Prefect.

With the Prefect badge came duties. I was in charge of 'Pink Dorm' and we had such fun. I arranged a farting competition where everyone had to lift up their nighties and point their bottoms towards the centre of the room and at the count of three...fart! Then I gave instructions that each girl had to steal something from the kitchen for our midnight feast. Word got around and soon all the dormitories were doing the same thing. I also arranged an escape committee and charged three pence for a hand drawn map of the area, a bus timetable and some biscuits. My first escapee was a girl called Mandy. I took her to the top of the fire escape and showed her with my torch which path to take, past the Science lab to the bus stop. We made sure she had a penny for her fare. At the time, I thought it was a good plan!

Great success, I thought and went back to bed. Poor Mandy was found crying under a tree and was petrified. My first proper business had failed. I was reprimanded and had a warning that if this happened again, I would be expelled. Another business was hair brushing; as every girl with long hair had to brush their hair a hundred times a night, I offered to do it for them whilst they read their comics. I made a tidy sum and that bought me more respect. I was flying high, and I was only ten years old. I was also put in charge of the five year olds and would make up stories every night, so they would go to sleep. I loved making up stories, but it got boring with the fairies. So, one night I told them that the hatch in the ceiling opened up every night, and giant spiders came out and walked all over them. They were terrified. It was great fun for me. Well, of course, I was found out, and the complaints from the other parents poured in. I received my second warning, and I was expelled. I left school with my head held up high. I had, after all, left my mark for the first time.

Once home, I never said a word to my parents as I felt I had nothing in common with them, which was sad in a way. I'm sure my parents didn't know what to do next, but they soon made a plan.

We were going to live in South Africa. Apparently, my stepfather had family there in a dreadful mining town called Krugersdorp. Uncle Dan and Auntie Helen owned the hotel there. So, all our furniture was packed up into a big Pickfords van, and the chickens were given away. We had our last meal at Windy Nook and it was delicious. Only at the end of the meal did my stepfather say, 'That was a tasty duck, wasn't it?' We had just eaten Alexandra. Once again, I was reminded that I hated that man with the big nose, my stepfather. I continued to dislike him all my life until he finally died and then I felt only relief.

We set sail on the Warwick Castle from Southampton. The band played Rule Britannia and I cried; I don't know why. I had my little brother's hand tightly in my hand and he squeezed it, which was the first time we actually bonded. The journey was very exciting, and we all had fun as a real family, the only time we ever had successfully together. There were fancy dress parties. I was a mermaid with a big flipper but had no liberty bodice, so my mother stuck my long hair down with bread and water glue over my flat nipples, which was very embarrassing. Then there was dunking in the pool by a 'pirate' when we crossed the Equator, or the line as we sailors called it! The boat wasn't very glamorous because it had been commandeered during the war, and it was filled with sailors. They were 'very rough', a 'troop ship', I heard my mother say. I loved them. Whenever I could, I would sneak off and duck under the 'out of bounds sign' and sit listening to the stories of their adventures They were wonderful, and I listened in amazement. They even signed my autograph book. My brother was a nuisance most of the time. His best trick was to drink a whole bottle of Syrup of Figs then climb up the funnel and be sick down it. Obviously, the Captain was not happy about this, and I remember he actually growled. I thought it showed Michael had a great sense of humour, even if he was so tiny! I loved him even more after that and realised I had to keep an eye on him as he needed me. I do still keep an eye on him as I think maybe he still needs me!

We arrived at Cape Town. It was hot and there was an enormous mountain called Table Mountain. It was covered at the top with cloud, which they called a tablecloth. We stayed only a couple of days. Then caught a train and went up the Garden Route, which I was too young to appreciate. Arriving in Johannesburg, we were met by our new family and their children, Helen and Elliot. Their hotel in Krugersdorp was a few miles away. We moved in, but my mother was crying again. I must say it was terrible. It was like a large tin shed with a corrugated roof, but I suppose it was a home of sorts. The bar of the hotel was 'off limits' as it was always filled with very drunk men, including my stepfather. Mind you, there was nothing to do in Krugersdorp except playing bowls and listening to the new Juke Box in the main dusty street, blaring out songs like 'Sparrow on the Treetop' by Guy Mitchell. The problem with that area in those days was that although every family had black servants, there was always a scary feeling in the air. I didn't understand it then, but I do now. Our servants were not paid much and had to work really long hours. I remember going down the main road in Johannesburg and seeing a young black boy trying to walk past an Afrikaans man; the man didn't like that and kicked him to death. It was my first experience of what life could be like, and the sight still haunts me today. Rumour had it that 'they' were cutting off servants' heads and rolling them down Sydenham Hill. Who knows, I didn't see anything, but there was an odd feeling in the air, which I could feel even though I was so young.

After that, Michael and I were both sent to boarding schools to keep us safe. I went to St Ursuline's Convent, where I decided not to be a ballerina, nor a drummer, but a nun. I did an awful lot of praying and had my rosary in my knicker pocket all the time. I fell asleep at night saying 'Hail Mary Full of Grace'.

The convent was very strict, and I spent most of my time there scrubbing the Chapel steps for my sins. When I had been particularly naughty, I was told that I would be in Limbo and never go to Heaven. I don't think I ever committed a Mortal sin, but somehow I seemed to be constantly in trouble. Ever Saturday night, we had to go to bed straight after homework, and we soon found out why this was; the nuns and the priests from Michael's school would meet up for a dance! We would creep along to the gym and watch them. They had only one record called 'Jealousy!' The nuns would lift their habits up and dance closely to the priests, why I had no idea, but it seemed to make them all happy! Meanwhile Michael was at a school in Rudesport, not far away. One day, there was a tornado right over the town, and everything flew into the air. I was devastated waiting for bad news or expecting him to fly past at any moment. But the Missionary school he was in was solid and all was well. We rarely got to see each other, but we passed notes via the Art master, who worked at both schools. Then one day we were told at prayers that the statue of Our Lady of Fatima was coming to the Convent. What an honour, we were told. We were all lined up, eldest first, then the middle school and then the juniors. Last of all were the school black servants. It was then that I was told that as I was such a sinful child, I would be the last to kiss Our Ladies feet! That was it. I wouldn't kiss her feet, and I would not become a nun after all. I was expelled again. The reason given was that Sister Stanislaw thought that I was too much of an individual to take advantage of anything her Sisters could teach me! Huh! St Ursuline's was closed down a few months later, perhaps someone had found all the confiscated letters that the pupils had written to their families saying how unhappy they were!

We left the area very soon and went to live in Durban, by the sea. I went to a wonderful school called Marie Stella Convent. It was in an amazing position overlooking Durban Bay. We even had our own caterpillars the same colour as our uniform, black and yellow. We had to be at school at 7am to learn Afrikaans. The first day I heard the most terrible screams, and I saw a young girl about my age being dragged up the hill by a nun. I had no idea what that was all about until 10 years later when I met the girl in London; she had become a mannequin just like me. She was called Aldine Honey. We worked together a lot, but she was always trying to get me to go to bed with her. I don't think she was a real lesbian, but she used to love to embarrass people, especially me as I was easily shocked then. At school, I made friends with a couple of sisters whose family were the Hinds family, a bit like Kellogg's here. I had the time of my life with them. Every day the chauffeur would collect the three of us from school and take us to their big house. The garage was filled with amazing cars, so we would use one each to pretend it was our home and entertain each other with pretend cups of tea and fairy cakes. My 'home' was an Oldsmobile, Megan's a Chrysler and Noel's the Cadillac, worth a lot of money then, but now they would be priceless. On rainy days, we read plays and acted on their stage in their playroom. Best of all was when we were taken to the Hinds' custard factory. We would climb up the chute and slide down it to land into a deep urn filled with custard. Can you imagine that special dried custard squeaky feeling? We put custard into bags and made trails all over the factory. Never have I had such fun. Even now I can't think of anything that has given me such pleasure. I heard many years later that Noel had been speeding along the coast route and had been involved in a crash; she was decapitated, how terrible. I never knew what happened to Megan, married with lots of kids, I suppose, and with lots of money.

My brother and I loved Durban because for a while we lived in a hotel on the beach called Edwards Hotel. There was a pool nearby, and we would swim in it almost every day. One day we were there, and there were some big boys there fooling about being noisy. I had just got out of the pool and turned to look for Michael as he couldn't swim properly. He wasn't in the shallow end. Then I saw him in the middle of the pool without his ring. I shouted for help and then dived in to save him myself. I had just passed my life saving exam. With lots of kicking

Edwards Hotel in Durban

47

and gurgling I brought him back to the shallow end. The boys just laughed at us, but I knew I had saved Michael's life and, again, I knew he still needed me.

After three years, we came back to Great Britain. How wonderful was that! We lost all the furniture as we couldn't pay the storage bill, but mummy was so glad to be home that she almost didn't mind. That was when my stepfather and Michael left to live in Earls Court in a room in Redcliffe Road, and my mother and I went back to the open arms of the Tucker family in Boscombe.

Going back to 762 was the pinnacle of happiness.

It was then that I decided I was not really very bright, but, in another way, I knew I had become 'streetwise.' I knew how to manipulate people. I learnt how to flirt with the local boys on my way to Church every Sunday and was beginning to have rather tiny breasts, which gives a girl even more confidence. So, in a way, at 13, I didn't feel I needed school anymore, so I shut my brain off and survived in my own way. The Wendy way. I went to another 3 schools, all boring, mostly Convents; they were inexpensive and better than going to a Council school I was told, so I went along with it. Who cared if I didn't learn anything? I was wise enough.

AN ASIDE

In 1954 Roger Bannister ran the 3 minute mile, and I was there at White City to cheer with the crowds.

ANOTHER ASIDE

Later in life when my daughter was eight years old, I thought it would be good to take her to the boarding school I had gone to, so she could follow in my footsteps. In the 'Pink Dorm', I pushed a bed to one side and found the loose floor board where we used to hide all our bounty from the kitchen, it was still there but empty! Sarah begged me not to send her to a boarding school, so she never went through that experience, which in a way was a shame, I think!

Chapter 2 part 1

Peter my first love - business college

I have no idea why we went to live in Ealing, but as there was no sight of my stepfather or brother, I remember thinking maybe we had run away. The owner of the house was a wonderful red haired chubby lady called Betty. She and my mother became friends, and while life was cramped in the little bedroom that we rented for £4 per week, it was stress free and I started to breathe properly again. Well, 15 is a difficult age to be, especially sleeping in a double bed with one's mum, and there was nowhere to be alone except in the toilet. I spent a lot of time in there and started to pretend that when I left home, I would buy a toilet and make it very modern with a push button for the bed to come down and another for the hob and another for the basin. It seems silly, but at the time it was all I wanted, peace and quiet and a home to call my own.

I had just discovered boys, and my mother found the whole idea of me growing up difficult to bear. She decided I should know a few facts about men, so she had drawn me a picture of a huge tall cucumber type thing with two round things at the bottom. I looked at her speechless, and I didn't dare ask her what it was. But seeing the look on her face, I gathered it was something unmentionable, so I fled with a red face. That was the beginning and end of the birds and bees for me. Consequently, I was totally unprepared for everything ahead.

There was nothing to do in Ealing Common except catch a bus into Ealing Broadway where there was a Lyons Corner House and a cinema. I would meet my school friends there on a Sunday, after Church. For some reason, I had been going to the Methodist Church on the common, perhaps because I was lonely, and I got free sponge cakes.

The talk around the table, at Lyons café, was always about boys, and who had done what. I think we made up a lot of stuff not wanting to be left out or considered unsexy. My own experiences were non-existent, but I could, even at the age, tell that some of my girlfriends were doing things that they didn't like or want to do because of keeping face. So, the cheek of it, I started my next business. Advice for Virgins (A 4 V). I charged a cup of tea and Lyons treacle tart, or 3 pennies, for a consultation. I made up all of it. I remember telling one of my best friends, Judy, that if she kissed her boyfriend 'down there', her lips would turn green and everyone would know. What? She actually got arrested kissing her boyfriend (on the lips) in their car in a public place a few weeks later; laughable now, but it was in all the papers. The headlines were 'Kissing in the car couple'. Poor Judy, her lips weren't green, but her reputation was ruined, and she left college early as all the boys were trying to get her behind the Gym hut to try to kiss her. Later, we heard that she and Alex, I think his name was, had got married a year later. Seems a nice end to the story. I closed 'Advice for Virgins' soon after that!

One cold Sunday afternoon, I met a boy called Ken, and he bought me a cup of tea and packet of crisps at Lyons, the way to my heart then. He lived with his mother by Ealing Common and was easy to talk to, not very interesting but neither was I then. We started dating. Well, he asked me to the cinema the following Sunday, and I said 'yes,' telling my mother that I was going with a girlfriend. We sat in the back row in the 1/6 pence seats, you had made it if you got to sit there on your first date, but I think it meant that you were an 'easy kisser.' Ken was the first man I had kissed, and he had thick lips like cushions. It was very nice, and I scanned the magazines for more adventurous things to do and practiced kissing on my arms. I became quite an expert!

The following week we entered the Ealing Common Kissing Competition and won it. 4 hours and 27 minutes, one kiss. Only because I needed to go to the toilet did we have to stop. So, my reputation was well established, but I was still a virgin. Not that Ken didn't try lots of tricks to get me to bed, like telling me to hide under the bedspread and he would come and find me; how does that game go I wonder? His mother came in just in time and I was banned from the house, but I was intact!

A few days later, Ken called to say he couldn't see me that night as he had another date. He suggested that I come along anyway as he had a new friend who was very rich and owned a Coconut Estate in Trinidad, and we could all go out together. I should have said 'No, thank you', but rich sounded good to me, and I was already a bit bored with Ken and his big lips. So, we all met at Lyons as usual. My date was called Peter. He was short, but he was very good looking and the evening went well. We seemed to hit it off, and he told me all about his Estate and his life in Trinidad. He was in Great Britain to go to St. Bartholomew's' Medical School, where his Uncle, Rodney Maingot, had studied and became their most famous Surgeon. We all went back to Peter's room, and he produced a large bottle of Rum. Well, it tasted wonderful, my first drink, and I was hooked. Ken and whatever her name was were tipsy, and I think they were getting on more than very well, but I dared not look. Peter suggested we sit down on the other bed. For some reason, I stood up and said loudly 'I am going home, thank you and goodbye'. Again, I left intact.

A few days later, Peter arrived with flowers for my mother and a magazine for me. That was it; my mother was head over heels in love with him. You could see her eyes light up, and her face beamed with delight when I introduced her to my 'new boyfriend.' Until my mother died, many years later, Peter was her hero. Peter was the one she wanted me to marry. Peter was a good catch. Peter would be able to take over from her in bringing me up. Peter had the right contacts. Peter was wonderful…

Yes, I too thought he was pretty wonderful, and we fell in love. My first love and my Svengali, he taught me many things; he and my mother had a plan. In fact, how my mother could have handed me over so completely to Peter I will never understand. I was too young to be taken over by a man she hardly knew. Peter always said, spend time wooing the mother and the daughter is all yours. Which was true, I suppose. Peter was deeply, deeply in love with me. He had found his love and decided to train me, so I was worth marrying.

Again, without me actually having any input, my mother and Peter decided that I should leave school, which had been, in fact, a total waste of time. The plan was to send me to Chiswick Polytechnic where they had a Business course, Shorthand, Typing and Commerce. I loved it but had a pretty bad time as I spoke properly and was quite a young lady. The rough boys had fun laughing at me but looking back, I suppose it did me good. There were boys of all sizes and shapes there, and I fell in love with a different one every day. The big love was David Best. He was the Basketball Captain. Every girl loved him, but, for some reason, he chose me, the plainest girl there! He asked me to meet him in class 5B after the match, and I was there waiting. Waiting for what, I wonder. He pushed me against the blackboard and kissed me in a heavy-handed way and then put his cupped hand over my breast. I was so taken back that I instinctively slapped his face. He left quickly, and I stood there covered in chalk and crying. I didn't tell Peter or my mother. Great! I had a secret all to myself! Looking back now, I wonder which way my life would have panned out if I had carried on with my Convent education. I bet I would have become a secretary and married the boss, ugh boring!

I passed all my final exams except bookkeeping, in which I managed to achieve 3%. There was no way I would get my Business certificate with that result so, after taking advice from my best friend Julie, I decided to go to the Headmaster and try to find a way to get the Certificate.

I was very honest and said how much I had enjoyed the course and that I planned to go into business for myself after leaving. I smiled and smiled at poor Mr Ashcroft, crossed and uncrossed my legs, showing the top of my lisle stockings. I think he was so terrified of me that he said that he didn't want to ruin my future, and he would give me my certificate. I came out triumphant, and, from then onwards, I understood that all men could be manipulated! Now I was almost a woman of the world, Peter was allowed to take me to stay with some friends of his in Devon. We went on the back of his motorcycle, an Aerial 500. Needless to say, we went straight to The Column Hotel in South Molton, booking in as Mr and Mrs Smith, as one did in those days, and there I lost my virginity. It didn't seem to be a big deal after all the stories I had heard about losing IT!

Peter moved into a flat that he shared with Mark Patterson and Gary Usher in Cromwell Road, Kensington. All 3 were going to be doctors; well, the other two did become successful doctors, but Peter was so besotted with me that he spent all his days and nights writing 40-50 page love letters. I didn't know how to handle such love and felt smothered by him. His mother blamed me for his failure at Bart's, but it was not really my fault; her son just loved me too much. We had some fun days, like the day Gary took us down to Henley Regatta in his little open top MG. Peter and I under the soft top doing all sorts of naughty things, a bit of a squeeze but interesting!

One morning I received a letter from the Polytechnic saying that I had an interview with the Director of a company at Number 1 Carlos Place WI. I didn't get the job because I got in such a muddle with the shorthand and left with my satchel filled with crumpled up paper! I only mention this as now when I go to Scotts for lunch or have my hair done at Nicky Clarke's over the road, I always stand and look at Number 1 Carlos Place and remember that dreadful day and my red face and those tears.

AN ASIDE

Yes, Peter was my first love, but his undying love suffocated me. Also, together with my mother, they killed off any special feelings I had by trying to make me perfect to marry. Every day Peter wrote me those long, long letters in tiny scrawly writing. I never read them as I was sure they would be scolding me and,

52

quite frankly, I was finding life a challenge without more negative vibes coming my way...

ANOTHER ASIDE

Much later in our relationship we had a wonderful baby daughter called Sarah. So, that great love we had for each other was transferred to our gorgeous daughter. Peter and I were never married. We were not meant to be Peter Pan and Wendy Darling after all.

Chapter 2 part 2

My mother and Peter had an idea - grooming I think it's called nowadays!

When Peter suggested that his friend, Dr Bramwell, had offered to introduce me to London society, my mother was 'over the moon'. Her dream of presenting me at court was getting nearer. Apparently, Dr Bramwell was one of those people that seemed to know everyone in the 'right' circles. He had the jewellery shop in South Molton Street and was a friend of Peter's family; therefore, he could be trusted to look after me.

I was told about this latest plan one evening and was very upset as I wanted to start making my own way in the world. Yet again in my life, I was handed over to a man, and my life was to take an enormous turn. The next days were spent at Debenhams in Wigmore Street being fitted for new clothes. Afternoon dresses, shoes and gloves. Where the money came from, thinking back now, I have no idea, and I suppose I will never know. Perhaps it was from Peter! It amazes me now to think that my mother and Peter thought that by introducing me to such a world would make me happy. I suppose then they could feel they had completed my education preparing me for life in the big wide world. I had my own plans, and they didn't include going to the right parties and meeting the right people. I just wanted to work, but, as usual, I went along with whatever was asked of me.

Dr Bramwell, true to his word, called my mother with dates of forthcoming tea parties. The first one I clearly remember as it was at the Ritz. It was just an informal get together for some of his friends, he said on the way there. Well, other than cramming my face full of cucumber sandwiches and fairy cakes, I didn't meet anyone of interest as everyone there was quite old and very 'fuddy duddy', I thought. After that, I was taken to the Snow Ball at Grosvenor House, which was more exciting, and I enjoyed myself. There were several good-looking men at our table, and they all knew Dr Bramwell. He explained that I was his ward, and he wanted to show me around. I'm not sure they believed him, and I did feel a little uncomfortable; but the food was very special, and I cleared my plate and asked for more! At least, I got to dance, and everything seemed a bit more interesting than the boring tea parties.

Meanwhile, my mother still worked every day at Harrods, and Peter stayed in bed until 2pm before having his lunch, generally a Wimpy and crinkle chips, and chain smoked. At the same time, I was beginning to enjoy all the attention, and my dinners out with my new friends would be at the Caprice or Quaglino's. I did love walking down that big staircase, and, really, it wasn't long before Peter and I seemed to have nothing in common. He hated music, except Mighty Sparrow steel band. He was from Trinidad, after all, but I was into Elvis Presley and was madly in love with Cliff Richard! I do think that their plan worked in a way as the more parties I went to, the more confident I became, and I could hold a whole conversation with someone without one stutter.

Later in my life, I looked back and could see that, in a way, I was being 'groomed', and I dread to think what people were saying about me at the time. But I was powerless; I just did what I was told. I was 16 and thought there must be more to life than party after party. There was nothing 'seedy' about it, and I was by now enjoying all the attention. However, none of the young men I sat with or danced with gave me a kiss! Perhaps they were told not to touch! Randall, Dr. Bramwell's chauffeur, ushered me into the Rolls. This was apparently a special night, so I wore a pink net dress with about 20 layers of net. I thought I looked like a fairy on top of a tree, but obviously 'they' were happy with my appearance, so be it! We picked up Dr Bramwell from his house in Phillimore Gardens and went to supper at my favourite restaurant, Wheeler's. I always had Lobster Thermidor, which was very fashionable in the late '50s.

I was told that we had been invited to Billy Butlin's big party for his daughter Cherry. The party was at the Albert Hall and when we arrived there, it was utterly amazing as it had been transformed. All the seats had been removed in the centre to make a ballroom. There were balloons and streamers and a wonderful band playing 'swing music'. Brilliant, this was going to be fun, I thought. And it was. I was introduced to Billy Butlin's son, Bobby Butlin and that was it. We danced all night; not only was he one of the most handsome men I have ever met but a wonderful dancer, so we twirled around the room like a prince and princess. We were definitely noticed by everyone, including the reporter from Jennifer's Diary, THE column to be mentioned in as everyone read it to see who was who and what was what. There we were, 'What a beautiful couple' people said, 'Was there any romancing?' No, he was working at the Butlin's Holiday Camps for his father, learning the ropes, and had to travel nonstop going to those dratted Balls. Honestly, he was very boring, and I think he thought the same of me. We had a few kisses, not bad, but he was not for me, thanks!

One day I got a call from Dr. Bramwell, I never did know his first name, and he said he was not well but Randall, the chauffeur, would pick me up and take me to Portman Square. A Major Sydney Rosette was throwing a party for all his American friends as it was Thanksgiving. Sydney (Tony) was surrounded by good-looking young men when I arrived. He saw me and came sliding across the room to greet me. I realised he was gay, but it didn't matter much in those days. 'Welcome, welcome', he said, 'I have heard so much about you and have been longing to meet you'. He grabbed a glass of Champagne as the waiter went past and handed it to me. 'Now let me introduce you to some marvellous young men.' Well it was a bit like a sweet factory; they really were good-looking, and I loved the American attitude to life, which seemed so much more romantic than our stuffy ways.

That night I met an interesting architect called Digby Bridges. His name was always cropping up; he was in that inner circle of debutants, but his life was a busy one as he was a highly respected architect, I gathered. I saw him years later being interviewed on BBC TV about life in the fast lane in the early sixties. Pity, he was very nice. There were a couple of fairly interesting men there but very few interesting women. They seemed to spend the whole times in huddles or in the 'bathroom' as the Americans called it. Out of the corner of my eye, I had been noticing someone for a while, and I gathered later when we were introduced that he had been doing the same. I had been warned that he was dating Ava Gardener, and there were rumours that they were getting married. So, I sort of tried to ignore him, but once we started talking, we couldn't stop; he was so interesting. His name was Frank Silvestri, and he was a doctor at the American Hospital in Rome, which is where he first met Ava. Reading between the lines, I think he thought her a bit of a drama queen but why not? She was Ava Gardener after all! We did go out a few times whilst he was in London, and we enjoyed each other's company.

One evening we went to dinner at Coq d'Argent, where the food was wonderful.

Frank asked if I would like to come to a private supper party given by Princess Margaret at the 400 club the next evening. I immediately said 'yes'; you can't turn down an invitation like that. My mother would be thrilled. We had to arrive at 7.30 and supper would be served at 8pm, but we were not allowed to sit until the Princess came and was seated. At about 8.20pm she arrived. She lifted her hand in a royal wave and then stood by the table, waiting for someone to light her cigarette, which was in her long cigarette holder. So, we stood and stood and glared, but she would not sit down. Finally, her escort Billy Wallace (a real Debs delight) pulled out her chair at the top of the table, and she sat down at last. We actually applauded, which was a bit frowned upon, but I suppose you are allowed to behave like that if you are Royalty. Not that Queen Elizabeth would have done that, I am sure. The evening was uneventful except for when Billy Wallace came over after the meal, and Frank introduced us. We chatted about nothing for a few moments, and Princess Margaret looked over and glared at me; she nodded to him and they turned and left. That was my royal moment, and it lit my mother's face up and she sparkled, which made me happy.

Ava had called Frank to come back to Rome. He kissed me and said, 'Come to Rome soon, little girl' and he was gone.

He left the next day. Well, not before he had been interviewed by all the London newspapers; I suspect it was a slow news day. He was asked why he was going back to Rome, and he replied that he wanted to be honest with Ava and tell her that their affair was over as he had fallen in love with a 24 year old beautiful young lady. He said he could not divulge her name as she was too well known in London society. She is from a wealthy family and he had to be discreet! Poor Frank, where he got his information from I have no idea, but perhaps he put two and two together and made 6!

The next few days were horrific for me and my mother as the press were relentless in their pursuit of a story. How could Ava Gardner lose her boyfriend to this young London girl...what did I have that was better than AVA GARDNER?...My mother was secretly happy about the whole situation, I think. I was just annoyed for as far as I was concerned, I felt Frank could have told me how he felt before he told the press.

I had a note from him a few days later just saying 'sorry.' The note came in a glove box filled with about 10 pairs of kid gloves in every colour and length possible from a famous glove shop in Via Condotti in Rome. I needed gloves like a hole in head!

AN ASIDE

I did go to Rome a few months later, and I think that was when my life really started...I fell in love but not with Frank!

I have one regret, well maybe two; perhaps I shouldn't have gone to Rome in the first place, but having gone there, I most certainly should have not come home as I came back without my heart! Thankfully, Peter hadn't seen the news about Frank and me in the newspapers.

Chapter 2 part 3

Two men in my life - well actually three!

Peter made a new friend, called Tom Hill, when he was at St Bartholomew's Hospital Medical School, and, in fact, that was, in part, why Peter failed his exams. They hit it off from day one, and as they were both going to be doctors, they expected to be friends forever. Both were as bad as each other; neither of them was very keen on getting up early for any of the morning lectures, so that was half the day gone. Then there was Squash. They played each afternoon and after that appeared in a lecture room to catch the gist of whatever was being discussed. Well, as Peter had mainly got his place because of his Uncle Rodney Maingot, who was one of Bart's most successful Surgeons, the Dean tried to overlook the odd missed lecture here and there, but as the other part of the day was taken up by writing long, long letters to me, or perhaps seeing me, he came to the conclusion that there was no time left for Peter to become a doctor. So, he suggested that it might be an idea to stop seeing me. Of course, Peter explained that I was the woman he was going to marry - one day!

We often went out the three of us. Now I think about it, we nearly always went around together. I found it much more fun with Tom (Tom-Tom) around as he was hopelessly in love with me. Every time we met, his eyes would glaze over, and I always felt he would just float up to Heaven if I smiled back at him. So, I played on it. I could wind him around my tiny finger and flick him away whenever he annoyed me. I loved the power I seemed to have over him. In fact, I had two men in love with me, which was glorious. We were a little gang, and they called me Bird. I lived in a Bird's nest, Tom always said. What with Peter's long letters and Tom's little gifts of miniature bottles of perfume. I was totally loved. I think every woman should have two or even three men in love with her; perhaps this way marriage would work for everybody!

We often went to Oxford to see Tom's parents. They were so warm and welcoming. His father was called Gunter, and he was a lecturer at Oxford University. They had so many stories of World War 2, which always fascinated me. It was amazing that they escaped after the failed plot to kill Hitler, but I gathered his mother still had nightmares about their narrow escape that night. In the evenings, we would go to a bistro; one of our favourites was called 'Fanny's Bistro' in Fanny's Road in Barnes. It was a take off of Luba's Bistro, but it was not on the 'fashionable' list as many people hadn't heard of Barnes. A year later, they had to change the name to The Bistro and even changed the name of the road to St Hilda's Road. You see how prudish, in some ways, we were in the early Sixties.

Tom's favourite club was Esmeraldo's Barn in Knightsbridge. I loved that I could get up and dance away all by myself as neither Peter nor Tom danced. Every time we met, we would go to eat at Dino's or Daquise in South Kensington (the Polish restaurant). Sometimes, we would go to the Troubadour coffee bar …still there now. It was a dark coffee house, but there was always someone playing the guitar. They didn't get paid, but it was somewhere for them to practice. You were seen as a true 'arty-crafty' person if you went there.

Tom's other friend was Marcus (Mouse). He was always around somewhere. He had a proper job and worked at Lloyds. He said he had a pinstriped suit and an umbrella hidden in his wardrobe, but I doubt it for Marcus was bordering on mad as well as being one of the kindest people I ever knew. He was classed as an 'artistic type,' which in those days meant that nobody understood him, a sort of odd type, if you know what I mean. He would come to pick me up from the station sometimes, and he generally had his shoes in his hands, or I would find him asleep in the drop down hood of his 'Beatle' car, oblivious of the titters from passersby. That was my Marcus! I secretly adored him, not in a sexy way I don't think. He was very rich and came from York or somewhere up there. He used to say to me that he didn't need money and he carried a suitcase around filled with the essentials in life, like a toothbrush, matches, an umbrella and spearmints. I think he was right; we all have so much baggage we cart around with us, keeping us from flying away and being free!

One day we decided to go to Majorca for a holiday, just Peter, Marcus and me. We spent most of the time drinking too much, especially Negronis, our newly found special drink. It was during a rather liquid lunch that we decided we would buy a piece of land and build a Bird's Nest on it! Well, we did buy about an acre of seafront land, the price was £800. The Notaire said we had to buy it through him as it was against the law for a British person to own land. So, we fell for it, and many years later when I tried to contact the Notaire, his son said he had retired and there seemed to be no papers in the archives. The lovely man who sold it to us was after all just a crook! It was during that holiday that Marcus opened up a little more. I suppose it was the wine, but I could see he needed someone to talk to. It seemed that, reading between the lines, he thought he was gay. Yet, he was telling me this as if he didn't believe it because he was in love with me! Well, I think that's what he meant. I never asked him, and he never told me directly, but I'm pretty sure that is what he was trying to tell me. But I was too inexperienced to sort that sort of problem out.

Peter had to go back to Trinidad as there was a problem with the manager of his Coconut Estate. Marcus called me and asked me to go to a party with some of his friends. I was interested in meeting them and thought perhaps it would answer some of my questions about my dear friend. There were not many people there, and it was more of a 'sit on the floor party' as we all sat on cushions on the floor discussing various subjects. I sat beside someone called Terence Conran who was going out with Fenella Fielding, and we all chatted about his idea of simple furniture that was not going to cost the earth. Furniture for the middle classes… and he was going to call his first shop Habitat. Well, his dream came true didn't it?

I didn't learn anything more about Marcus. I always felt he was on the verge of telling me something, but he just looked at his feet and said nothing. I know he admired Philip Larkin but little else.

Terance Conran as a young man

In time, something in Marcus's life would change my life completely. I will tell you later, but it is a terribly sad story.

AN ASIDE

Life was pretty good although I still hadn't achieved anything to make me really happy or fulfilled. I appreciate now that having three men in love with me was very special, but, of course, we take things like that for granted when we are young - I should be so lucky now!

ANOTHER ASIDE

Apparently, the club Esmeraldo's Barn was owned by the Kray twins...we never saw anything shady there. It was very upmarket, we were led to believe.

Chapter 2 part 4

My best friend Tom - the July plot to kill Hitler

I have a picture of Tom. Looking at him, you might say what a boring looking guy. Of course, he was anything but. Well, maybe a bit, but his family was far from it. Let me tell you about him first. As I have already mentioned, Tom was Peter's best friend at St Bartholomew's medical school, and they spent the entire year at Bart's playing Squash. Peter fell in love with me and so did Tom. So, they both flunked out of their first MDs and blamed me the rest of their lives!

Tom became a Probation Officer and was pretty high up the ladder, apparently. I flirted with him, and it drove him mad, poor man. I know he never stopped loving me, but he was not the man I was looking for.

Neither Tom nor his father had a German accent. Only his mother, a tiny German lady who made wonderful Marble cakes, still had a heavy German accent. Dolly, was Tom's sister and her husband, Mr Kaufman, was the something or other head of the British Museum or was it the V&A? I realised that the family were German and Jewish, but, in truth, they were more British than I was, in a way.

One day in London Tom asked me to come to tea in Calthorpe Street, a house that he shared with Marcus and Bob who worked for BBC on the music side. On the round Mahogany table, tea had been laid out, silver tea pot, bone china cut and saucers and a plate of Rich Tea biscuits. We drank tea and talked about the latest bits of gossip. Then Tom stood up and said, 'Follow me'. He took me into his bedroom, took my hand and said, 'Look at this painting'. It was beautiful, and I knew from my History of Art classes that this was Degas' Blue Dancers. I was so close, I could touch it, but I just stood and stared in bewilderment. Still holding my hand, Tom said, 'If you marry me, I will give the painting to you!'. I thought for a while and then slowly and in a very grown up voice said, 'No, I don't love you enough to marry you'. I didn't have to ask if the painting was real. I knew it was and I knew that I had walked away from a fortune, but, hey, you can't marry someone for a Degas, can you?

On the other hand, I couldn't really just forget the Degas. So, I started asking a few questions here and there, and when I saw Marcus one day at a coffee bar in Swiss Cottage, he told me the story. Tom and his family were German Jews, which I knew anyway, but I didn't know that they were connected to one of the families that had organised the plan to kill Hitler. This was later known as the 'July Plot'. It was decided by some of the Generals, high-ranking officers and wealthy members of society that Hitler had to be dealt with as he was out of control. With great precision they planned the assassination, and the date was set for 30th July as they knew Hitler was to be at a special secret meeting that day.

It was obvious that the wives and children of the 'would be assassins' should not stay in case the plan failed, so a few days before the planned plot, the underground movement smuggled as many men, women and children in case there might be reprisals. By 29th June 1945, the day before the plan to assassinate Hitler, many escaped via the French underground movement, but some of Tom's family didn't make it. When Claus von Stauffenberg placed the bomb, which was in the briefcase, at Hitler's feet, there was hope that that would be the end of the out of control Hitler. Unfortunately, when the bomb exploded, it did not kill him. Some said there was a window opened while others said the briefcase was in the way, so it was moved to the other side of the room; nobody is absolutely sure. Over the next few days, Hitler ordered several Generals, and anyone connected with them to be brought to justice. Even Rommel was implicated in the plot. He was offered poison to kill himself or face a Court Marshal. He chose the former and died quietly, and Hitler gave him a State funeral, which had been agreed if he took the poison.

Thankfully, some of the families had already escaped, including Tom's father, mother, sister and Tom himself. Tom's father, Gunter, was devastated that his brother and sister died alongside the Generals. Nobody talked about the incident. It was all part of their war effort that went wrong. Soon after the war, Tom's aunt Barbel von Haeften, she was Lieutenant von Haeften's wife, was found living in a little village. She had somehow managed to avoid being shot, but Count von Stauffenberg, her brother, was shot, and Hitler continued to rule although most of his Generals were dead. I met Barbel in Heidelberg when I went on a walking holiday with Tom and his family. They were truly wonderful people, and the whole family had tried hard to rid the world of a truly dreadful Dictator but failed. No one mentioned the war.

Tom and his whole family changed their name to Hill. After the war, the Germans began to identify the paintings that had been seized by the Army when they took over wealthy Jewish homes, and slowly the wonderful paintings were returned to their rightful owners. Tom's family were reunited with a couple of Lautrecs, the Degas, a Monet and many others. The problem for Tom and his family was that the paintings were so valuable that they couldn't afford to pay for the insurance, so many were given to galleries and others were just stacked in the kitchen. One Lautrec, the carriage with the dogs running behind, was in the loo, and the sun was directly on it; it faded, which is so sad.

AN ASIDE

Tom and I remained close friends for many years. In the end, he married a nice quiet girl, more suited to him. They had two children and lived happily ever after. Well, not really… Poor Tom contracted MS and died a horrid death, but dear Auriel, his wife, nursed him to the end. I wouldn't have been so good at that. At his funeral, I was so distressed, I couldn't control my grief. Auriel came to me and said, 'The family are leaving now, and we want you to be with him on your own as he loved you so much!'.

What an amazing gesture. I was glad he married her, not me, as she was stronger than I would have been.

Sometimes, I realise how rubbish I am.

Chapter 2 part 5

Profumo Scandal and a narrow escape from Cliveden

At one of the parties I went to at Major Tony Rosette's flat, I remember meeting a young good-looking man. He was short and had a roguish look about him, just my type then! He was very well connected, apparently, and had an Austin Healy (although I preferred Triumphs). Anyway, he seemed to have a way with women and as I was so naïve, I fell for everything he said. His name was Arthur, the same as my stepfather, not a good start, but I avoided calling him that as much as possible. He had some great friend in the country, and he asked my mother if I could have lunch with him one Saturday. He promised to get me back home by 9pm. As Peter didn't wake up until about 4 pm every day, I thought I could get away with it. My mother said, 'Leave it to me', so I did! We arrived at 11am to his friend's house, Cliveden, near Taplow; it belonged to the Astor family. It was a huge house, but that was not where his best friend,

Stephen Ward, lived. He had a wonderful little cottage in the grounds. The main room had a wonderful painted ceiling, and I wish now I could remember what the subject was. I think there were cherubs of some kind. Stephen was charming. He was an Osteopath, apparently, but he was also always drawing. In fact, every time anyone

Cliveden

popped in from the big house, he insisted that he had to draw them. His pencil sketches were really good and always very life like. He did a couple of me, but I threw them away as I didn't like them. He sketched one of Arthur, which I still have today. I wish I had kept mine as they are now worth £600-700 each. Why am I so vain, I wonder! Anyway, Stephen asked us to do something towards lunch as he had to go to collect his girlfriend from the station. Arthur and I laid the table and peeled potatoes, but we couldn't find any food, so we were hoping he would bring something with him. When he arrived back, he had his arm around one of the most beautiful women I had ever seen. Her name was Maggie Brown; she was an American model and very famous.

Well, they did bring a couple of pheasants back from the big house, so we were all set for our lunch party. After lunch, we girls did the washing up. I had put on some false nails - I still bit my nails, so this seemed the best idea. Maggie, of course, guessed about the false nails and insisted I did the washing up. 'What a cow' is all I thought at the time as my nails floated in the washing up bowl! Afterwards, Stephen said, 'Come on, we have to go and buy a double bed for Maggie and me'. So, we walked into town and bought a bed, like you do. When the store man said it couldn't be delivered until Monday, Stephen just said, 'Don't worry. There are four of us'. So, we carried it back to Cliveden! I remember we were all laughing so much, it took longer than we thought. We lifted the bed over our heads, and we trooped down the main road; cars were tooting at us, but Stephen just waved them on. Most people thought we were just students being crazy. We had a cup of tea and some scones that we had bought in the town and threw a log on the fire; everything was lovely - a real country house afternoon.

Arthur suggested he should call my mother to see if I could stay the night as there was going to be a big party at the house tonight, and we had been invited. Well, of course, my mother said 'no', and, sadly, I was put on a train and sent home. That turned out to be a close shave as the next day the papers were full of a police raid on Cliveden in the early hours. Rumour had it that

John Profumo

John Profumo and Stephen Ward were arrested as well as the two girls, Stephen and the two girls, Christine Keeler and Mandy Rice Davis. The charges slowly unfolded over the next few days about Lord Astor's party at Cliveden that night.

Apparently, amongst the guests at the party was the British Secretary of State for War called John Profumo, then a rising 46 year old Conservative Party politician. It seems he was introduced to 19 year old Christine Keeler by Stephen. They said Stephen had contacts in both the aristocracy and the underworld, but that was true of lots of people in those days. At that same party was a military attaché, Eugene Ivanov, who was Christine Keeler's lover. John Profumo began an affair with Keeler, and rumours of the affair started to spread. In 1963 John Profumo lied about the affair in Parliament, stating that 'there was no impropriety whatsoever' in his relationship with Christine Keeler. This was not true, of course, and later he apologised to the House of Commons for his lies with deep remorse. So, as the story was growing each day, it seemed only proper that John Profumo resigned. Prime Minister Macmillan continued in office, but within a few months the Conservative Party was defeated, and Labour won the election. The powers to be tried to argue that Ivanov had intended to entrap Profumo or to use Keeler as an access agent but could not prove it.

Stephen Ward when he was arrested

It all seemed like a film to me, especially when they continued to accuse Stephen of procuring not only those two girls but other girls for the high-ranking men, in other words being a pimp.

Then the press turned on poor Stephen; word got out that he arranged parties and provided a certain type of women for the parties and many other unsavoury things. I didn't believe any of it. He wasn't like that; he did just know a lot of people. What made me really sad for him was that Maggie disappeared back to America the moment there was any mention of trouble, and he was on his own. She deserted him and he needed a friend. It got worse for him as people started making up stories, and the girls gave statements about the antics that went on at the big house; things seemed to get more and more incriminating day by day.

The press became determined to make a big story out of a small story. Finally, Stephen Ward, nice Stephen, a brilliant Osteopath and fine artist, was to go before a judge being accused of procuring and various other things that were made up to make sure the blame was all on his head. Basically, I think we all realised he was being made the scapegoat. Someone had to take the blame, so the problem would go away. The Government had been rocked and that wasn't in the rules.

He beat them all and committed suicide before the Court case. I hope everyone involved felt good about that. I hope Maggie can live with herself too.

Christine Keeler made a fortune selling her story and was famous for a while. Mandy Rice-Davis, another girl at the party, did the same but, of course, if it had been today, it might not have even reached the back page!

AN ASIDE

How lucky John Profumo was to have Valerie Hobson, the wonderful actress and his adoring wife, standing by him through this dreadful case. His career as a Politician was in ruins, but I know his marriage survived, and he was eternally grateful to her for her support.

Chapter 3 part 1

My first job in Tin Pan Alley

I think the narrow escape I had from the Profumo drama taught me a lesson. Perhaps I should not have strayed into a world that I didn't understand. A few days later, I received a letter from my College to say that there was vacancy in a company called UMP - United Motion Pictures. 'Wow' that was for me, I thought, a career in films; well, actually, a telephonist, but everyone had to start somewhere.

I went to the interview and to my amazement they hired me. I did feel they were desperate, but I was over the moon. I was to be in charge of the telephones and do the filing. The manageress's name was Miss Remington. She was terrifying, but I was determined to make a success of my new career. I tried really hard to be good at my job, but I seemed to get in a terrible muddle with the wires. It was one of those plug in old fashioned phones; I got the first bit right by saying a cheerful voice (no stutter) 'Good morning UMP can I help you?' Then, after that, I went to pieces. I got away with murder by smiling and saying 'sorry' rather a lot. That worked for a while, but soon my sweet charm wore thin. Paramount got put through to the kitchen and Warner Brothers got cut off, three times!

I enjoyed going to work in Denmark Street as it was full of interesting companies like Noel Gay, who were involved in the music business. Nowadays, it would be a very 'cool' place to work, but at the time it was a bit of a nightmare for me, especially as I realised I was not managing particularly well at the new job. Soon, I was dreading going in to work, which was not what I expected from my new career.

Every day something important seemed to happen at UMP. It was where Frank Phillips, with his wonderful voice, would do various documentaries. He was the voice of Pathe News for the cinema. He was a lovely man too; a real gentleman, my mother said. I would take him a cup of coffee in-between his broadcasting, and, often, he asked me to sit down beside him and we would talk. That was long before all the accusations about young girls and older men were ever discussed. He used to tell me not to despair; I was so pretty, so, perhaps, I should think of another career.

In fact, everyone working at UMP seemed to think I should become a mannequin. It was finally a man called Forbes Taylor, the cartoonist, who came to my rescue. He took me out one lunch time and bought me some nylon stockings and a pair of Stiletto shoes from Lilley and Skinners in Oxford Street. Well, there was not much telephone work done by me over the next few days. Actually, I had lost interest. I tried hard to come to terms with the challenge of high heels as I had only walked in Cuban heels before. Miss Remington continued to frown at me, but one day she came into the office with a Woman's Own magazine. There was an article about 'walking like a man', and that's how I learnt to walk with attitude. Very important. No more mincing girlie walk for me. Later, when I became a well-known mannequin, I was known for my slinky slide!

The next step was to apply to Lucy Clayton agency. I would not have been brave enough to apply, but Frank with his famous voice called them and suggested they should see me, and, of course, they had to see me.

I remember I was wearing my best Wetheral suit and, obviously, my new shoes. I glimpsed at myself in a big mirror, and I looked 'the bee's knees'. My appointment was at 3.15, and I went to Selfridges to check my make-up in their ladies room. Then as that big Selfridge clock struck 3, I walked very slowly over the road to the Lucy Clayton offices.

They hated me. I was too short neck to waist (not sure what they meant), had bad legs and no confidence, good walk, but the answer was big NO! When I got back to the office, there was a letter on my desk. I had been fired, so that was the first of many job rejections in my life. BUT as I walked towards to the tube in Bond Street, I decided to sit in the garden in Hanover Square before going home to Ealing to tell my mother about the dreadful day. I was sitting on the wooden bench looking at my feet when I heard a dusky voice saying, 'Keep your heels high and your spirits even higher darling… and never look down!'. I looked up and there was a cuddly looking man with a large pimple on his nose clutching the lead of a big white bulldog. He was to be my saviour, but I didn't know it at the time.

He sat down and we started talking. I told him what had happened, and he shrieked with delight. 'Darling, it's fate meeting like this. My name is Michael Whittaker, and I am setting up a new agency, and you must be my first mannequin. We are going to set the world alight. You will be part of a great new agency, so I insist you join Michael Whittaker Enterprises. Together, you and my girls will conquer the fashion world; don't miss this chance darling!'

I was smitten; he seemed so kind and so dedicated to his idea. Of course, I did completely forget what my mother had said about talking to strangers, but I believed this man was genuine and over the next 3 years, I knew my first impressions of him were correct.

He wrote down his address, 33 Brook Street, top floor, just off Bond Street, and gave me his phone number. We arranged to meet in a week when he had moved into his new offices. Meanwhile, he suggested that I should go to a proper hairdresser's like Rene on Hay Hill, off Berkeley Square, and then to call Tom Hustler, the society photographer, to have some pictures taken for my portfolio. He also said to tell them to send him the bills – 'Remember Whittaker Enterprises!' He left in a 'swirly way', which I understood later was the way he left every meeting.

By the time I went into the tube station, I was on cloud 9; what a day! I went to the phone box the next day and booked an appointment with Rene, mentioning Michael's name. It was as if I had said the Queen had sent me. Thank goodness I had saved a little from my wages and although Rene waived the charges. I thought I had better go to Fenwick's to buy another pair of silk stockings and some make-up, so I would be prepared for the future. I must tell you at this point that during the early 60s, Fenwick's was THE place for mannequins to go and spend a penny and redo their make-up. The attendants were wonderful; they were excited if you had got a booking and sympathetic if you had no work; they were truly our only support in what seemed a very hard business for young girls like us.

I telephoned Tom Hustler, and he booked me in for a photo session the next day. I remember it clearly as I was so agitated, knowing that I was not an easy person to photograph. Even I could tell that I might be better as a catwalk mannequin as opposed to a photographic model. The photos were not amazing. I still have them now; you could see I was pretty but not model material. Well, Michael saw this and decided to make me one of the best mannequins that there was.

He recruited a beautiful mannequin called Hanneli Dane, and she took me under her wings. I adored her, and she was very flattered. I remember she asked me to walk and turn. 'Right, well, the walk is fabulous, darling, but the rest of you is a disaster. A real challenge.' She worked with me every morning for 2 weeks. I walked up and down the catwalk, twirling and twirling, not as easy as you think, but by the end of my gruelling training, Michael and Hanneli were very pleased. I could sit gracefully, get in and out of a car as if it was a Rolls

Hanneli Dane

Royce and I owned it. They tried to get me to adopt a snooty look, but then they decided that I could be their giggly pretty mannequin. Michael chose music for me and insisted whenever I was on stage, this music must be played; 'Younger than Springtime' from South Pacific was the tune, and it brought me good luck and a very successful career in the end.

AN ASIDE

Most of my friends envied me as to them, being a mannequin was very glamorous. They would ask me all the time where I had been and what shows I had been in. I suppose it was a bit like that; yes, when we travelled, we naturally travelled first class everywhere; we stayed in 5 star hotels and ate at all the best restaurants in town. But it wasn't all glamour; there were endless fittings where you were put on a chair and pins would be stuck into you, sometimes on purpose, I think. We had to stay skinny, although we all ate like horses, and most of all we had to look beautiful at all times when we slid up the catwalk. I can tell you that the shoes we were made to wear were crippling, and we all had corns; lots of us had varicose veins through standing for so long, but a nicer bunch of friends you could not wish for. If anyone had boyfriend trouble or felt unwell, we would work doubly hard to cover up for the girl in trouble. Boy, did we get up to tricks; we never missed a thing. In fact, I am sure sometimes I got bookings because I was always up to something! Being away from home for weeks on end was not really fun, so you had to laugh your way through everything, and the friendships made during those years were very strong and lasted for many, many years.

Chapter 3 part 2

Becoming a mannequin NOT a model

Everyone who was anyone was at the opening party for the agency. The press cameras clicked at anything moving, and the flash bulbs flashed away nonstop; it was like the Oscars in America. We were all interviewed by the BBC and, of course, by Tatler and Queen Magazine. That was the first time I met Vidal Sassoon; he had been dragged along to Michael Whittaker's new venture, and I could see he was a bit grumpy. After all, he was on the 'A' list in those days and had to be seen at all the big events; even if they weren't big now they could be big later, and he, like me, had to be 'exposed' as much as possible. Vidal had a small hairdresser's in Grosvenor Street, upstairs with Leonard. Later, when I knew about things like that, I thought he was the better hairdresser. Vidal, Leonard, Gerrard and Eddie Morris were four hairdressers from the East End who all made it to the top in the early sixties. To be recognised, you had to have your hair done by one of those hairdressers; you also dined at the same group of restaurants and just waited until your look came into fashion, or somebody somewhere liked your look and booked you. It was a waiting game for us all.

I met some lovely people at the agency. The men were generally bit part actors, who, for a laugh had signed up to be photographic models to add to their income from acting or being a waiter.

Me

the mannequins at Michael Whittaker Enterprises

As it soon became apparent that Whittaker Enterprises was going to be an important agency, I thanked my lucky stars that I had joined it that miserable day in June. There were about 20 girls on the agency's books. We had a head booker called Carla, who was very elegant and had been a mannequin in the 50s. Celia was her understudy but seemed to do most of the work whilst Carla sat behind her desk looking beautiful. Then there was Bill, who was Michael's 'partner'. They all looked after us so well. They were there to cuddle when the audition went wrong and also be ready with champagne when it went well. We were like one great family of beautiful looking human beings.

Every day before we went to our auditions, we would meet up in Fenwick's ladies room to 'put on our faces' and to catch up on all the latest gossip. There was a lot to talk about, which was to be expected with so many sexy young girls and handsome young men just hanging around waiting for something to happen. Actually, it was really quite innocent; we would chat about a new boyfriend or a new film we had seen. Sex wasn't really discussed then, and, compared with the talk nowadays, we were little angels, well some of us were! Before you got your first booking, you went through hell. You had no money, even for 10 Senior Service cigarettes. We all smoked in those days, sometimes with a long cigarette holder like Princess Margaret, and we were always hungry. I was lucky because I still lived at home, so there was always food there and plenty of crinkle chips when I was with Peter. Michael warned all his 'little girls' that things would be tough, but we had to be patient. Any day now, the phone would ring, and you would have a booking. Whilst you were waiting for that call, you had to keep yourself in tip-top condition, always ready for the big break. Nails had to be polished, eyebrows trimmed and teeth whiter than white. Michael would say, 'Just remember that you are a Whittaker girl, stand straight and look to the future'. But we were all eager to get on with our new careers as well as being hungry all the time!

My moment came when Louis Rubens and Lou Rawlings, owners of a very successful trendy dress company called California Cottons, were walking along Grosvenor Street. They stopped and looked

California
COTTONS
2nd Floor

at the Whittaker Enterprises smart new sign. I came out that very moment and they asked me if I was one of Michael's mannequins. I said I was, and they said they would go up to congratulate Michael on his new venture.

An hour later, I got a call from Michael to say 'darling you enchanted Louis and Lou. They want you to start work at California Cottons at once. You will be paid £5 per week as a house mannequin, 5 days a week'. Well, that was it. I had made it, fame at last!

I started the next day and spent the following 3 months putting labels on the backs of the dresses and making cups of tea for everyone. Bored doesn't even come close to how I felt. Was this my life?

I think at this point, Louis realised I was bored and disappointed. One day he came into the dressing room to tell me that there was a very important buyer called Miss Peacock, from Richard Shops, coming to see both collections, and I was to show the collection to her with another mannequin that had been booked to help me. I was pretty nervous. My face had turned bright red, and my skin went sort of blotchy on my chest and arms. It was nerves, I suppose, but I did look at bit odd. Everything went well for the first half hour, and I was beginning to relax. We had to change quickly as there were only two of us. We had no dresser, but we worked well as a team. I twirled around the showroom under the big chandeliers and began to enjoy myself. Miss Peacock seemed to look straight through us, but, after all, we were just moving hangers to her.

All of a sudden, she shouted very loudly, 'Louis get rid of that girl. She's too thin and too young!'. I was devastated and as I was in the middle of my twirl, I nearly fell over. Louis rushed over to catch me and whisked me off into the dressing room. 'Sit,' he said, and I did.

Later, when the buyer left, Louis came to me to explain why Miss Peacocks had been so rude. She was always like that, apparently. She was jealous of young thin mannequins and as she was such an important buyer, with a large 'open to buy' budget, anything she said was like the Holy Grail. She insisted I should be given my notice before she would come back into the showroom, so sacked I was. But not before Louis suggested that I showed the California Cottons collection to the customers who lunched in the restaurant at Swan and Edgar's, the big store at the end of Regent Street. 'It will be a good move for you, and you will gain confidence,' he said. So, I thanked him and the next day I went to the store where I was treated like a Queen. I had my own little dressing room. They brought a rail of dresses in and some accessories and explained that all I had to do was to walk up and down the aisles holding my California Cotton badge; I still have it now. If anyone wanted to feel the material or ask how much it was, I had to discuss the merits of the dress and, hopefully, they would go after their lunch or tea to the department and buy one. Well, I was a hit, and sales were really good. The head of the department came to say how pleased they were, and Louis called Michael and said what a great success I was - my first appearance in public and I was a success. There was no way they could stop me now. Here I come. Little shy Wendy Lewis was about to tackle the world! (I had changed my name when I became a mannequin to my father's name as Cowen didn't sound very theatrical.)

Chapter 3 part 3

Peter always waiting – my Svengali

As I became more and more successful as a mannequin, I had to go away on trips and was always abroad or locked up in rehearsal rooms late at night. Peter went along with it for a while, but I think he felt we were drifting apart. I knew we were, but there was little I could do about it. Peter had dug a hole for himself; he never got up in the mornings until 11 or 12 o'clock, sometimes even later, whilst I was up and off most mornings by 8am. I didn't live with Peter but with my mother in Ealing where I had a little room at the front of the house. Next door lived, I thought, one of the most wonderful men in the world. He was also training to be a Doctor at Bart's; Peter had already been asked to leave by then. His name was John Bench. He slept in the next room in the next house, so in my juvenile mind we were almost sleeping together; after all, there were only a few bricks between us. At night I would lie in my bed thinking of him and having make believe conversations and bit by bit, all one sided, I fell deeply in love with him.

Remember, I was not supposed to look at anyone else. I was earmarked to be Peter's bride, but I was young and a little attractive by now, and men did pay me a lot of compliments, which I enjoyed. Peter was always very serious and didn't believe in trivial talk; it had to be a discussion. Having worked hard all day, I would go to see him, and he would talk for 4 or 5 hours, always very serious subjects and way above my head. He would drive me back to Ealing before I fell asleep. This was the case most nights. So, whilst all my new friends were being wined and dined by various men about town, I was just sitting and listening to Peter and his views. He never asked me if I had any views; perhaps I didn't have any, but it would have been nice had he asked me. Our sex life was very regimented; we made love a couple of times every time we met. Every 'session' lasted a long time and I don't think he thought much about my pleasure. I thought that was what 'making love' was all about.

Anyway, one night when I got home, I saw a note pushed under my door. It was from delicious John next door! Would I, Wendy, like to come to Bart's wine and cheese party with him on Friday? How the hell was I going to get out of seeing Peter? The next day, in the dressing room, I asked the girls what I should do. One of the older mannequins, said at once, 'Don't worry. I will cover for you. I will call Peter, he likes me I think, and ask him if you could help me with a dress

I'm making and to allow you to stay the night'.

It worked and he agreed. So, wearing one of the samples from Polly Peck collection where we were working that week, and taking extra care with my make-up, not too much though, I caught a taxi to the City. John was waiting for me, and the evening was a great success, I think. We discussed his dreams and mine. We laughed at some of my stories. It was very late, and John drove me back to Ealing. Without thinking, I turned to him and planted a big juicy kiss on his lips! John pushed me away saying 'no, no', and he turned and left. I have no idea why I kissed him, but, in a way, it seemed natural as in my mind, we had been sleeping together for months. But he had no idea that I felt that way, and even I had to admit there was a great big wall between us! So, for the first time, I had been personally rejected. I continued to love him, but we never went out again. So, back to Peter and those long boring evenings.

I asked Peter if he could teach me to drive as I was saving for my first car. He agreed, but it was not as I expected. He made me sit in the passenger seat with my eyes closed and told me to listen to the noises of the engine. He started up the engine. I then had to tell him if there was anything wrong with the engine. Listen for each noise and explain each one. Only when I got everything right, several days later, did he put the car into gear, and I had to tell him when the 'revs' were right, so he could change gear. Bloody boring, I can tell you. It was 6 months later when he said I could go to BSM and take lessons. I think my instructor was mesmerised by the fact that I immediately told him that his crank shaft sounded suspect!! I passed first time, naturally, and bought myself a bright blue Standard 10 van, which had been in a 'right off' and was covered in blood and chicken feathers inside! It cost me only £187, feathers and all! I know how much Peter loved me, and I was very young, but I had not had much fun in my life so far. Still, I didn't dare to say that I would like to stand on my own two feet and neither my mother nor Peter seemed to take me into account. I felt like a dummy that they tossed around. 'Go to this ball,' or 'wear this dress,' 'don't go out with your friends'. In other words, I was restricted in everything I did. I began to realise that my love for Peter was dwindling. I knew I loved him, but I needed to breathe on my own. The world now was opening up, and I wanted to fly; but my wings had been clipped, and I wasn't man enough to stand up for myself.

I think I had been so brainwashed that I believed everything Peter told me. He never came to see me on the catwalk, so he could never say 'you looked lovely' or 'what a stupid outfit you were wearing'. So, there wasn't much we could discuss as far as my life went. I spent the weekends in his hot bedroom with the gas fire on and the windows sealed up with tape, so no air could get in. He hated the cold. The room always smelt of Swarfega (a green gel that mechanics used to clean oil of their hands) as now he had decided to become a mechanic. He spent all his time on his Ariel 500 motorbike or was under the bonnet of one of his friend's cars. So, I too became a car buff and bored everyone I met by talking about De Dion back axles!

AN ASIDE

I'm sure that in those days I really loved Peter. He was my first love, after all, and I knew he loved me. But if you have nobody to make comparisons with, how do you know if he is the right man for you?

I knew it would make my mother happy if Peter and I married, but I wanted to make my own choice, and so I stuck my heels in.

Chapter 3 part 4

Men in raincoats

Being a mannequin was fun and hard work all at the same time. The hours were erratic and so was the pay. I think now, looking back, that Michael was finding it more difficult than he thought to run an agency. The clients didn't pay quickly, and so he couldn't pay his mannequins regularly. Thus, I was always broke. One day some of us got together in the ladies at Fenwick's to air our views. This couldn't go on. We would go together to confront him, so we walked down Brook Street, all 6 of us, and up 4 flights of stairs. Michael was at the top, arms crossed and waiting for a fight. He had heard about the unrest and was prepared for a fight!

Needless to say, when it came to confronting him, the other girls slipped behind me, and I was left to be the spokeswoman alone. I told him how unhappy we were and how difficult it was to work hard and seemingly never get paid. Of course, he was very sympathetic and understanding. He told us about the slow paying clients and his cash flow problems. Then I came up with an idea. Perhaps he could work on a plan to pay us all a basic minimum 'wage' to cover our costs like rent, transport and food, and then when the client paid, the agency would take their cut and pay us the balance. The idea went down well, but I had to have the last say as usual, so I added, 'if you don't agree we will all leave and go to another agency'. Michael went berserk. 'How dare you stand there Wendy Lewis and stamp your foot at me, after all I have done for you!'. I remember it to this day. He was right, and I was wrong, but my only wish, at the time, was that the floor would open up and swallow me whole. I never crossed him again. He did, in fact, take on board the method of payment, and soon other agencies followed suit, using the same system. So, I sort of won, in a way!

So, back to work. A booking came through for 3 girls from the agency. I was one of them. The client was a very popular group of stores called Fifth Avenue, a Jewish company who were very up to date and popular with the 20 - 30 year olds. They had the brilliant idea of making the window a stage. There were 3 big windows and the 2 main ones were on Regent Street, at the Oxford Circus end and, therefore, very busy with passersby.

Everything worked very well to start with, but as word got out that there were live mannequins in the windows, the sleaze started. You would be twirling around the floor and then perhaps stop for a moment so the customers could see the whole outfit clearly, and at that point, the men in the front row would open their raincoats to reveal various naked parts of their bodies, especially those 'little bits!'. At first, it was a shock; then it was quite funny, but in the end it was so disgusting, that the directors had to put members of the staff outside with long sticks. They would tap the 'raincoat' on the shoulder with the stick and nod knowingly with a menacing look.

I think one of my favourite memories was of the 'cow shows'. We called them that but, in fact, they were fashion shows put on by either ICI, British Nylon Spinners or Wool Secretariat. The venues were around the country, in the summer, at the Agricultural shows. There were generally about 8 of us that were booked for the shows. It paid well, and we were totally spoilt as Michael made sure of that. First class from day one. We were issued with wellie boots and rain hats. At first, we wondered what the hell we had let ourselves in for, but after the first show at the Bath and West farm show, we understood. The rain, the mud and the smell of cow dung was everywhere, but who cared? We had so much fun, it didn't matter. Perhaps it was the genuine kindness of the farmers who thought they had gone to Heaven with so many pretty mannequins around. We had to go on a press call most mornings, generally cuddling a cow or feeding a goat. I suppose, it was meant to make some sort of statement, but nobody seemed to know if the public were buying more of their fabrics. The fashion shows were full every day, so we must have been doing some good somewhere!

On one occasion, we were asked if we would mind being in an experimental film, so that the cameramen could test the film in different lighting conditions.

Whilst most homes in the 60s had TVs, many were only in black and white. Of course, we agreed; anything for a bit of publicity was our motto. Somewhere in BBC archives is a picture of me talking and stroking a cow whilst standing in a field. The results were hilarious; my face was bright green like the grass in the field and the cow and brown with green patches. It was so funny, I wish someone could find it and let the world see one of the funniest programmes ever made by BBC.

As far as Peter and I were concerned, it was agreed that I was to be allowed more freedom. He understood I needed my head and agreed to let me be away a lot during the summer months at the 'cow shows'. He thought there was no danger that I would stray when I was away with 8 girls travelling around from show to show.

He was wrong. I met someone called Alan Davidson. He was very good looking, but he was an alcoholic. We were really good together until the booze took over. I think that was because he thought I was beautiful and out of his reach, so the more he drunk, the easier it was for him to believe that I loved him. Actually, I don't think love came into it, but I was young and free, for the time being anyway. Sometimes, when he was in London, he would arrange to come to see me after his meetings, but by that time he was so drunk, he had to be put in a taxi. He would turn up, fall out of the taxi into a heap and say, 'Wendy, Wendy, I love you' in a loud voice and then pass out. It happened many times, and I would get calls from his hotel concierge saying that he was at the desk crying for me or other desperate cries for help... I must say it was a real turn off, but when I saw him again at the next 'cow show', that boyish grin just melted my heart, so off we would go again.

One night after a rather boozy meal with the 'gang', I put my key down on the table so that Alan could see which room I was in; then I said 'goodnight' to everyone and went upstairs. I was lying on the bed with not much on. I had my back to the door. I heard the door open and expecting that it was Alan, so I turned over saying something like, 'Darling, I need you,' in my sexiest voice. Well, when I turned over, it was not Alan standing there but Philip the MD of ICI....I screamed. He said, 'sorry sorry' and backed out of the room looking confused for he had thought the key thing was meant for him. Alan never showed up, and the next day I was dropped from the team. I was very sad that it had ended, but I think for Alan's sake it was probably for the best. I never saw or heard from him again. Only when they play 'our' tune on the radio do I think of him. The Righteous Brothers 'You've lost that Loving Feeling'.

Chapter 3 part 5

Pinewood Studios…my own dressing room

By now, I was earning quite a lot of money and beginning to understand what I wanted in life. However, I was still doing the rounds of parties and balls with Tony and still seeing Peter the nights I was around. I did miss going out with my friends as I used to do when I was at college, but it seemed ungrateful to put a stop to all the endless parties when it was so important to my mother. I had become used to my new expensive lifestyle. So, my life was split in two, really, the 'show off' balls and pretending I was something I wasn't and the utter spoiling I received from being a mannequin, then back down to earth with the Wimpy and crinkle chips with Peter.

Every opening of every restaurant or club, I was there. I appeared weekly in 'Jennifer's Diary.'

I loved working with the male models; they had my sense of humour, and 80% of them in those days were not 'pansy boys' as my mother called them. They were just good-looking young men and generally 'would be' actors. One boy called Steve was the rugged type and got lots of work doing road drilling adverts or truck drivers. He wasn't like that at all; in fact, he was

IN LONDON LAST NIGHT

Miss Wendy Lewis at the May Fair Hotel last night. She was one of the guests at the St. Mark's Ball.—See WINNERS.

me in Jennifer's diary

a pussycat deep down. We had a sort of fling, well a lot of kissing in the front room, with my mother calling out, 'I know what you are up to!'. So, nothing really developed with him, which was a good thing really as I'm not sure he was going places, and I was!

Make a note: 'need flat of my own soon!'. Living with my mother was very convenient as she did my laundry and cleared up after me. Poor mother worked all day and cleaned all night. We never heard from my stepfather, and I was thankful that at last my mother had come to her senses. I hoped she could have some peace now instead of the drunken abuse she received from my stepfather. I was told that my brother was working on a farm and was very happy, but I missed him. Soon after that we found a flat in Chiswick with 2 bedrooms….at last a room of my own…but she waited up for me every night, and I let her do my washing, of course! My mother now worked at Harvey

Nichols in the lingerie department. Her favourite customer was Princess Alexandra, she always asked for my mother to serve her, which naturally made my mother very proud. They both had a love of delicate lingerie and until she died my mother always had beautiful underwear, unlike me as nothing ever matched and often, I never wore any anyway!

As I was well established in the fashion world by now, I was booked for all the main fashion shows at Harrods, Simpsons and Harvey Nichols. In between the shows, I would go and do a season and special press shows. This means that you go to work as an in-house mannequin for 5-6 weeks and they had various important buyers in and the press always wanted a story. There was generally some story around me, so they always hung around just in case. The press and the audiences liked me because I was very glamorous as well as a bit giggly and, of course, I was seen on the town with the most delicious males, none of which broke my heart, but I remember them with a warm smile. It was alright having a bit of 'hankie pankie' with them but never anything serious as I knew I belonged to Peter. I never stayed out too late with any man but sneaked out at every opportunity to go dancing or to eat, my two passions in life then. I went out with a man only if he could afford to take me to Wheeler's or Prunier's for Lobster Thermidor. I ate a lot of Lobsters, I remember!

My agents Michael and Celia, she had been made a partner by now, decided to promote me more by sending me to auditions for Film and TV commercials. Well, it proved an excellent decision as I got one commercial after another. I was 'the girl next-door type' and pretty silly with it, so I was always chosen as

I fitted in with the director's idea of the 'girl next door'. The other mannequins always stuck to their snooty look; pity, really, as I was making the money. I was asked if I had an Equity card, which you should have if you were going to speak in any of the commercials. But I flatly refused to speak as I was happy clowning around, and the thought of speaking in public reminded me of that chair and the poetry that I was made to recite as a child.

It seems funny now, but when TV was in its infancy, the film and TV companies had to be very careful with what they were allowed to show or do. I think Mary Whitehouse was around then, and she vetted everything, making everyone's life a misery. I remember my first commercial was for Tetley tea. I was supposed to be a wife and John, a model friend, was to be my husband. He looked about 18 in his striped pyjamas and dressing gown, and I looked nearer to 12 in a flannelette nightie with bows on and a sort of shawl thing in case any flesh showed. There was a problem, as we were supposed to be married and in bed, a double bed at that, and it was a bit risqué. The director thought they would not get away with it, so they put a big bolster down the middle of the bed so we didn't touch each other. I saw the rushes and I looked pregnant as the bolster was so big. Anyway, it was very funny. My husband had to yawn and stretch, without showing any flesh, and say, 'How about a cup of tea darling,' and I just had to smile and say 'Tetley's?' and he said, 'Of course.' Then a little jingle was played, and that was it. One hundred guineas just like that AND repeat fees, which meant every time the advert was shown, I got 2 Shillings or something like that.

Hey, I was on my way to being rich!

I loved working at Pinewood best as they always sent a car for me at about 5 am and the chauffeur would wrap a blanket around me and say, 'Go to sleep Miss. We will soon be there'. When we arrived at the gates, the doorman would salute, and I would just nod. My dressing room was fit for a Queen. A Chaise Longue if I was tired, an amazing dressing table brightly lit with light bulbs around it. In the corner, I had my own Avocado coloured wash basin. Make-up and hair was first, and this was done whilst you looked over the script, wordless for me.

I remember one particular advert was for Sketchley Dry Cleaners. I had a tan colour frock on, and I was supposed to be waving at someone. Wardrobe had a problem, and so did I, for the lights were so hot and I was so nervous that I had big sweat marks under my armpits. They tried fans to cool me down and kept drying the dress, but my nerves got the better of me, and I was near to tears. All of a sudden, someone who had been watching my pitiful efforts came from behind the cameras with a glass of water and a pill. 'Take this dear. It will calm you down. Don't worry. I take them all the time.' It was Norman Wisdom. In half an hour the dress was dry, and I was calm, so calm I could have said one or two words if pushed.

During my lunch break, I went and thanked him, and he gave my hand a little squeeze and winked at me.

Now, lunch breaks at Pinewood were special as whatever scene you were doing, you stopped when it was lunchtime. The crew and actors all flowed into the big dining hall and soon everything was silent except for the clatter of knives and forks. The funniest thing was that at the table you could have two Roman soldiers talking to a brain surgeon or perhaps three gypsies and a couple of fairies chatting over a chocolate sundae. I was having my lunch one day when I was joined by Stanley Baker (a film star in Zulu), Dirk Bogarde with his new boyfriend, who was also his cook, and Cliff Richard. He didn't know it, but I loved him, and I stopped eating as my mouth was hanging open. Cliff turned to me and said, 'Can you pass the salt'. I froze like a statue, so he came and took it out of my hand! Like all girls of my age, I loved our film stars and even if I was pretty grand myself, I still asked for an autograph, although not this time as I think I just melted into a puddle at their feet…I was invisible!

My most successful commercial was for Windolene window cleaner. The advert was such a success it was shown at all the cinemas around the country and on TV. Soon, I was noticed by everyone and people would stop me and ask for my autograph as if I was a film star. I would be walking down the street and look up, and people would see me and start the 'wipe it on wipe it off' action that I had to do. It was rather nice although I did pretend it was nothing special as if I was indeed a film star. All I know is that for months after the last filming, I had huge muscles from the wiping off the Windolene under the hot spotlights in the studios. I had to pretend it was easy to wipe it off, but it dried so quickly, thus the biceps!

One day I was booked with my girlfriend Jill Pengelli to work with Tom Jones at the Shepherd's Bush Empire. All we two sexy little girls had to do as Tom, who was pretending to be a cameraman, moved the camera to front of screen as he sang, was to jump up and down with balloons. Easy, but we got carried away and jumped up and down in front of Tom and nobody could see him! We were sacked!

It was a good year for cars. British cars seemed to be taking over the market. I was booked along with Raymond Baxter, a commentator who specialized in promoting cars. The first commercial we did was for The Truimph Herald, square looking car, nice engine, and its only gimmick was that the bonnet opened up away from the windscreen in one piece.

Then I was booked for a photoshoot to introduce the new Standard 10. What a boring car! But I suppose I should have been grateful for the work, and I enjoyed being around cars and talking about cars. Peter had drummed it into me, so I lived and breathed cars. In those days pretty girls were supposed to just smile and be 'window dressing'. Of course, it helped that the famous car correspondent, Raymond Baxter enjoyed my company, so work poured in and I was 'in the money'.

AN ASIDE

Many years later I went to a party given for one of my daughter's friends 40th birthday and for some reason I was asked too. When I went into the house I squealed with delight. The house was owned by J. Arthur Rank and he had let his niece, I think, live in it as long as nothing was changed. In the house were the exact basins I had in my dressing room at Pinewood, the avocado ones, and the same dressing tables. It was like going back 40 years, wonderful! Actually, I think they found it a bit difficult living there as every now and again Mr Rank would appear to check everything was in its correct place and move things about a little to make a statement.

Chapter 4 part 1

My darling Jean - she was like a sister

AVEDON

When Jean and I first met at Polly Peck, the fashion house in Conduit Street, we were mannequins and had been booked for their press show. We didn't expect to become such great friends, for when we first met we didn't like each other very much.. It's strange how first impressions aren't always right. I do it all the time. I say, 'It's easy to sum someone up at first meeting'. Wrong! I do talk rubbish sometimes. I jump to conclusions about everything; perhaps it's my pig headedness, who knows? Jean's face appeared in all the glossy magazines; she was a photographic model and at a different agency, Jean Bell. She had been married before to lovely Les Condon, who loved her more than himself, such a sweet man, but he played trumpet at Ronnie Scott's, so he was asleep all day and worked with Ronnie all night. Jean hung around the club, but it was inevitable that she would stray. They divorced, and Les never got over it. Many years later, he died alone in a basement room shortly after Ronnie Scott committed suicide. Actually, it was really sad in the case of Ronnie's death. He had a habit of calling his daughter saying he was going to commit suicide, but it never happened. This time, his daughter thought it was just another 'cry for help,' and didn't rush over as she usually did. This time it was true, and he did manage to kill himself.

Jean went on holiday to Marbella after Les died and met Philip Levene, the writer who wrote some of the Avengers; he was such a kind man. He used to say to me, 'Wendy, you will never write your book if you don't get a work plan'. He was right. Many years later, I am still struggling with my work plan. I wish he was here to guide me. He had his Genizah, which was his good luck charm. He left that to me in his will. When he died, in the Marsden hospital, he left a lot of money to a friend and also to Jean, but it seemed to disappear, who knows where. Jean never had a penny, and Philip has been dead for 30 years! After Philip's death, Jean went to work in New York with Whilomena's agency, and she was photographed by Avedon, the famous American photographer. I have the original hanging in my hall, so beautiful. She didn't stay long. Mainly, although she had a beautiful face, she didn't have that willow type of body that was in fashion in New York at the time.

Some time ago, I had met a racing driver at one of Tony Rosetti's parties called Michel Urman. He gave me his card and said, 'call me if you are ever in Paris'. I called him, and he said Jean and I could stay with him in his gorgeous house on Avenue Victor Hugo. He asked if we could help him with a dinner party that he was throwing later that week. That will be fun, we thought. Well, not really fun, but interesting if I remember correctly. Michel gave us a shopping list and a bundle of francs. Great, but he was French, and we were English. I could cook spaghetti al Burro and Bolognese, and Jean could make coffee! We managed somehow. We put chunks of fresh baguettes in a basket and then plonked a load of Pates which we bought from a local deli. Then there were 2 huge bowls of pasta and my two sauces, and finally, we bought a selection of pastries from Fauchon. It went down really well. I think it was so different in those days when the French ate meat with a sauce of some kind, always with unpronounceable names!

After the meal, someone played guitar and we sat around smoking, and it was very relaxed. I asked Michel where Jean and I could sleep, and he showed us to a bedroom with a single bed in it; to get to it, you had to go through his room. Once we went to bed, we realised that Michel had picked one of the girls at the party to go to bed with Fine, but then both Jean and I needed to go to the loo! No way was I going to interrupt Michel's love making... there was nothing else we could do, so we opened the window, perched on the sill and peed out of the window. Thank goodness it was late, and there was nobody in the street! We fell about laughing. Michel came in to see what the problem was and asked us to join him. We declined!

Jean and I stayed on for a few days. Nothing was mentioned about the party. We continued to laugh, joke and generally make a nuisance of ourselves. I always had so much fun when I was with her; she was like a sister to me, and I loved her to bits.

I'm not sure she understood my relationship with Peter, but she never said anything, and they seemed to put up with each other. Everyone liked Jean, but as Peter only wanted to talk about cars, or have a serious discussion of some kind, they rarely talked to each other. Jean didn't do serious!

An old friend, Brian Morris, a photographer, phoned me one day to ask if Jean and I would go to New York for him to sell pages in his famous Photographers Book. He had no American photographers in the book, and he decided to do a section of the book of top US photographers. Actually, I think he fancied Jean, and it seemed a good way to get to spend time with her. It never happened. Brian was not her type in many ways. We went to New York and stayed with Brian's rep out there. I am messy at times, but the room we were given was disgusting. They had had tiny black rat type dog called Mighty Mighty. They loved him so much, he was allowed to do anything that took his fancy. So, he fancied doing his poo in my bed! I ticked him off, and they heard me. They suggested that if we complained again, we could find somewhere else to stay. Well, the atmosphere was not brilliant as you can image. Our hearts weren't really into this cold sell business. We went to lots of studios and sold a few pages, but I don't think we even covered the expense of the two flights. Again, we just laughed our way through each day, mainly because we kicked poor Mighty Mighty every time we saw him! Thank God dogs can't talk!

I don't think we were very popular with Brian when we got back, but, honestly, if he could have seen the room we were supposed to live in, perhaps he would have understood. We were just happy to have escaped from the whole Brian is no longer a friend I suppose, not because of that episode but for another reason which I prefer not to disclose, which is sad after so many years of friendship. A missed opportunity on my behalf or perhaps a lucky escape, I realised later on. Maybe I will tell you why later in the book or maybe not, let's see! Whilst we were in New York, Jean and I decided to give up smoking when we returned to London. For Jean, it meant stopping smoking a packet of 20, but for me, it meant giving up 60 cigarettes during the day and another 40 if I went out in the evening, in other words 100 a day! So, we made plans. First try Acupuncture. Well we made an appointment the day we returned to UK for both of us, and we had high hopes. The Acupuncture session, well, that was useless, they put pins in our ears and I found if you twiddled the pin whilst having a cigarette, it was really satisfying!

Then we tried Hypnotism. Well, I tried, I really did, but the man kept saying, 'You are going now, you are going away'. But I wasn't, and I started to giggle, and he washed his hands of me; that cost me £100! By this time, Jean had stopped smoking, but not me. I think I was a lost cause. Then she came up with someone who guaranteed success, Gillian Riley; I think she was American. There was a weekend course, so I went for it, my last effort. All on my own, with a packet of ciggies hidden in my knickers, I went to Abbey Road and holding very little hope, I paid my £125 and waited for the miracle. Day one, Gillian talked about giving up, and we smoked throughout and there were ashtrays everywhere. 'I like this course,' I thought to myself. The next day, I arrived and lit up immediately, then looked for an ashtray; there were none. 'Gillian there are no ashtrays,' I said. 'That's right, Wendy. You don't smoke anymore!' I remember I stood there, tears running down my face. I just stood all alone, realising everyone was looking at me. Gillian stood up and said very clearly, 'Wendy, come up here, and I will give you your money back. We need to move forwards, and you are holding us up'. How did she know how to handle me, I wonder? Of course, I shook my head and went back to sit down. I gave her first a pathetic Wendy look, then one of my 'don't mess with me' looks.

I left the course clutching a packet of Senior Service with a message written on the front. It read 'YOU CAN HAVE ONE IF YOU WANT ONE!' It worked; I quit, and for 25 years I had my packet of ciggies in the glove compartment in my car. Occasionally, I would take a peep, but I never had another cigarette. Sometimes I think that that was most probably the only successful thing I've ever achieved in my life! Five years ago, I had a car crash and wrote off my little Mini . I was whisked off to hospital. I lived, but I never saw my packet of cigarettes again; it had done the trick anyway.

Jean was with me through most of my adult life, and we opened a business together called Secrets. It did rock our friendship. We smoked 'pot' together. We never took hard drugs; we were too nervous. Actually, we were just pretty girls who were great to be with, and we didn't need drugs. But I'm glad we tried the 'pot' thing. I have a piece still in my memories box, but, like me, it's a bit past its sell by date. Maybe tonight I might try grating a bit and having a go. Could do with a laugh today!

Several years later, when I opened my boutique called Harriet, Jean was my first mannequin. Here she is wearing one of my best sellers called 'Rosie'; every

debutante in London bought one at the time.

Some of the men Jean went out with were really nice. I remember David Sharp, lovely man, in advertising. Then there was Ronnie; he was very tall with buck teeth. One day, he brought his toothbrush with him and put it in her bathroom. There was rapid knocking on the wall. I rushed in thinking she was in trouble. 'Get his toothbrush out of here.' That wasn't easy, but I just whispered in Ronnie's ear something about it being too soon. He nodded and that was done!

Another time she went out with someone new, and she was really excited. They spent most of the time listening to Jazz and eating popcorn. Eventually, they

went to bed, quite normal you might think. But no, he bent down and unscrewed his leg and hung it on the bedstead at the end of the bed. It wasn't funny, really, but the way she told me about the crucial timing was hilarious. Apparently, he saw the funny side too, so they made love with the leg rattling at the end of the bed!

This is my favourite photo of us together; we were both a little tipsy. Jean rarely drank, but we were going to see Barbra Streisand at Wembley, and we met in the carpark where we ate salmon sandwiches, she hated salmon sandwiches, and we also drank half a bottle of Champagne to celebrate. The fact that I managed to get Jean across the carpark and into the loo was a feat and a half. Then she slid to the floor and intended to go to sleep. With the help of a couple of young men, we frog marched her into the auditorium and plonked her in her seat. She did wake up when Barbra came on stage, so she didn't miss anything. But I decided that was the last time I would drink with my darling Jean; coffee only for her in future!

When Frank Sweeney, the man Jean was so mad about back in the Polly Peck days, told me he was getting married to Carol, another photographic model, he asked me to design her wedding dress. I knew Frank would like something different, so I designed the first trousers suit to be allowed into a church. She looked stunning, and this picture always comes up when you Google it. Jean came into the boutique and chose a white dress in spotted muslin. I tried to talk her out of it, but Jean was Jean and would not be persuaded to wear another colour. So, in every wedding picture, you can see Jean in the white dress behind Frank. Her plan worked! The marriage only lasted 3 weeks, not my fault. Carol decided she was still in love with someone called Mike and left!

The wedding breakfast was at The Hungry Horse, in Fulham Road. There Jean met Stephen Brind. They hit it off straight away. One Saturday morning soon after Frank's wedding, I received a call. It was Jean. 'What are you doing today darling? If you are free, can you come to the registry office as I'm getting married!' Typical

Picture of trouser suit in every newspaper at the time...

94

Jean. Of course, I was there. We drank Champagne from the bottle in the street and generally behaved badly, what's new!

Jean and Stephen had an up and down life. Perhaps things weren't always good, but sometimes they were great together. The problem in those days was there was so much fun to be had, and they were both very attractive. I loved them both, and later when I met Dawson, the four of us were inseparable. We had holidays together, we smoked 'pot' together...you name it we did it! Always laughter, always a drama just around the corner; it's how we lived then. Much later, they had a lovely daughter called Samantha. She's my goddaughter and very pretty. Very like Jean in many ways.

VOGUE

THE NEW BIG VOGUE NOVEMBER 1963 THREE SHILLINGS

Here is a beautiful picture of Jean on the cover of Vogue...

AN ASIDE

Many years later, when Jean was dying of cancer, in New Zealand, I went over to be with her. We watched Cabaret several times, singing loudly along with 'I'm going like Elsie'. We listened to our favourite singer Barbra Streisand and drank a lot. To hell with doctor's orders. She asked me to deliver a message to someone when I went home. 'Tell him he was the only one.'

I delivered her message on the day we had a party to celebrate her life back in the UK.

I gave him the message, and I could see from his face that it was a very moving moment for him. He had been her secret lover. I didn't say anything more for I, as many others, didn't approve of their relationship.

Jean's presence is always with me, but she is not there to tell me how wonderful I am! I have very low self-esteem, my daughter says. One day, Jean filled a big empty box of matches with tiny bits of paper and wrote all my achievements on each piece… there were a lot, and nobody was more surprised than me. But I, of course, I am a nonbeliever in myself.

Chapter 4 part 2

Crazy Chrissie - a love hate relationship - living in a brothel!

I remember clearly the day I met Christine Harris, Chrissie, as we all called her.

My mother was now working in the lingerie department at Harvey Nicks and as I had to go there one day for a fitting for a show the following week, I thought I would take my mother to the cafe on the third floor for tea. The lift stopped on the second floor, and a skinny mannequin slid into the lift. At first, I thought it was Audrey Hepburn, but, no, it wasn't. My mother beamed and proudly introduced me to this tall graceful vision. 'Hello Chrissie, can I introduce you to my daughter Wendy. She is also a mannequin and is doing the show with you next week.' Chrissie looked down at me, and I visibly shrank as she looked me up and down. Then she turned to leave the lift on the fashion floor and as the doors began to close, she looked at me and with a blank expression on her face and said, 'Hello'' and slid away. I was deeply hurt and cross as I could see my mother was feeling the same. Funny girl that Chrissie, but years later I learnt to love her to bits!

We worked together in most of the shows, the important ones. We were both on the plane that nearly crashed over Zurich airport. Somehow Chrissie and I had many, many near misses, which you will hear about later in the book. I don't think I really ever got to know her; she was so complicated. But bit by bit we learnt to be friends. She had a sharp tongue and many a time she made me cry. I had to hold back the tears as she would hate me showing emotion...that was Chrissie being a bitch...then there was Chrissie being kind, but you always had to be on your toes as any minute she could turn into a 'bitch' again.

We slowly started to appreciate each other. She was amazing on the catwalk and had a very funny way of walking; we all called her the 'mincer'. One day after a big press show lunchtime, when we had just finished an important Press show at Quaglino's for Polly Peck, we realised we were starving so we went to have lunch at the Stockpot, cheap and cheerful and very popular with us girls. She started to open up and told me about her affair with Oliver Reed. They went to art college together and he sounded pretty crazy even then. If we were not working together, we didn't see much of each other. When we did catch up for a coffee or something, she was always eager to let me know about her latest lovers, perhaps to check my approval. No, I don't think that was true; you see, Chrissie did as much as she could to shock everyone. That was her. She used the 'S' word and the ''F' word continuously. I was still saying 'damn' and 'blast' in those days, and she shocked me by using such words. She didn't care a damn about what we all thought.

There was very little work around for Chrissie and I, so we decided to go to Paris for a little holiday and some window shopping. We went by car as I had just bought a new car, a Spitfire sports car. It was not exactly 'new', but a wreck really. I had bought it as a 'right off' from my local garage. Mechanically it was fine, but the bodywork was a bit of a joke. It had been smashed into a brick wall, so it looked horrific. However, as I said, it was sound, and that is all my £400 would buy. We didn't have a lot of money, so we decided to take some food with us, bit like taking coals to Newcastle, really. So, we bought 4 tins of beans, 4 tins of Sardines, 2 tins spaghetti and 2 Fray Bentos steak pies. That was the sort of food we ate then, rubbish!

We had a good trip and reached Paris at dusk. We thought we had better start looking for a hotel before it got dark. Chrissie studied the Paris map and decided that we were in the expensive area and she suggested we move to another cheaper arrondissement. We were moving very slowly, and I suspected that we were caught up in the evening rush hour. All of a sudden, the car behind us bashed into the back of my car. 'Bloody male drivers,' I shouted as I got out of the car. A man from the car opened his door, and I made a note that he was very good looking! Thankfully, he spoke perfect English. He was joined by his passenger, also very dishy! 'I am so sorry. We were moving so slowly, I think I must have nodded off for a second. Please, let us have your names and which hotel you are staying at, so we can arrange for your car to be picked to have the bumper mended.'

They seemed really upset and when we told them that we had no hotel yet, they said they knew one very close that always had the odd vacancy. The eldest, who was called Herbet, suggested that we should follow them, and they would introduce us to the owners. So, we did. The hotel was a bit seedy, but they had a room for us. The two guys suggested they took us out for a drink to say sorry for all the trouble they had caused. Free drinks always were acceptable.

Free drinks turned into supper and more drinks. There was a man playing piano softly. Andre (the passenger in Herbert's car) and Chrissie were enjoying themselves dancing, well smooching more like. We finally went back to the hotel at 2 am, utterly exhausted. It had been a long day.

The next morning, when we were having breakfast downstairs, I picked up a local paper and nearly chocked on my coffee. The headlines were 2 BANK ROBBERS ESCAPE WITH PAINTINGS WORTH MILLIONS and have totally disappeared! There was a picture as well…it was our 2 guys from last night! Had they stolen the paintings and then bumped into us? Or did they do the robbery after they dropped us off! They were pretty laid back. I would have liked to have known more about the robbery.

Our little hotel turned out to be a brothel. Every evening before going to bed, we had Pastis in the little bar, and it was then that we started to notice waiters walking around one minute with a tea towel on their shoulders then other times without a tea towel. I asked the young girl, who spoke a little English, what that meant. 'That is to let the men who come in here for good times. It tells them when there is a vacant room where they can find pleasure!' I'm not

my darling friend Chrissie

sure, I grasped what she meant but then, when we went to bed and switched the light off, we understood exactly what she was trying to tell us. The noise of love making through the thin walls was almost impossible to block out. I can't say we got used to it. The problem was that it went on all night, and we were terrified someone would take a wrong turning and end up in our room! So, we put the chest of drawers over the doorway and went under the blankets.

In my kitchen now, I have a cushion which I had printed with the address of our little brothel. 6, Cherche du Midi. It brings back some amusing memories as you might imagine!

Chapter 4 part 3

Trying to Move on

I suppose I was just, at this point in my life, going through the motions. I was still living with my mother, and I was still seeing Peter most nights of the week, so, generally, I seemed to be stuck in a rut. I had expected by now to at least have my own home, but I was working hard and playing hard which left little time to find a flat. Well, that is what I told myself!

Peter seemed quite happy with our relationship, but me, well, I think we were just waiting for something to happen, and nothing ever did!

Perhaps then it was up to me to make a move. I wish that I could have talked to my mother about this situation, but she was still blinded by Peter's charm. He really did turn it on for her. I hoped that she would say something to Peter about marriage or come up with a plan for my future; surely, I should be involved!!

I was working really hard as there seemed to be plenty of work around. I was fussy about the assignments offered to me. I wouldn't do lingerie shows or bathing beauty shows. I was always in charge of my work, but my personal life was rubbish. Now looking back, I should have made my mother understand that I didn't want her to arrange all those balls and dinners. I wonder now what people must have thought about me. I was still shy and nervous except when I was on stage, strange isn't it?

My hidden life was pretty good. I had learnt to be a really clever liar, and Peter and my mother seemed to fall for everything I said. That way I could get away with murder; well, maybe not murder but at least I managed to get out with my friends whose lives always seemed wonderful to me, whilst they, of course, thought my life was all glamour and sparkling ball gowns.

Peter seemed to be enjoying his new venture and spent most days under the bonnet of his car and he smelt of oil and petrol. His hair was thick grease. He always said it was bad to wash your hair more than every 3 months. But you see, I was living in another world where men went to hairdressers, had manicures and saunas. He wouldn't come to any of the events that was asked too, saying he couldn't see the point of standing talking to somebody about the weather. So, I had to go on my own but, quite honestly, he wouldn't have fitted in.

I would have liked to have gone on a holiday, but Peter couldn't get a new passport. His old one was out of date, but he was scared to renew it in case they called him up. He was in hiding as there was still National Service call up then. I began to wonder what sort of person I was tied to...I don't think I ever understood him, and he definitely didn't understand how a pretty girl like me wanted to go to parties.

Then one day, I decided to see if I could leave Peter and I went over to Chrissie's to stay. I didn't have a plan, but I needed to think about the relationship. I needed to rethink my life for I was feeling like a caged animal.

So, I took all my few belongings from Peter's room and left a note to say I needed to breathe and not to worry. Peter got on the phone to my mother and all hell let loose. She called Chrissie to see if I was there and said that Peter was going to commit suicide. Later he had broken down on the telephone to the Samaritans, and they called me to say I was playing with somebody's life. I told them why I had left, but they wouldn't listen. They just repeated that I should go and talk to him to explain how I feel. But nobody knew Peter like I did. I knew that if I went to talk to him, I would never escape. So that was it. I went back, but I wouldn't get into bed and I sat in a chair for weeks. It was the only thing I could think of doing to show how upset I was. A few weeks later, he was eating an ice-cream when he had a sharp pain down his left arm and numbness. He self-diagnosed, declaring that he had had a mini stroke bought on by the stress of my behaviour! Well that was it, my mother was furious, and I was accused of being heartless. Helen, his mother, called from Trinidad and gave me a lecture, her poor son, nothing about me as she would never think that her lovely son would do anything wrong.

So, I said I would stay. It seemed to make everyone happy - except me, of course. I just stayed, just my body, I continued to lead a double life. As long as I didn't actually leave and close the door behind me, Peter was happy. I didn't want to hurt him as I knew that I loved him, but I felt trapped. I flapped about like a caged bird.

AN ASIDE

In fact, in the end, Peter left me. We were obviously not supposed to be Peter Pan and Wendy like the fairy tale. Our relationship was so depressing sometimes, we never gave it a chance. It was my fault, I think...I was too busy trying to please everyone. Peter was simple, not complicated like me. It's sad, really, as in the end he hated me as he thought I had ruined his life...maybe I did. Who knows. At first, I did love him; then because he and my mother seemed to take my life over, I fought back as I couldn't breathe...

Chapter 4 part 4

A different club every night – introducing the MORRIS MINI to the world.

I still did the odd 'season' work. I found it quite refreshing, staying in one place for a while. We had to put up with quite a lot of bad behaviour from the men in most of the houses. I think they thought they had bought us not only to show their clothes, but also to flirt with us. Together, we were pretty scary; we didn't stand for any 'monkey business' as we used to call it. They all used the same remarks when they walked into the mannequins dressing room saying, 'Oh dear, girls. I'm sorry. I didn't think you would be undressed'. It's called a dressing room!

This was the time that I seemed to see Jean quite a lot. We were booked for an important fashion show at the Talk of the Town in Leicester Square. It was the first show that we had been in that allowed us to do more than walking up and down a catwalk. So, Jean, Chrissie and I worked out a sort of a dance routine. I cringe now thinking about it, but it went down wonderfully with the audience. We started a trend; no more snooty mannequins walking up and down glaring at each other. 'Younger than Springtime', my theme tune, was playing, and the audience clapped enthusiastically which gave me enormous confidence. Who would have believed that little Wendy Lewis was up here on this huge stage enjoying herself…not me!

When I was booked for the fashion extravaganza at THE TALK OF THE TOWN in Leicester Square, I was told that I had been chosen to introduce the new Mini to the press. The climax of the fashion show came when the car, which was below stage, came up through the trap door onto the darkened stage. On went the spotlights, and there was the first MINI with me driving it! I drove the car to the front of the stage and seconds later, 6 very skinny model girls climbed out of the car. The swearing from the girls in the car would have shocked even today!

The audience stood and clapped and whistled, and we knew then that this little Mini was a special car and would be here to stay. Everyone, at some time in their life, has owned at least one of them, including me. And when the Mini was 50 years old, a couple of years ago, I decided to buy another one to celebrate. I thought they might give me a discount, but they didn't! Sadly, I didn't have it long as you know already. I wrote it off, nearly wrote myself off too as I went through a brick wall!

Thinking back, I'm amazed at how hard we worked. Fittings, hair styles, make-up, rehearsals that sometimes went on until 2 am. Then the real show, which was quite demanding. Not that we complained; after all, work was money, and we always needed money. There seemed to be less time to dance on the tables. Now I still dance, but by myself or with my cocker spaniel Harriet.

The clubs were amazing in the sixties. THE SADDLE ROOM was one of the first to open and was mostly supported by debs and their delights, as we called them, all very proper. I loved going to John Mills club at LES AMBASSEDERS. Poor John, he was never given a British passport, and when he died, his friends buried him in a special bespoke coffin and dressed him in a shirt and suit by TURNBULL and ASSER with a tie that had FUCK IT printed all over it. Another popular club was The Crazy Elephant, CRAZY E. Then there was DOLLY'S.

I loved the EDMUNDO ROSS club; the music was new and exciting to us. Then there was THE MARQUIS; I never went there. The 400 club where Princess Margaret always went with her escorts. Then a little later came ANNABEL'S. I used to go there with Gordon and Pat, we would eat copious amounts of Caviar, and dance till dawn, those were the days. There were many nightclubs, but we only went to the ones that were IN FASHION, those were the ones that you had to be a member. The dances at the time was the CHA CHA, THE TWIST, THE JIVE, THE LOCOMOTION, THE MASH POTATO and of course, ROCK AND ROLL.

We didn't need to run a marathon or belong to a gym to do Aerobics. We were just fit.

In Soho we had SCOTCH. I have some crazy memories there; wish I could remember them! I'm not sure I remember the order of their openings, but SPEAKEASY was around that time and then AD LIB at the top of the building with an express lift to the top. I can remember going up but not going down, I wonder why? The AD LIB was my club. I danced on the tables with VIDAL SASSOON, did the Congo with JOHN LENNON, twisted the night away with many stars of the time. Then of course, there is TRAMP, fifty years old this year owned then by Johnny Gold and his wife, my dear friend Jan de Sousa. She worked for me and Mary Quant as a model.

In Paris, there were many clubs, but the only one I remember belonged to REGINES. She was the queen of clubs, and everyone always wanted to copy her. She did, I believe, open REGINES in London but it failed, no idea why.

In NEW YORK there was CLUB 21 , HIPPOTIMUS and STUDIO 54. And many more, but I wasn't really into the New York scene in the sixties...too busy working and dancing!

Chapter 5 part 1

Running away to Rome - a beautiful experience

Work as a mannequin was at last starting to pay off. All those days when I nearly threw the towel in, all those days when I had to walk to every audition as I didn't have the bus fare. Now, all that seemed worthwhile. I had plenty of bookings with some of the top fashion houses, such as Susan Small, Frank Usher and Digby Morton, as well as several commercials on the go. These were not just fun to do but also very lucrative as the repeats were paid in a lump sum every month. So, by now I was quite a high earner. However, it wasn't enough money as far as I was concerned as I was accustomed to a certain standard of living. An expensive one. I was used to being wined and dined in all the best places and also loved being recognised. I suppose like many pretty young girls, I was spoilt, but why not? Grab it whilst it's out there. Sadly, it's something that has stayed with me all my adult life.

I don't do poor!

I was doing a 'season' at Polly Peck. That means you have a block booking for 4 -6 weeks and can't do much else workwise. However, Polly Peck was a well-known fashion house and it was yet another feather in my cap. The Zelker family, who owned Polly Peck in those days, before they sold out to Nadir Adir, liked me and, whilst I was flavour of the month, I could do nothing wrong. It was quite nice being in one place for a few weeks and, being a regular, you got to wear all the best clothes before any of the new girls. Jean and Chrissie were also booked for the 'season', and it was lovely to be working with friends. Although we had to work long hours, always looking beautiful and never complaining, the three of use enjoyed every moment of it. Our friendship was the most precious part of my life then. I was still with Peter, and he still controlled me. My friends thought it would work out in the end, but it didn't.

There was another mannequin, called Jennie, (can't remember her surname… maybe it was Cahill, yes it was!) She was nice and very beautiful and looked like Grace Kelly. I remember she always wore beige, before beige was in fashion, and in fact everything about her was beige, her clothes, her hair and actually her personality, if you know what I mean. We were total opposites but for some reason we seemed to just 'click' and soon became firm friends. I suppose it was because we had one thing in common, we both wanted to run away!

I had never been very good at saving, so when I looked in my post office book, I could come up with only £25. Jennie said she could match that, so where should we go? At the station, we had a choice for £25 one-way ticket to Naples, Milan or Rome. We didn't have any idea which would be best, but Jennie said her mother had lots of friends in Rome, and I also still had Frank Silvestri's contact details; not that I really wanted to see him again, but, apparently, Ava had finished with him, so perhaps he would be happy to see me. And it might be good for a free lunch or two! So, decision made, two single tickets to Rome leaving next Tuesday morning at 10.20.

Neither of us wanted to discuss the matter with our families. This was our decision and after all, we were both old enough to leave home. I didn't tell anyone, which gave me a feeling of power at last. I went to Smiths and bought a copy of Hugo's Italian course (1/6), which I still have by my bed. I mean to learn Italian and perhaps one day I will, but meanwhile I can't bear to throw it away as for me, it was the start of a new wonderful adventure. Still many years later when I wake in the morning, it is there, on my bedside table, and it never fails to make me smile! I feel as if I can actually speak Italian just by looking at it! I left a note for my mother, who was still working at Harvey Nichols. I promised to call her when we had arrived. My poor mother. She would be so alone. My stepfather had buggered off some time ago. But I was bent on saving myself. I had to get away before I suffocated. I telephoned Peter from a telephone box on the station, Jennie made me do it, I was too scared, but she was right. He was furious, then calmed down and said he would come with me! So, I lied. Polly Peck has a new store opening in Rome and the Zelker's had decided to send the two of us off at the last minute. I would call when I had a hotel and I put down the phone. Then I was sick. I had escaped. I was scared but free at last. Free from my mother and free from Peter; for the first time in my life, I was my own person! Nobody would ever be able to manipulate me again... sadly, that was not the case but then I didn't know what the future held for me. The train journey was a story in itself, never to be forgotten. We had not anticipated such a journey. It was meant to be an adventure, but we soon realised that we hadn't thought it through properly. When we climbed on board our train, the Milan express (we had a connecting train then on to Rome), we were not prepared like other travellers. They had drinks and sandwiches, books and puzzles as well as rugs and pillows; the journey was about 11 hours long. We had little spare cash for food or drink, so we learnt the hard way. But perhaps that's what standing on your own feet is all about.

If you haven't ever been on a long train journey, in a third-class compartment, going to Italy, you haven't lived. What an eye opener. We hadn't been able to afford a couchette, so we had to sit upright in a hot overcrowded carriage. Everyone smoked, including us. There was no air conditioning, which was not unusual in those days. This was OK to start with, but once we turned right to go down to Milan, we all started to sweat. The toilets got bunged up, and the pee dribbled down the corridor. We both began to wonder what we had done. I had thick dungarees on, no denim jeans around yet, and a cotton starched shirt which scratched. The only time it was bearable was when the train stopped. Then we would jump down to the platform from the high train and stand on the station, breathing deeply. Mulhouse, Lugano, each station had its own smell. I can close my eyes and smell it now, and the pee! We both had our diaries with us, and I wrote. 'Just went to Lugano but didn't stop long!' It made us laugh and kept us going.

We had some coffee in the restaurant car, which was all we could afford and sat watching the twinkling lights of the little Swiss villages rushing past, a sense of excitement started to build up inside me. When we got back to our carriage, we thought it might be an idea to try to get some sleep as it was 3 am and everyone else was asleep. They were sort of flopped in odd positions which was quite funny. We managed about two hours catnap, but then there was a big commotion as the border guards came on board at the Swiss border, and we all woke up. Shortly after that, more commotion, guards shouting out something or other. All the people from our compartment had now left the train. At that point, the lights went out and the shuddering train went silent. It took us a few moments to understand what had happened. It was only when we leaned out of the window that our train had gone into a siding and there was nobody on the train. In the distance, we could see the platform and a sign saying MILANO. We realised at the point that we would have to run down the train line and clamber up onto the platform. I'm sure we would have treated our tourists differently; somebody might have tried to explain. Well, it didn't match our idea of swanning into Italy with our sunglasses on the ends of our noses and swinging our bags over our shoulders like Audrey Hepburn did in Roman Holiday.

Having found our platform for the 'Roma Express', we sat on our cases on the platform, and I smoked the last of my Senior Service cigarettes. Another problem. We needed the rest of our Lire for the Pensione, so it meant no food, no ciggies. Our sense of humour was rapidly disappearing. Things cheered up a bit when a group of young Italians came onto the platform. They were obviously talking about us, and one of them whistled at us, just like the builders do in UK. That made us feel at home. Then one of them came over and said something, but we just gaped at him. 'Ah Inglese!' he shouted over his shoulders to his friends, and, at that moment, as I turned away, he pinched my bottom! We had heard that the men in Italy do that, but it was still a shock, almost without thinking a said sharply 'basta', which I think meant 'enough'. He laughed and walked away saying 'that won't work in Italy little girl' in perfect English! So, into the diary FIRST PINCH ON BOTTOM...rather nice!

Two hours later as our train steamed gently into Rome station, we watched from the window as it jolted to a stop. We had arrived at Rome station rather the worst for wear, and we were very tired. All I could think of was going to bed. Luckily Jennie's mother had arranged a little hotel just off Via Veneto for us to stay for a few days whilst we were looking for work. We had the address and had practiced our Italian for the taxi, 'can you take us to Pensioni Mascarelli in Via Sicilia. How much? (quanto costa) Thank you! (Gracia)'. I had a few other phrases, such as pronto, forte, piano, Buena sera, vino and gelato, but that was it. Typically British, I expected everyone to speak English! Thank goodness we were also going to be met at Roma station by some friends of Jennie's mother, so hopefully everything would work out and we would be safe.

We slowly dragged our bags down the platform, a little dazed I remember. My mind was a total blank. I didn't care where I was, I just wanted a ciggie and a bed! All of a sudden, five young men came down the platform waving a union jack and shouting 'Jennie, Wendy, we are here for you!' It was quite embarrassing as they were kissing us and saying how wonderful it was to see us in their beloved Roma. I think they must have been quite disappointed as we were smelly and bleary eyed and looked very white. We didn't need to say anything as they talked non-stop to each other in very fast Italian, but it was very welcome, really, as we were past being tired. They took us to the Pensione, dropped off our bags and said they would come back tomorrow and show us their Roma...buone notte...and they were gone.

That's the day my life started for me...

True to their word, the young Italian men arrived at the Pensione at 10 am. The owner of the Pensione came up in the beautiful ancient filigree lift to our room to announce their arrival. She seemed quite flustered. We realised why when she handed over their business cards. Young Italian men in those days always presented themselves with a slight bow and their card, and maybe still do.

When we looked at the five cards, we realised why Signora Caldi was so red in the face. The first card was from Count Maurizio Piscelli, the next was Giovanni Bulgari, then Franco di Menerbi, Prince Frascati (the wine family) and then there was simply Paolo Ajroldi, Baron di Robiatte. We had not realised that we were being escorted by the sons of some of the most important families in Italy. I think Signor Caldi's attitude changed towards us after that, and she was very helpful in many ways now that we were part of the very important families in Rome.

In broken English, one of the boys explained that they had made a plan for the day. First, a drive around some of the important monuments in Rome, a visit to St Peter's, then lunch and then a siesta. We did explain in very slow, but loud English (we all did that in those days as very few people spoke any other languages, but it was common knowledge that if you shouted, the 'natives' understood!) that we had to find work as we had enough money only for one week at the Pensione. I'm not sure that they understood, but it was Saturday and, obviously, we would not find work at the weekend. So, we smiled and enjoyed being escorted by such debonair young men.

The day was magical; everything we had hoped for: the Colosseum was larger than expected, the Fontana de Trevi was filled with coins and St Peters was more beautiful than one could imagine. I think both Jennie and I were a bit overwhelmed by it all. Lunch was in Via Condotti, a little typical Italian ristorante where we had Calzone and a glass of Verdicchio, which was THE drink at the time. What with the sun and the heat and the wine, I think Jennie and I thought we had arrived in paradise. We went back to the Pensione at 2.30 exhausted but elated. We had made the right choice after all.

The boys picked us up again at 9pm as they had promised, and we went to have a pizza in Piazza Novana. It was a proper Pizza, thin and delicious followed by a gelato, also in Piazza Novana - the best in Roma. Later Paolo, who had not said much all day, suggested that we went to the newest trendy club in Rome, which was called Il Pipistrello, the bat, to dance. I realise now that young Italian boys always ended the evening with a dance. That was their plan, and then depending on the girl perhaps they would be lucky and go the whole way! The club was dark and full of young somewhat tanned young men all clinging on to very pale young English girls. We sat down and the band played a typical Italian smoochy tune. Everyone jumped up to ask Jennie for a dance. Then Paulo asked me to dance. I could tell he had set his heart on dancing with Jennie, but I was second best and at least he was on the dance floor! We danced in silence. Then they played the most popular tune of the year in 1955, Come Prima; it was a winner...those slick young men had the girls swooning in their arms. I can still hear the melody; it's imprinted in my memory. Paolo held me close and it was nice. He was a large man (perhaps a little fat) and although I was pretty tall, I felt small and comfortable in his arms. The dance ended, and we just smiled at each other and that was it.

Chapter 5 part 2

Paolo my new love - lovers and friends forever!

The following day Paolo called to ask if I would like to go out with him to have lunch. He also mentioned that his aunt owned the fashion House in the Piazza de Spagna called Carosa. Her name was Princess Giovanna Caraccido of Carosa. He suggested that it might be a good idea for him to speak to her and see if there was a chance of me wearing some of her dresses at the Palazzo Pitti. This was the most important fashion show of the year in Milan. Wow! That would be amazing. So, of course, I agreed. He said he would pick me up later and arrange the meeting.

You know that sometimes your mind goes back in time, and you relive a scene over and over again. Well, this is one of those scenes. I heard my name being called, and I opened the shutters and looked down to see Paolo leaning against the smallest car in the world; I think it was called a Fiat Topolino. A quick thought flashed through my mind, how the hell were we both going to get into his tiny tiny car! It was at that precise moment looking down from my bedroom window that I fell in love with him. Yes, that does sound rather silly, but later he told me it was the same for him. We often spoke about that magical moment years and years later, and here I am, sixty years later still remembering that moment!

I also remember we hardly spoke. I asked where we were going and he said, 'mare' and smiled then started to sing. I laughed and was completely relaxed as everything Paolo said or did seemed magical to me, apart from his dreadful singing voice. I can be thinking of my darling, perhaps an Italian tune is playing on the radio or just a view of Italy, and I close my eyes and pretend I am there. THEN I hear Paolo singing, generally 'Solo Mio', and I freeze. How can you be in love with a man that sings the same song over and over in a flat voice. No way…but I know I am, and I always will be!

The day that I met his aunt, the Princess, was important for me; not for her, of course, as she had met, I gathered, several of Paolo's girlfriends in need of work and she was kind and helped them, for her nephew's sake. So, I was nothing new. Paolo whispered in his aunt's ear, and she turned to look at me with a little smile on her face and gave a nod to me. I was to start work the next day with fittings for her new Carosa collection. The collection had to be ready by the start of the shows in Milan at the Pallazo Pitti. This was the most important date in the Italian calendar when the Italians try, year after year, to be better than designers in London and to shine brighter than their arch enemies in Paris. It never happens, but the stakes are high; and one day they will be the top Couturiers in the world. Meanwhile, they must trail behind as always. Not the case nowadays, I must add!

After the meeting, Paolo and I went out to celebrate. We had an espresso at Doney's in Via Veneto, standing at the bar as to sit down costs extra money, and it was then I realised that Paolo too had no money! Typical, I had the Italian with a title, who lived in a beautiful house with his aunt in total decadence. He had only a very small allowance, and we had spent that already at the club on that first night. How funny that when you are young, you don't need money; you sort of get by. We never had money at the beginning of our love affair. Later, we were both very successful, and money was no issue. Thankfully, his aunt had obviously made a few arrangements with certain restaurants around Roma, so as long as we went to those, we could eat… well, get enough food to survive, just. I remember going one night to Romulo's, which was down a little alleyway. It was typically Roman, buzzing and had a wonderful Mediterranean smell of Basil and garlic, you know that smell I'm sure. We were greeted with outstretched arms and ushered to a rather dark table for two, obviously well-known here too I thought! Without being offered a menu our meal arrived. Plain boiled spaghetti with a chunk of butter on top. Paolo scattered Parmigiana cheese over it as the butter melted and plenty of pepper and salt. That was my first Spaghetti al burro and for several years I would always turn to the same dish when I was in need of comfort food, either because of a broken heart or a seemingly overwhelming problem. It always works a treat. Paolo, being a good Roman, ordered the Trippa (tripe); as none of the tourists ordered it, Romans ordered it to help the owner out!

When I was on my own during my days off, I would sit outside with a Cappuccino in either Doney's or Cafe de Paris, both on Via Veneto and just around the corner from my little hotel. It was like sitting on a film set as there was always some celebrity hanging around and always ready to chat a pretty girl up. It was here I met a really nice man called Brioni, a famous men's designer. We talked sometimes for hours, and the Cappuccino's turned into Campari sodas, he paid! One day when sitting outside the Café de Paris, one of the men that had come to the station came past and was pleased to see me. He sat himself down and chatted away about himself for an hour. I did tend to glaze over from time to time but then he said, 'I'm flying down to my vineyard this afternoon, come with me if you like!' He was, of course, Prince Frascati, but the thought of his boring chat and then how would I tell Paolo that his friend had been chatting me up. So, with a beaming smile I said 'Oh, Paolo and I would love to!' I have never seen anyone move away so fast, his tail between his legs. I never told Paolo as I knew he would be jealous. I often wonder what would have happened if I had gone with him. Now, I just drink his wine and remember that although the wine is good, he was not!

I also felt a bit guilty too when I phoned Frank as I thought it would upset Paolo; Italian men do get so worked up about things. Frank was over the moon when he heard my voice, 'Darling, is it really you? Why didn't you tell me you were coming? Meet me for lunch at Georges and we can catch up'. So, we met, and it was surprisingly nice to see him. He was obviously well known in this restaurant, I supposed because he was generally with Ava Gardner. Still, I was only too pleased to eat a decent meal. I think Frank must have realised I hadn't eaten for a while, so he over ordered everything, and I stuffed it in. Most girls in my business were known for their enormous appetites and most men taking us out had to have a very large wallet! Lunch, I clearly remember, was Vittelo Milanese and a cold green bean salad followed by a fruit salad (Macedonia del frutta.)

When the bill came Frank suggested we went back to his apartment for coffee and more catching up. I was a bit tipsy and very full, so it seemed the natural thing to do. He made some coffee and we talked about his affair with Ava. Well, I thought it was an affair, but what happened next threw me a little. He leaned over and kissed me very gently. It was a nice kiss but not a very nice kiss, and I think Frank could see the look in my eyes. 'Darling Wendy, you are such a sweet little girl, so full of life and so trusting, but I have to tell you that I am gay!' At that moment I grew up a little.

ENGLISH HERITAGE
AVA GARDNER
1922-1990
Film Star
lived and died here

Of course, that was what that kiss was. How to deal with the situation, who knows; I had no idea. But it didn't matter, really, as I was not even vaguely interested in Frank... but I wondered why Ava went out with him as she was so beautiful and had the pick of every man in Rome, maybe they were just friends.

Jenny, meanwhile, was dated by several of our lovely young Italians. We didn't see much of each other as I was either working or with Paolo. We did have a big problem, though; Jenny had a pair of beautiful beige stiletto heeled shoes whereas I had only a pair of now rather shabby Dolcies shoes. She kindly leant her beautiful beige ones to me to go to Carosa for my fittings. If she had an interview, we would meet on the street corner and swap shoes. Jenny was doing the rounds of photographers for she was more of a photographic model. Although she got a few bits of work here and there, she decided to go back to UK, with her shoes! It was then Paolo came up with an idea he would go to the beautiful shoe shop on Via Condotti and try to strike a deal with the owner. It worked, and when he told me what he had done, I was embarrassed but 'over the moon' all at the same time. He had suggested that I should wear several of their top sellers of shoes around Roma and have a photographer to take pictures of me wearing their shoes. No fee, but after one week I could have my very own beige Stiletto heeled shoes. So happy!

Chapter 5 part 3

Filming Ben Hur - Paolo versus Peter

Rome was alight with excitement. The film BEN HUR was to be made at the Cinnecitta studios. Auditions were to be held at the Excelsior hotel in Via Veneto. Every bit part actor, from far and wide, flocked to the city, and everywhere was buzzing. Everyone wanted a part in the film, however small. Days before the filming started, the main stars, Charlton Heston and Stephen Boyd, arrived and the party people started to filter in, always ready to party even if they were not in the film. Every night, Paolo and I would amble down Via Veneto to check who was in town and hope to get an invitation to one of the huge parties that happened every night. We managed to get into Perry Como's party, the best of all. That was when I danced with Harry Belafonte and was chatted up by Johnnie Weissmuller (Tarzan). Later, Stephen Boyd tried to get my telephone number, but Paolo puffed himself up to look threatening, so Stephen disappeared. Pity, he was very sexy! During the time they were shooting the Chariot race between Charlton Heston and Stephen Boyd, many of the bit part actors put bandages on their arms and legs pretending that they had been wounded in the dangerous scenes; everyone grabbed the moment to show that they were part of the race.

Gina Lolobrigita threw great parties, but we couldn't get into any of them as there were so many guards. Jayne Mansfield floated about being Jayne Mansfield all big tits and red lips. She was everywhere, draped over American cars or wriggling around a lamp post. In 1967, sadly, she was involved in a terrible car crash, and, apparently, she was decapitated. How terrible… she was so beautiful.

The film was finally finished, and Rome went back to just being Rome. I wonder if it was ever the same again! Actually, I think they made La Dolce Vita there soon afterwards. Rome had a rather wicked name by then.

Paolo took me to the station a few days later as the time had arrived for the fashion show at the Palazzo Pitti in Milan. I was very nervous. When I arrived, I gathered there was a problem. Although nobody spoke English, there was a nasty feeling in the dressing room. No smiling faces from the other mannequins. I went to where I could see my name WENDI written and sat down ready for the make-up girl to come, but I noticed I had no garments hanging on my rail. Finally, someone from Carosa came to tell me the problem. The Collection had been stolen, so I was not needed. Then there was shouting all up and down the dressing room. The Italian mannequins were shouting at me. It turned out that there was a rebellion amongst the girls as they were fed up with English and German girls coming over and pinching their bookings! One called Sophia had a knife and waved it at me. I left without a word, glad to be still in one piece but really shaken by the whole nasty experience. Great relief when I jumped aboard the train back to Rome. One journalist had asked me for my point of view, but I had none. It was not my place to say anything; it was their country after all. The next day the papers were filled with the pictures of the girl with the knife and one of me looking like a trapped rabbit! Not exactly the sort of publicity that Carosa needed, but at least I got them mentioned and their name was in the headlines!

Back in Rome there was no chance of Paolo and me being on our own at any time, but we managed quite a lot of what, in my day, they called heavy petting. Really difficult in that silly car, I can tell you. We used to go up to Monte Mario and sit under the stars always talking, always cuddling and kissing. I think he also knew that we had something special. As we wanted to be together completely, Paolo bribed one of the maids at his aunt's house and she let us into the kitchen entrance, where there was a spare bedroom. At last we were alone. I think the excitement and anticipation didn't help matters. We tried to make love, but poor Paolo couldn't manage it; all would be OK another time, I thought. There was never another time until the end of our affair in Rome. Motto here maybe, 'don't ask for the moon when you have the stars!'

I know that Paolo felt he had nothing to offer me, no money, no home and no prospects. So, one day, we decided to go to the library and try to find ideas for a career, as you can't be a 'beach bum' forever. That was such an important day. We came up with the idea that Paolo should get involved in the latest new craze. Advertising. We collected all the books we could carry and drove to Monte Mario to read them. Yes, this was the right career for him, we were sure. I played the part of the client, and he was a Count Executive. It was the first and most important decision Paolo had made. He made it for us, so that one day we could be together like a real couple. This was the decision that changed our lives completely.

When one Saturday Paolo suggested we should go to Fregena and swim, he asked me to catch the coach from Roma terminal to the beach. I managed it but fell asleep and missed my stop. Well, what a display of temper we had but never mentioned again. When we got to the beach, instead of going to the smart paying beach, we went to the free beach. I presumed it was because he had no money, but it was actually because I was so white, he didn't want to be seen with me until I was brown. Honestly,

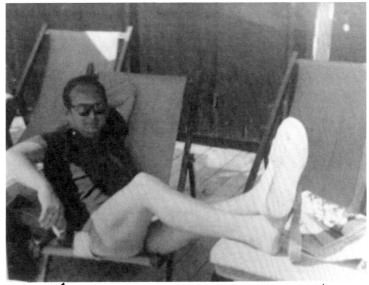

My very own beach bum!

Romans, they are so vain! We swam and lay in the sun with me covered in Olive oil, which was going to make me brown quickly, or fry me! Later we sauntered to the Conchiglia, a little bar and family hotel that played music. In our bare sandy feet, we danced slowly, just feeling the warmth of each other's bodies. It's still there now. I went there with Jean years later, and one of the waiters remembered Paolo, but not me.

Well back to reality. My mother wrote every day and Peter wrote twice a day. He wrote 20-30 page letters, but I never read them. The next morning, a telegram arrived saying, 'MARRIAGE IMPOSSIBLE. MEET ME IN LUGANO.'. Now what was I supposed to do! Paolo being more sensible than me said I should go and tell Peter face to face and work something out. It was only fair. He was right, but on the other hand, he didn't know what control Peter and my mother had over me.

That evening Paolo and I went to Conchiglia for our last glass of wine and spent the whole evening dancing, well standing, on the dance floor. When the bar was closing, the waiter put on the record 'Arrivederci Roma'. As we walked out, I looked back and somehow felt I would not be back. My heart seemed to beat fast and heavy for I knew that tomorrow, when I went to Peter, I would indeed not come back.

I know now that I didn't have the guts to change my life, and it was many years before I did. I regret that evening and often say to myself, 'If only'. But I suppose we all have things like that, and maybe it was just not meant to be.

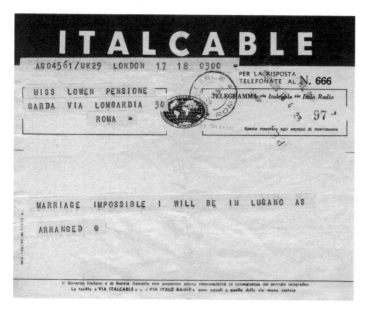

ITALCABLE

AG04561/UK29 LONDON 17 18 0300 =

PER LA RISPOSTA
TELEFONATE AL N. 666

MISS LOWEN PENSIONE
GARDA VIA LOMBARDIA 30
ROMA =

TELEGRAMMA via Italcable via Italo Radio

3 97

Spazio riservato agli estremi di ricevimento

MARRIAGE IMPOSSIBLE I WILL BE IN LUGANO AS

ARRANGED

Il Governo Italiano e la Società Italcable non assumono alcuna responsabilità in conseguenza del servizio telegrafico
Le tariffe « VIA ITALCABLE » e « VIA ITALO RADIO » sono uguali a quelle delle vie meno costose

The next day at the Statzione Termini, when I boarded my train, we just held hands and looked into each other's eyes. I thought I would burst. I thought I would just die there and then, but I didn't. I just clung on to his hand and as the train slowly moved away, I looked back at my darling Paolo, who stood there unashamedly crying. 'Goodbye Pipi Paolo, goodbye.' Later that day, I don't remember the journey at all, there was Peter standing on the platform, his eyes filled with love for me. He seemed so slight and short after Paolo. At that moment, I felt as if I was being hauled in and I hung on to the rail very tightly thinking, go back, Wendy, go back, but I didn't. Peter was hugging me and whispering my name. I have no idea how I got through the next few hours. My mind went blank. He chatted away, first scolding me and then declaring how he couldn't live without me. He had promised my mother that I would call when I arrived, so I did She just said, 'Oh darling, I am so happy you are back with your wonderful Peter. He loves you so much'. She didn't need to say more I just shrivelled up and got on with Peter and Wendy, like Peter Pan and Wendy. I wrote to Paolo and said I was sorting things out and would call shortly. I told him I loved him... Peter and I stayed away for a month, driving into Spain and staying in Benidorm in the only hotel on the beach. Unbelievable when you see it now!

We never mentioned Rome and, to be

Picture of me on a deserted beach in Benedorm... So sad

honest, we didn't do much. Every day we took pictures and went sightseeing. We went everywhere and we didn't stay in any hotels. Instead, we blew up two Lilos every night and slept in the TR2. Very hot and cramped! Thankfully, we couldn't make love, so I felt I was honouring Paolo in a way. Apparently, Peter had brought 100 Durex with him; the custom men had said 'Bon chance' to him and waived him through! I wonder what they would have said seeing him coming back with the contents of that suitcase untouched.

Back in London, very brown all over and plenty of work lined up. The press got excited about my arriving back from working in Rome. Had I seen Frank? Had I heard from Ava? 'A slow news day', I suspect. Work seemed to be the cure for this predicament and there was plenty of it.

Chapter 5 part 4

British Fashion Week in Paris - Duke and Duchess of Windsor

When Michael, my agent, called to say I had been chosen to go to Paris for British Fashion week and that the Duke and Duchess of Windsor would be there. It was a big fashion moment. Press made the most of it, and the next morning we were in every important paper and magazine, in every country. We had 20 garments each and so there were many many fittings. Chrissie was chosen too and Aldine Honey, the school girl that was at my school in Durban, Jackie Bowyer, Hedda Marks, Jan de Sousa, Cynthia Poole, and many more. We took off to Paris with newspaper men virtually running down the runway. It was such a big deal. When we arrived, there was a red carpet and trumpeters dressed in full regalia and Busby's to boot!

The show was amazing, more trumpeters, more flashing lights. My dresser zipped me into my stunning Dior pink satin gown, and as I looked in the long mirror, I said to myself, 'This is it. You have made it kid'. At that moment, I also saw my silhouette. I had always been flat chested, but this dress emphasised my flatness, so as I started to go towards the top of the stairs, I grabbed 2 pairs of gloves and shoved them down my front. At that same moment, Rene, the most famous hairdresser at the time, was putting the final touches to my huge 'beehive' style hair. So somewhere out there is a photograph of me as I look down to check the stairs. To my horror, at that moment, I saw was not exactly

easy as I had very high heels on and three pairs of extra thick eyelashes on! The trumpets blared out and as I reached the bottom, there were the Windsor's sitting in pretend thrones. I slightly curtsied and then turned right and swept down the catwalk. Then I

me

heard Chrissie loudly whispering, 'Wrong way!' So, there was nothing else to do but a sort of double twirl and sweep down the other way. The audience loved it and clapped like mad! Later the Duke and Duchess came backstage to talk to us. Well (Mrs. Simpson) the Duchess really wanted to put her name on some of the dresses, which I suspect the manufactures will give her. She came to chat to me and whispered that she had noticed the gloves popping out of my dress. All I could do was blush and say I thought I had got away with it! She went over to one of the manufacturers, and I was left talking to the Duke. We talked about his garden, and all he wanted to do was to leave and go back home to water the plants! He indicated that SHE seemed to like to drag him along to these fashion shows even though she knew how much he hated them. I suggested he should be brave and dig his heels in and stay away; he looked doubtful. (Must call my mother to tell her!)

After the show, I sat at my dressing table. I looked into the mirror and as I peeled off my numerous eyelashes, I vowed that was my last show, go out on a high they say, and I did!

I wrote to Paolo that night to tell him the news.

On the plane coming back from Paris, I started to put together some ideas for a new venture. I can't say I had a firm plan, but it wasn't long before I did. I think it was just luck that I came up with the idea of being a dress designer! Rather like Paolo and his advertising career, being a dress designer was also the latest craze. First on my agenda was to tell my agent. I walked up the three sets of stairs in Brook Street to his office and told him that I was going to retire. I was 22 years old and had had enough of catwalks. I was fed up with smiling at lots of faceless people in the audience. I think Michael was quite amused but said he would take just well paid bookings until I had something up and running. Thank goodness as I did have the common sense to realise that I would not start earning for some time.

My first move was to call my friend Jill that I was depending on to help with the patterns and some sewing, to discuss where to start. I decided I was going to be a dress designer and open a Boutique to sell my designs. The name came to me as that is what Dior called his shop where he sold accessories in his Avenue Montaigne Boutique. It was the name that soon would be found over every dress shop in the sixties... Boutique! Jill and I had several meetings to discuss my new image, to establish the kind of clientele I wanted to target. She agreed to be my first machinist, and we both felt great excitement with such a big challenge ahead of us.

Every evening when I went to bed, I wrote to Paolo, and every day I received a letter from him. Sometimes when my mother went out, I would call him, but in those days telephone calls to Italy were a big deal. It was a Trunk call, and the operator had to connect to the Italian operator and then you would get connected, if you were lucky!

If my mother was in, she could hear everything as we lived in a tiny flat in Chiswick. I was wonderful to hear that Paolo was fascinated with the new world of advertising. He was so motivated and had already been for various interviews with the local advertising companies, but he was now a high-flyer and was waiting to see if he could get some sort of work with Y&R or perhaps C.P.V. He was prepared to sweep floors just so he could put a foot in the right door. That was the right attitude, so I was so proud of him.

My paolo in winter clothes in Venice

Several weeks later, I had an exciting call from him saying that he was starting as a junior executive with Y&R and had already made friends with another new recruit called Alex Brodie, an American. That turned out to be a great contact, and it wasn't long before both of them were asked to go and work in the new Y&R offices in Frankfurt. As Paolo spoke German, that was another feather in his cap. They had been given a company flat, and life was good for them. With the help of Chrissie, I found a way to go to visit them in Frankfurt. I lied and told my mother and Peter that I had a show to do in Germany, and it was easy. Chrissie confirmed that she was going to be in the same show, so all was OK. She was a very convincing storyteller!

As we landed in Frankfurt, I realised I was nervous, no idea why. Life was getting so complicated that I wondered if perhaps I was making a mistake. But when I saw him at the barrier, I knew I loved him, and as we hugged, I melted in his arms. I was home if only for a few days, and I let out a sigh of happiness. Paolo and I met as often as possible. This photo of him in Winter clothes was quite a shock as I had only seen him in summer gear or bathing trunks. He looked even larger, but nothing could take away his beautiful smiling face. How wonderful to see him; my life was back on track, and my heart was filled with love again. At the flat, I met Alex and his new girlfriend Ursula. I think we all realised the moment we met that we would be friends for years to come, and we were. Supper was ready and for the first time I met Elena. She was Italian, and she cooked for the two men. She was just a wonderful cook and over the years she never left Paolo's side. She cooked for him all his favourite food and travelled wherever his work took him. I vowed one day that when Paolo and I married, she would move in with us; she was, after all, part of the family. I realised when I left that I had two men in my life, Peter and Paolo; they both knew about each other, but the matter was never addressed. In a way, it might have been better, well simpler perhaps, if I just stop seeing both of them and started afresh! Well, that was too big a decision for me to make. So as often as I could, I went to see Paolo. He travelled a lot, so we met in Paris, Milan or Frankfurt. He and Alex became pretty important in the advertising business, and they both worked really hard.

When I got back, I had lunch with Marcus, Mouse; he was spending so much time meditating which seemed abnormal to me. He looked as if he was getting deeper and deeper into himself, and we wouldn't be able to get him back. In fact, only a few weeks later, he was arrested at a bus stop in Leeds, when he was trying to give all his money away to the people standing there. I think he just wanted to be free as he always said, 'You need only one suitcase and a few pounds to be happy,' and he was quite rich, family money, of course. So, I think that was what it was all about. The Police decided he was 'crackers' and he got locked up in Leeds Mental Hospital. The first I heard of it was a card from Marcus saying, 'Dearest Bird, they have locked me up. They think I'm mad. Please come at once and tell them they are wrong. Come quickly please. Love, Mouse'. I telephoned that day to say I was coming up to sort things out and arrange a meeting with a senior member of staff. The next morning, I got a call from one of the nurses to say that Marcus had escaped, climbed over a wall and disappeared. I didn't know what to do next but knew Marcus would phone me or something. No, not a word, not a word for about 10 days. Then I received a post card from Finland. Somehow, he had ended up in Finland. He had met someone, and he was going to marry her. He said he was sorry that it was so sudden as he would have loved me to be there, but it was sort of spur of the moment decision. That was an understatement! Peter, Tom and I were thrilled he had escaped but worried about him getting married to someone he hardly knew. Well, Mouse would always be Mouse, so life went back to normal. We presumed sooner or later we would hear something from them in Finland.

A few weeks later, Mouse and his new wife Carola did, in fact, arrive from Finland. The whole situation was really strange. Mouse didn't want to discuss his odd behaviour, nor did she. So, we kept our silence, hoping that one day, we would find out the truth!

Chapter 5 part 5

An Important Booking in Zurich - and a near miss

Plans for my new venture started to take shape. Not quite sure I was very organised, but it was difficult having not had any experience in retail, nor, of course, dress design. Thank goodness I learnt the basics for opening a business at business school. Also, my stepfather's wheeling and dealing had rubbed off on me, I was sure.

Out of the blue, I got a call from my agent. Work was scarce on the ground at the moment, so it was a pleasant surprise. I had landed a fantastic assignment, the British week in Zurich; same set up as Paris, minus the Duke and Duchess of Windsor.

I did my usual preparations, a leg wax, wash hair, nails and packing. The client told us all to be at Charles Jourdan, in Bond Street, tomorrow to collect our shoes, six pairs in all…yippee we get to keep them afterwards, one of the perks of the business.

A car would pick me up at 9am on the Saturday. Great, there would be no expense spared, obviously. That's what I loved about being a mannequin, one was treated like royalty. But it also spoilt you for normal life, and I learnt to expect VIP treatment as the norm.

I hoped to open the boutique for Easter. I had bought several lengths of fabric from Derry and Toms, the zips and buttons. It wasn't going to be a big deal designing a collection as there were only 2 shapes and Jill had her worksheet, all under control. Hopefully, there would be some ready for me to see when I got back from Zurich.

My limo arrived on time and on the way to the airport I read the 'call sheet'. Press call at 10.30, girls outside plane, 11 am girls on steps of the plane waving, the usual rubbish. Lunch on board. Arrival 3pm. Hotel 4pm. Official banquet 7pm. More pictures with German something or other. Nothing different, just the same set up as always. Photos non-stop, so we had to be sure we looked beautiful all the time and to smile, bloody smile, the whole time.

When I arrived at the airport, I could hear squeals of delight coming from the departures lounge. It was always wonderful to catch up with all your old friends. Thank goodness it was the same bunch, all my friends. It was like an exclusive club; we knew we were very privileged to be there. We also realised we had reached the top of our game, and fees were steadily going up at last.

The first day would be trying on our clothes and sorting out the accessories. Then a photo shoot, first of many. Michael, my agent, was there with his partner Bill to produce the show. You knew the show would be very theatrical as that was Michael's style. Bill followed behind Michael tying up all the loose ends. There were a few tense moments when Michael lashed out at one of us, but we were used to that and he meant no harm.

The next step was with the hairdressers and then make-up. We each had our own dressers and you generally spent time together to work out how you wanted help. I was very quick changing from one garment to another, but I needed a good dresser to be there ready with shoes and gloves. Hairdresser standing by. A complete change from a suit, with hat, shoes and gloves took 3 minutes. I can still get ready at home within 3 minutes and go to the loo in 2 minutes...

The show was a hit. Everyone enjoyed it, even us, and they laid on a banquet for us. The wine flowed in abundance, the food was wonderful and that was all we were interested in.

We had an hour to look around the town the next morning. It was always the same, we never had time to do anything for ourselves. We travelled around the world and rarely saw the city we were in. Instead we bought postcards as that was the only way we could make a note of where we had been.

The trip was over, and we were back at the airport. My relief to be going home was immense as whilst away I thought of a million problems about the boutique. Perhaps I had made a mistake, perhaps I had taken on a bit too much. I realised I was just panicking, but I needed to get back as soon as possible. The Boeing looked huge as we boarded and, for one moment, I was nervous, and a chill went down my spine.

Of course, we were photographed climbing up the steps, waving and smiling. I was sitting beside Eve Lucet, not a great buddy and always a bit stuck up. I knew she thought I was beneath her, but it wasn't going to be for long, so I didn't bother to swap seats. I waved to Chrissie a few seats away. Then a nice take off...nothing to worry about, order a Dubonnet, home next stop. Well, in theory, but, actually, the plane started to judder, and there were some strange noises coming from under the plane. Nothing to worry about, after all this was a British Airways flight, so we were safe.

The captain announced we would be landing in eight minutes, 'fasten your seat belts please'. Then another message from the captain, 'Please take up the BRACE BRACE position, we have been unable to lower the under carriage, so we will be landing on the belly of the plane. Please stay calm'. We rushed to look out of the windows. What we saw didn't make us stay calm, believe me. There were 6 fire engines lining the runway and foam all over it. Well, that was it. Many of the girls on board changed from being cool and aloft into crying screaming wrecks. One girl tried to get out of the plane, and she tore her nails off trying to get the door open. Another one sobbed and then screamed, changing into a raging bull; it was a terrible sight. I managed to get some of the girls into their seats and put seat belts on; they sat and whimpered. The stewardess slapped one girl to calm her down and it worked - she just collapsed in a heap. I must say it was a terrifying experience.

The noise of scraping and the smell of burning rubber was the most dreadful sound I had ever heard. But we survived.

Of course, the press were at Heathrow. The headlines the next day were very dramatic.

MODELS IN COMET EMERGENCY
BRITAIN'S TOP MANNEQUINS NEAR FATAL ACCIDENT

Wendy Lewis reported that everyone was very calm on board, which of course was far from the truth. But I was very proud of myself as I was in complete control of my fears. Others commented that I was the star, and I think I went up a notch or two in their eyes.

Chapter 6 part 1

Paolo a star - Harriet my first boutique in 1963

After the Zurich incident, work seemed to pour in; even though nobody had died, we were treated like heroes. In a way, it was annoying as I really wanted to get on with my new venture, so I was very fussy about the bookings. I accepted a few, of course, as I knew I had to earn money for the new business. Having already managed to persuade Jill to be the first seamstress, the next step was important; I needed a trading name as Wendy Lewis was not 'catchy' enough. I had all the forms ready to fill in for the new Company but still no name. I took the bus to Companies House and on the way I noticed the name Harriet Hubbard written on the side of the bus; then I saw another bus going the other way and written on its side was HARRIET HUBBARD, a well-known brand of cosmetics. Yes that's what I will call my boutique, just 'HARRIET'. So, from that day onwards, the boutique and I were known as Harriet; now I am no longer designing, my Cocker Spaniel is called Harriet.

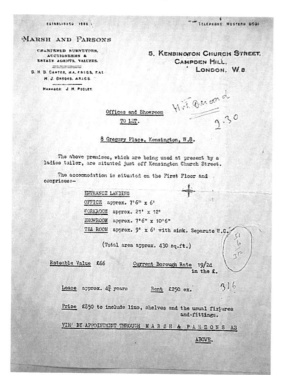

Next, all that I needed to do was to find some premises. Remember we had not made one garment yet! I decided Kensington Church Street was the right pitch, so I went into Marsh and Parsons, the estate agent, still there now. A lovely man called Mr Marshal listened to my plight; I only had £500 and needed about 500 sq. feet. He said there might be a chance that Distinctive Trimmings, the shop a few doors down the road, might be coming up, but it was £8000 a year. Well, that was no good, but Mr Marshal suggested a little loft he had in the mews just off Holland Street. It wasn't actually a prime position nor was it in a secondary position, but I loved it. It was in Gregory Place, and, up a flight of stairs, there was a big room then a smaller one, a little kitchen and a loo. Yes, this is perfect, I thought. If I had been streetwise, I would have tried to find premises that had at least a shop front but, actually, as it turned out, Harriet became so well known that people found us even though we were tucked away. The rent was £5 per week...great.

So now all I had to do was design my first collection...easy!

Meanwhile, Tom painted the main room, and my friend Gavin Robinson and I went to the Lacquered Chest in Kensington Church Street to buy some furniture, a beautiful huge 3-fold mirror, and two chests of drawers to hold fabrics. My friend Denis Norden gave me a pretty little buttoned sofa, and Marcus had lent me a Grandfather clock a few months ago, so that is where we decided to keep the tin with the takings.

harriet...

.... is a new boutique with new ideas.

You won't find one quite like it anywhere in London. Or, come to that, anywhere else.
Harriet is run by model girls who *know* fashion. *Really* know fashion. From the inside.
So, at harriet, you will (of course) find chic, up-to-the-minute clothes designed by us, ready-to-wear and inexpensive.
Or, if you like (and this *is* new) we will design especially for you. *You* choose styles and materials to suit *yourself*. And it won't be expensive. A suit absolutely exclusive to you would cost from about £15.
Or, again, you could come and browse about our SWOP SHOP: model clothes, from some of the best Houses in London, worn maybe once or twice, and at *really* low prices. Or, if there was something you just wanted to hire, you could do that, too.
Jewellery we don't do ourselves. But Paris House do. . . . And we stock it. In Kensington.
We can also give you advice on hair and make-up. Free.
We're at 8 Gregory Place, Kensington Church Street (there's a map on the next page).
So come and see us. You'll probably find just what you're looking for. And you wouldn't find it anywhere else.
And even if you don't, we think you'll have fun looking.

I went to Derry and Toms to buy a Simplicity basic pattern and several yards of fabrics. So, now Jill and I had our master pattern made in cardboard marked 'cut here for style 1' and 'cut here for style 2', we were off. What excitement! Jill never stopped for a moment; the rattling of her sewing machine could be heard all over Chiswick. The plan was to have just 2 shapes to start with, a sack dress with no sleeves and then a sack dress with sleeves. We made 12 dresses in various fabrics, all in my size, which was a size 10, but we could make other sizes to order. The prices varied from 6gns to 7gns.

I wrote a few words about Harriet Boutique's opening, and the idea was that we would put a copy in every big expensive house around the Holland

Street area. It was the first of many good ideas we had. The area was filled with rich women, and several actresses lived nearby; they were hungry for a new place to buy their clothes, especially virtually custom made. That was to be our strength.

At last the Boutique was ready to open. There were 12 dresses hanging neatly on the rail (a broomstick actually) and fabrics neatly folded on a shelf beside that. The idea was that customers could choose a fabric they liked, and we could make one of the styles in their size. A neat idea, I thought. Paris House in South Molton Street lent me a beautiful gilt edged, glass topped, padded box, which was filled with the latest chunky jewellery. There was a coffee table in front of the little buttoned sofa, where I had all the latest copies of Vogue and Harper's. This was where a customer would sit, with a cup of coffee, whilst I suggested various designs for her to choose from. All very civilized.

I decided to be the only person at the opening; although Jill would have liked to be there, I felt I needed to clear my head. Also, I thought that if nobody came, I would die of embarrassment if she was there.

I opened the door and checked the HARRIET BOUTIQUE sign was still hanging over the door. The colour scheme was navy and white and, yes, it worked; crisp and chic all rolled into one. I made a coffee and sat at the table in front of the Grandfather Clock and waited and waited. By 11 o'clock there was no sign of a customer; another coffee, rearrange the fabrics, plenty to do, keep busy. I must not cry, I must not cry.

Then I heard someone coming up the stairs. I quickly put on a Tony Bennet record, my favourite at the time. I moved to the top of the stairs, and there she was, my first customer. She was 5'10" and a heavy size 14, my biggest nightmare. Her name was Miss Tanner, and she was one of the kindest people I have ever met. I showed her the styles and the fabrics and, whilst she sipped her coffee, she decided on 3 dresses. I casual dress, a formal one and a long one for evenings. Three! I took the measurements and we laughed ourselves silly. As I was so nervous, I kept making mistakes, but she was enjoying herself so much she didn't care, bless her. We never did know her first name, but she was our first customer, and, over the years, she brought all her friends in. I made her wedding dress... Wherever you are, Miss Tanner, thank you!

Word about the boutique soon got around, and people started to climb up the stairs. I think it must have been quite daunting, but soon the casual approach won everyone over. Every day was like a fun day. I made lots of mistakes, but nobody seemed to mind. Soon, people came to see what was happening, to have a coffee, to meet me to hear all my funny stories about being a mannequin. I was quite a star. I began to realise I needed help as I had to go out to buy fabrics and then get them over to Chiswick to Jill's workroom, which meant closing the boutique. So, I asked my mother to come in two mornings a week. She was amazing as she was, of course, used to dealing with her regular customers at Harvey Nichols. My mother also had a very special relationship with Princess Alexander, the Princess always insisted my mother should serve her and they became friends. She was a born salesperson, and she brought in the older customers, all of them had daughters and they brought them in to buy their complete wardrobe for their Season. So, gradually, Harriet became the place to buy something different, something especially designed for each occasion. They didn't seem to notice that I had only that one style … sack dress one and sack dress two! The debutantes kept climbing those stairs. So, I had to rethink my approach. I needed a pattern cutter. I needed another machinist. I'm not sure I was making money as the richer the customer, the slower they paid! To hell with it. I was on a roll.

Harriet boutique – 8, Gregory Place, Kensington Church Street, W.8

Costings for outworkers	£ .. s.. .d
Simple shift....no extras	1 .. 0 .. 0
Cutting out	2.. 6
Overlocking and finishing	3.. 6
Putting in zip	2....6
	£1 .. 8.. 6
Simple shift with sleeves	1.. 7 ..6
Cutting out	2... 9
Finishing off	5.. 0
Putting in zip	2.. 6
	£1.. 17... 9
Simple suit	£3 .. 0 .. 0
Cutting out	4.. 6
Finishing	7.. 6
Buttonholes	2.. 6
	£3 .. 14.. 6
Slacks	£1 .. 0... 0
Cutting out	2.. 6
Finishing	4.. 0
Putting in short zip	2 .. 0
	£ .. 8.. 6
Coat with no collar	£ 2 .. 0 .. 0
Cutting out	3.. 6
Finishing	5.. 0
Machined buttonholes	2.. 6
	£2 .. 10 .. 0

First fitting bus fare 1/- and final fitting bus fare 1/-

I decided to put an advert in the Evening Standard. A freelance pattern cutter required for small busy boutique. Telephone FLA 1234.

Then another one. Wanted machinist for small busy boutique part time. Telephone FLA 1234.

By the end of the week, I had a lovely pattern cutter called Violette. She worked at Bus Stop, which had just opened. She was going to charge £2.10s for each pattern and 10/- for each grade up or down. I had a portfolio of some designs, so I gave her one to make as a test. She passed with flying colours; she had real flare. Meanwhile, I had some calls for a machinist but not the kind of people I wanted. In the afternoon, I had a very special call. 'Good afteroon. This is Sister Stanislaus from the Convent in the Boltons. I have a Sister who is a very accomplished machinist, and she has asked permission to work in the morning after her prayers and again, if needed, in the afternoon, after her duties. I have agreed that she can come and see you. Would you be interested in meeting her?' That sounded great. The next day, I met Sister Mercedes for the first time, and I fell in love with her. She was perfect. She could do everything: buttonholes, smocking, pleating. She was a real find.

Now we were a proper working team, two machinists, a pattern cutter and two salespeople. I was really enjoying this fashion designing business. all I needed was some working capital, then more customers. I decided to go to my Barclays bank on the corner of Kensington High Street to meet the new manager, Mr Birdseye. He offered me a glass of Sherry and asked what I needed. I showed him my plan on the back of a Senior Service packet! He was very impressed as he listened to my plans. I showed him our sales figures to date and without further ado, he asked how much I wanted to borrow. When I said £500, he agreed and added, 'I expect to see Barclays investment grow and grow, good luck'. For years my account had a note about me liking Sherry. Not now, of course, no sherry and no bank manager!

I was still going to various Balls at Grosvenor House or The Dorchester, so I never missed the opportunity to hand out my Harriet cards. I made sure that the workroom made me some stunning dresses, so I was generally featured in Jennifer's Diary, and to all the debutantes and their mums, Jennifer's Diary was what it was all about. So, soon we started to get big Roll Royces trying to drive down my little mews and chauffeurs arriving to collect my customers. At teatime, I would serve special little cakes, and it soon became THE place for tea, gossip and to buy one of Harriet's latest creations!

I still spoke to Paolo on and off, but every evening we wrote to each other, we had both achieved so much. Well, I wasn't making big money like Paolo. Every day was a challenge but always fun. I worked so hard, I never had time for anything else.

One evening I was going out to a party at a friend's flat, but I was feeling very tired, so I called my friend and said I couldn't go 'Don't you let me down. You promised to come', she said.

The party was filled with lots of people I knew already, and I felt relaxed. There were a couple of film stars there, James Coburn and Lee Marvin (Wandering Star!). I had a brief chat, but they were pretty boring and better on the screen than in real life. I was about to leave when I noticed a short, very good-looking man staring at me. He sort of ambled over to me with a swagger and a very naughty smile. Someone whispered in my ear, 'That's Eddie. He's a crimper, nice guy'. He was easy to talk to and we chatted for a while, then I said I was leaving, and he said, 'Ah dear, I thought we were getting on rather well!'. I smiled and said, 'Yes, we're getting on rather well. Maybe I will come to the salon in Dover Street and have my hair done. OK?' I did make an appointment to have my hair done with Eddie, and sometime later, we had a very crazy fling!

Chapter 6 part 2

Photography Place - could write a whole book about this studio!

When I first met the photographers at Photography Place, I never dreamed that they would play such an important part in my life. Jean introduced me to one of the photographers called Frank Sweeney, the man she met in the record shop when we were working at Polly Peck and fell in love with. They seemed to be very much in love. I think, looking back now, that it was music that kept them joined at the hip! Another photographer within this group was Jerry Mason. I didn't know him very well in those days. He always drove a Ford Mustang and wore cowboy boots and a baseball cap. He seemed to travel a lot and always had a glamorous model hanging on his arm. He was very sure of himself, I thought at the time. Then there was 'The Brain Surgeon', Jerry's assistant. Actually, he was a 'stills' photographer and pretty good, but a bit of a disaster in many ways; too much drink and too many women, perhaps. Then there was David Finch, married and a good photographer. He was the first one to die, far too young.

They had an agent/manager, called Ian MacDonald. He had been educated in a Quaker school and had quite a few hang-ups; all the years I knew him, I didn't really understand him. When I first met him in 'Hadies' in South Kensington with Frank and Jean, I gathered he had been married to Beret, a Swedish model, very beautiful, but they had recently parted. I suspect Ian was still in love with her, but she, I think, was on the way up and he was not part of the plan! Ian seemed to know lots of rich people. He was from 'up North' and had been trained as an accountant. I think all the photographers thought Ian would be an asset, and he was in a strange way. Ian's problem was he put people's backs up. Somehow, if any of the photographers needed money for a project, Ian would march into a big bank, regardless of which one, and come out with the loan! Who knows how he did it, but he did! There are many funny stories about him. One of the funniest I can remember was when he was having lunch at The Casserole in King's Road. Beret came in with her new husband and came over to say hello to Ian. When she moved to her table, Ian turned to Frank and said, 'Who was that? Do you know her?'. Frank replied, 'You were married to her for 7 years. She was your wife!'. We all laughed at these stories, but he never really understood why!

It seemed the right time for me to start looking for a flat as living with my mother in her tiny flat in Chiswick was difficult for both of us. I found one easily in Clifton Hill, near Abbey Road Studios. I was very happy there as it was very trendy, and it was great to feel free again. It was very easy to get to my bookings and things slotted in around my new little flat. It was little. I had a 2 ring Belling hob which sat on a plank of wood over the bath. I'm amazed I didn't gas myself when I had a bath, but, when you are young, safety doesn't seem to be high on your list of priorities.

Jean called one day and said the studio was throwing a party next week and hoped I would come. Of course, I love a party.

Well, what a party. I think it must have been the best party given in the 60s. Everyone was there, I mean everyone. The Moody Blues played the music. I danced myself silly. At one point, I was dancing with someone and only halfway through did I notice the man was dancing on his hands, a handstand in other words. His name, I found out later, was Long John Baldrey!

Ian had invited Prince Adan Bourbon de Parme, who was supposed to be 4th in line for the Spanish throne. I don't think Spain needed anyone like him. I remember he asked me to come and sit on his lap, and when I did, he opened his legs and I fell down on the floor. I felt such a fool, but he just laughed. He was one of the rudest men I have ever met, heir to the throne or not! Everyone drank far too much and. in those days, we did tend to drink sprits instead of wine, which had not really caught on yet. I remember getting into my Triumph TR2, I think it was mine, and driving home. I had the roof off and was singing when a policeman drew up beside me on his motorbike. He leant over and said, 'nice party then?'. He was smiling. He asked, 'Where do you live?' and suggested that he went first and I should follow him at a short distance, preferably on the road not the pavement! Driving was so laid back then, especially as the roads were pretty empty late at night. Most of us were fairly drunk from lunchtime onwards. I think there are more accidents nowadays, well possibly not, but we were never told the figures. So, perhaps we never owned up to the accidents. I remember lots of us used to leave the clubs late at night and race along Western Avenue to go bowling at Tolworth roundabout. My TR always did the tonne, and I won most times. Could I see the road…NO!

Of course, I fell in love with Ian. He was a rogue, and most women like that in a man. He didn't love me, and he didn't behave very well. He broke my heart, and it took some time to get over him. It seemed everything I did annoyed him. I remember, several months later, when I moved into a new flat in Chelsea, I asked him over for supper one evening. I couldn't cook then but made a spaghetti al Burro and bought a bottle of rather expensive Chanti. I had no furniture, just a fridge in which I kept my silk nightie and a bottle of Champagne! I also had a single bed. That was it. We ate supper on the bed. He said he would stay the night. He did, but I wish he hadn't. He complained about the pillow, he only liked Dunlop pillows, not feather; the pigeons 'cooed' too much and at about 3 am he stormed out. Well, I got rid of the pigeons, bought a table and a Dunlop pillow, but he never came again! He slept with most of my girlfriends, and I pretended not to know… but I did!

He married 4 times in the end. Mandy was wife number three, I think, and they almost opened a club in Ibiza called Mandy's. But as usual, something went wrong, and it never opened. I still have the tee shirt though! Then he joined forces with Tommy Yerdi, and they bought an island called Grand Exuma, or was it little Exuma. They were going to build a village but didn't realise that every high tide the island submerged under water, wrong again!

Ian had a daughter with Mandy, but I only met her at his funeral; I don't think he was a very good father. Sadly, Mandy died a few years ago. She had Alzheimer's. The trouble with Ian was that he was always ill. He was a bit of a hypochondriac, but as he looked so white, well grey, he looked as if he was about to drop down dead at any moment! Although we all laughed about it behind Ian's back, we always kept an eye on him.

One particular day, we knew he was going to go into the London Clinic for an exploratory procedure, so in the evening we decided to all troop into the hospital to see him and eat his grapes! When we got to the Reception at the Clinic, we asked which room he was in. We were told, 'He's gone!'. Not sure what the receptionist meant. We just looked blank and said, 'Gone where?'. For a moment, I thought he had died, but then the girl said, 'Mr MacDonald didn't like our wine list, so he went to the Wellington Hospital!'. I know how silly that sounds, but, of course, for us it was typical of Ian. We just went on to the Wellington Hospital as if it was a usual thing for a patient to do!

Ian's last wife was Veronica; she was French and had four children from a former marriage. He ruled those kids with a rod of iron, but I think they loved him. By this time, I had met a new man. He was called Dawson, and you will find out who he is later on. We used to see them quite often in their flat in Bayswater Road, London. We played Bridge together. Ian was a good player and even better at Brag because of his glum face!

In Bridge he had a habit of saying halfway through the game, 'I think the rest are mine!'. They were, generally, but it was rather annoying at the time. One weekend they came down to stay with us in the country. They were unpacking, and I was cooking the supper. I heard Dawson say something like, 'There isn't a God, especially in this house,' or something stupid like that. Ian slammed his suitcase closed and grabbed Veronica by the arm saying, 'We aren't staying in this house any longer!'. I said something about Dawson just being funny although I knew he meant it. Veronica stood ashen faced, then grabbing her coat she followed Ian down the stairs. I burst into tears. Ian came back to say sorry to me, and then they left! That was what Ian was like, always a short fuse. We would catch up with them in a couple of weeks later and the incident was never mentioned again!

Our Ibiza experience…I remember, Ian, Frank and Jerry bought a boat in Ibiza. So, we would all leave work on a Friday lunchtime and catch the afternoon flight. The fare was about £19 return, those were the days. We discovered Ibiza and we had so much fun. We would stay at the Fenica hotel in Santa Eulalia if there was no room on the boat. We just spent the days on the boat or swimming and the nights drinking in all the harbour side bars. We didn't do drugs, but we did do drink, plenty of it. We didn't do anyone any harm except perhaps to ourselves.

Veronica called me one day a few years later and said they were renting a house in the country and asked us to come and see them. When we got there, I could see something was wrong. Veronica suggested Ian and I went for a walk around the garden whilst she made some tea. When we were far enough from the house and near a bench, we sat down. Ian turned to face me, and I could see he was upset. 'I have skin cancer and it's terminal'. I was silent. Don't cry Wendy, I said to myself, he doesn't need that. I couldn't think of anything to say, so I just hugged him. Actually, I think that was the right move, as he collapsed in my arms and let out a sob. We stayed motionless for some time, and that was it. We walked back to the house and had tea. Nothing was mentioned anymore about the cancer. He died shortly afterwards.

AN ASIDE

Although I feel sad when I think about Ian, I do also remember those awful times when I cried myself to sleep night after night because he didn't love me. He couldn't help not loving me, but it did change my life. He hurt me by sleeping with my friends, and I wasn't able to cope with it. I can smile now when I realise that in the end, when he was dying, who was with him...me!

Chapter 6 part 3

Eddie the crimper

One morning, I got a call from the estate agent Marsh and Parsons telling me they had a flat to let across the road from Harriet. It had one bedroom and a pretty courtyard garden with parking in the front. I went to see it at once, and it was a dream come true. Jean helped me move in, and she also rented the flat next door, flat A and flat B Mount Carmel Chambers. It was one of the happiest times of my life. We had many parties there, lots of laughter and quite a few tears, but I was so so happy there. I don't remember really going to bed… who needs sleep anyway!

I'm not sure why I started to have my hair done at Andre Bernard's in Dover Street. I had met Eddie at a party a couple of weeks before at my friend Pat's party and I was curious to meet up with him. I thought making an appointment to have my hair done was the way forward. Apparently, there was always a nice friendly atmosphere at the salon, and Maud, the cloakroom lady, was always ready for a good gossip. So, I made a booking with Eddie.

Eddie liked to call himself a 'crimper.' He called most of his clients 'Fred' and had a funny habit of flaring his nostrils, which he thought was funny. It wasn't, but nobody would ever have told him for he was a very dear person. Eddie came from Hackney and together with Vidal Sassoon and Gerald Austen at Carita, they virtually took over the hairdressing scene in London in the 60s.

After a few visits, Eddie and I started to go out together. Why? I don't know… as he was not my kind of man, but it just happened. He said, 'Would you like to go out to diner one evening,' and I said 'Yes'. So we did. Eddie had a set pattern with every girl he took out, I think. He would suggest a restaurant, perhaps San Lorenzo's or Trattoo in Abingdon Road, High Street Ken. This was near my home and his, so we would generally meet there; he never picked me up. He always stood when I walked into the room, a thing of the past, shame. I would drink wine, and he always drank whiskey. I remember after going out with him for a while, I dropped the wine and joined him with the whiskey. It was the start of my heavy drinking. You could never keep up with Eddie, but I tried hard! After our meal, the waiter would bring me a plate of Cape Gooseberries with pink icing on the top. I loved them, and most waiters in London knew the way to my heart.

IN MY VIEW . . .

NOEL WHITCOMB TALKS TO EDWARD MORRIS

When a titled lady enters the lush Mayfair hairdressing salon over which Edward Morris presides, Edward looks up and calls, "Hullo, Fred!"

"I call all my clients 'Fred'," he said, with a grin. "Duchesses, models, girls from offices—I treat them all as women instead of according to their status. That's the secret of dealing with women, I find."

Edward is 31, a bachelor, and has the dark handsomeness of a French film actor, with a touch of Sammy Davis vividness; in fact, he is a Cockney who started shaving dockers in an East End barber's shop and graduated accidentally to Mayfair by way of being a seaman in the Merchant Navy. Today he is a top hairstylist, and director of the swish Andre Bernard hairdressing business.

I went to see him because he is the sort of man who is an instant success with almost all women, and I wanted to find out whether this is a gift a chap is born with, or whether there is a formula for it.

"I think," said Edward, "it's something you can learn by experience. To start with, you have to realise all women are basically no good."

"I'm sure all the women you know will be delighted to hear that," I said, "although it might not be a bad idea to invest in a bullet-proof waistcoat in preparation for the moment when your remark is published. But, seriously, do you really *believe* that?"

"Well . . . not in my heart," said Edward. "The fact is, a man ought to give women the impression he suspects they are no good, because that, oddly enough, is privately flattering to a woman, although she might slosh you with her handbag if you came right out and said it.

"Women are such funny creatures. Although they are all the same in a way, you have to treat every one of them subtly different. And the more you see of them, the more they make your eyebrows rise in surprise. It's the top-bracket ones who really like to relax and let their hair down, astonishingly enough."

"But," I said, "isn't life pretty tricky at times in your job? I mean, if a woman is being extremely matey, you surely have to watch your step pretty carefully to make sure you don't say anything that will make her suddenly freeze up and give you the icy look?"

"Sure," nodded Edward. "You have to watch that. But it becomes second nature after a time when you deal with women daily. You sum up every woman from the start and try to assess what goes on inside the brain-box under the hair-do.

"I used to be terribly shy of women when I was a lad, but I gradually discovered one of the most important things to remember is that you must never be frightened of them. If you ever let a woman think you are nervous of her, she immediately realises she is in a position to treat you in any way she wishes—and sometimes does. Because, no matter how sweet women are on the surface, underneath they are cold and

calculating. Everything they do has a reason."

"It sounds," I murmured, "as though you have been given a bit of a going-over by the odd girl or two."

Edward grinned. "You're right," he said. "I nearly got married about three years ago, then it just . . . fizzled out. But it taught me something else about women. They are never exactly what they seem to outward appearance. When I see a woman for the first time now, I look for the real woman behind the act she is putting on. Very often she is trying to appear the sort of woman she would like to be, instead of the woman she really is. But she is usually quite relieved if a man sees inside the package, and treats her as the kind of person she truly is. Then she can relax and be natural. If the man accepts the act instead of the reality, he's lost."

I said it must be easier for a hairdresser than for most men to figure out these subtleties. "Oh, sure," agreed Edward. "As a hairdresser, you have such a personal relationship with a woman because you are actually touching her even before you've been introduced. You see her half-undressed and you don't take any notice. You see her at her worst, without make-up, and she takes it all for granted just as she would with her doctor. Those facts break down quite a few barriers for a start.

"The moment a hairdresser puts his hands on a woman's hair, she senses whether or not he knows his business. Also she knows instinctively something about the man himself—whether he is afraid, or shy, of women.

"If she realises you are not afraid of her or impressed by her outward act, she immediately relaxes—and that goes for any man. In a hairdressing salon the situation is simply magnified, because once a woman relaxes, she begins to set up a personal relationship with her hairdresser which invariably involves the exchange of confidences.

"Women tell their hairdresser absolutely

everything about themselves. But they expect him to be equally frank about himself—it's a sort of protection, because secrets shared mean neither side would ever dare be indiscreet. That's the way a woman's mind works. Pretty primitive, when you examine it."

Edward is a strange, likeable, eccentric character, but the oddest thing about him is that he has achieved this big acclaim as an international hairstylist in such a happy-go-lucky sort of way.

"I didn't set out to be a hairdresser," he smiled. "I didn't really care what I did. My parents were quite poor. I had an uncle in hairdressing, and my mother thought she'd like me to take it up, so she sent me to the Polytechnic in Regent Street to do a course. This didn't cost anything.

"I loved it. There were jazz-concerts every lunch-time, and I played basket-ball the rest of the time. So when I finished there, all I could get was a job in a barber's shop, shaving dockers. A real tough school, that was. You need a steady hand when you're shaving dockers. If you give them a nick, they are likely to jump up and nick you back!

"After that, I did a couple of years' national service in the R.A.F. and then got a job for a month doing women's hairdressing, but I was chucked out because I was no good—I'd no experience. So I joined the Merchant Navy and sailed round the world."

It was through meeting, when on leave, a girlfriend who worked at Andre Bernard that Edward tried his luck at the salon and landed a job there. Four years later he was a di....

In those early days Edward often used to get called into the office and told off because of the stunts he got up to. "But I was just doing what came naturally," he said. "If a woman came in with long hair, and asked to have it cut off, I used to take out a big saw, and maybe a hammer and chisel, and I'd say, with a completely straight face, 'Right, just hang on a minute. This won't hurt.' Some of them used to believe me and get up with a shriek. Then we'd all have a laugh.

"Mind you, you don't do that with everyone. You judge your client. I've got a staff of seventy-five to control now, so I tone it down a bit. But I still stay natural, and that's the biggest secret of all when dealing with women. I'm a Cockney and they know it. If an important lady comes in, I'll probably say, 'Hullo—you here again! Righto, me old bottle—sid-down. Jump in the basin and we'll get started.'

"If I started putting on an act, women would see through it right away—it's only the people who are phonies themselves who are impressed.

"What most men do wrong is try to act a part they think women want them to act, but reality is what women want most of all. They are very close to reality—closer than men—so they put on a veneer of sophistication to conceal that fact. A man who looks beneath the veneer, and is natural himself, automatically becomes a friend on an equal footing.

"There's only one other thing a man has to remember when dealing with women," went on Edward, smiling. "That is, what a woman wants most is the thing she can't get. Once you learn that, the rest is simple."

"Hm," I said, thoughtfully. "You wouldn't be kidding yourself, by any chance . . .?" **END**

Then, when Eddie had paid the bill and flared his nostrils at the check-out girl, we would fall into his MG and head for one club or another. Our favourite one was the 'Ad Lib' in Charles Street, at the top of the building. Once we were nearing the top floor in the lift, we could hear the noise of music and smell the smoke; everyone seemed to smoke in those days; it was what we did. When you stepped out of the lift, you really just switched off your brain and let the music take over. The music was too loud to speak, so you made your way to your table, ordered more whiskey...and danced!

Eddie danced with a little wiggle and, basically, didn't move a lot, but he stayed very cool. He was a follower of Tony Bennet and Frank Sinatra. He often danced with a cigarette hanging out of his mouth in a nonchalant way; it was his image, and he had perfected it. Dear Eddie! He loved going out with me as I was game for anything and often danced on the tables with Marilyn Rickard who was a good dancer too. They say she had an affair with Peter Sellars, but it may have been just gossip. I gather she had a bit of a drink problem, like we all did then, but now she is not in good shape.

The club was run by a nice man called Brian Morris. He liked Eddie and always made sure he had the best table, the one on the right when you came out of the lift. That was also the table the Beatles always sat when they came to the club. So, if they were there, we moved over to the next table. Ringo always called me Madam; he was very polite. I think the whole scene was bit beyond his comfort zone, but he and his girlfriend, Barbara or was it Maureen, occasionally got up to dance. A funny kind of dance. He seemed to be pretending he was a boxer and punched as if he had boxing gloves on; it didn't catch on! John Lennon spent the evening jumping up and down, he was quite restless, whilst George Harrison was always grumbling about having too much money and was often near to tears with the worry of it all...but nobody seemed to care about it. We just wish we had that kind of money.

One evening, Eddie and I were well into several whiskies and having fun. I was dancing around the club as usual, and the Rolling Stones came in. In the past, Brian had always kept them separate from the Beatles. They were seated in the opposite corner, not that there would have been trouble as it was not that sort of club, but better to be safe than sorry was Brian's plan. That night, everyone had been drinking a lot, and it was about 2 am when all of a sudden someone shouted, 'Congo,' and we all held on to each other and started kicking our legs out to the side. Then someone pinched my bottom and whispered in my ear, 'Pass it on'. Of course, I did; the man whose bottom I had pinched turned to me with a big grin on his face, 'I liked that,' he said, 'Do it again'. Obviously, I did, and everyone was laughing. Then I realised it was John Lennon's bottom I had been pinching! We continued up the corridors and through the club. It seemed funny then, but I suspect we were pretty drunk. John and I collapsed in our chairs, and I asked him to pass the menu as I was starving.

The Ad Lib was the darkest club of all, which is why many celebrities went there. They could party without fans watching. As I couldn't read the menu, I asked John if I could borrow his glasses. He handed them over and disappeared. So that is how I ended up with a pair of gold rimmed glasses. I kept them in my knicker drawer for 20 years and only recently I decided to part with them. I sold them for £10,000, but it makes me sad that they are not there anymore.

Out of the blue, the manager of the Ad Lib, Brian Morris left the club to work in a new club in Los Angeles. Shortly afterwards he died; none of us ever knew the truth behind his death, such a nice guy, such a pity.

The whole time Eddie and I went out, we were both in love with someone else. I was still in love with a man who didn't love me, and it was so distressing. As there was no way I could make him love me, I tried to drink and dance him out of my mind. Eddie was the right person to help me to do that. Meanwhile, he was madly in love with a model called Julie, who apparently looked like me, so that's perhaps why we got together. But both of us were so wounded, we didn't think of our relationship that way, I suppose.

One of Eddie's clients was Ursula Andress, hot from her role in the James Bond film where she came out of the sea with a bikini on and a knife tucked into it... you know the picture. Well, Eddie fell head over heels in love with her, and although he was only half her size, the flaring nostrils seemed to work, and they got on like a house on fire...only as friends I must add.

After a few months of going out together, Eddie told me that he had mentioned to his partners at Andre Bernard (a chain of successful hairdressers) that it would be a step forward to ask Harriet boutique to open a branch at the Bond Street salon. After signing lots of complicated contacts, Harriet opened the second boutique within the hairdressing salon. He then set up a meeting with Julie and himself with the view to setting up a franchise business with Harriet. It never came to anything as I think Eddie couldn't bear to work with Julie. A few weeks later, Eddie phoned me and told me Julie was getting married to Evelyn Rothschild. She told him she was doing it for the name only and didn't intend to consummate the marriage! What a strange set up. I could hear from

Eddie's voice that his heart was truly broken.

One evening I went to a friend's flat, girls only, where the hostess made a list of all the men around at the time and we girls had to say if we had slept with any of them. Well, guess who was top of the list? Eddie! He had slept with most of her girlfriends, so I decided to move on! I just must add that all the girls gave him 5 stars for being 'good in bed'. Although he was not well endowed, he was always fun, and we were all very fond of him!

Naturally, Julie's marriage didn't last long, and once the divorce came through, she married a man called Stephen May. Poor Eddie went to work in a new branch of Andre Bernard in Tokyo. Who knows what happened there, but perhaps Sake was swapped for whisky because he continued to drink? When he returned to London, he was in a sorry state, but he still smiled and still flared his nostrils, bless him. I gather that he used to spend his evenings across the road in the little club in the basement, drinking and playing piano with Alan Price, one of my favourite musicians in the 60s.

Finally, Eddie did get married, and I went to see him in his flat in Kensington to congratulate him. He was there, she was not, but she had left her dog with him. I could tell that the marriage was over, but I didn't say anything. That was the last time I saw him.

A few months later, the papers were all filled with the death of Julie, or as the papers called her Jeanette May. Apparently, Julie, who had changed her name by now, and a friend had been buying antiques and smuggling them back to London. The Mafia were supposed to be involved. They didn't want Italian antiques to be taken out of the country, so the next thing we all heard was that Jeanette and her friend were found outside Rome in a shallow grave. I couldn't bring myself to call Eddie. A few months later, he died of Cirrhosis of the liver. So very sad. The little crimper was dead, but maybe it was what he wanted if he couldn't have his Julie!

I have found a few facts about Julie's death…it may not be the actual facts, but from what I know from the family, I think it is not far off the truth.

One day in 1980 Jeanette May and her friend Guerin, who had two children and was known to be frightened of the dark, drove to Sarnano in the hills outside Rome. Jeanette had bought a farmhouse there. Later that day, they drove out into the hills despite the warning there was going to be snow. When they didn't return to the farmhouse, the police sent out search parties. They found the Peugeot 104 snowed in, but when they tried to start it, it started at once, which meant that the women hadn't run out of petrol. The car was filled with antiques, various valuables, clothes and a stereo. The search party found nothing in the two days.

It was disclosed that Julie had a large life insurance...

In desperation Stephen May offered a $150,000 reward for any information leading to his wife's disappearance. The women's bodies were found by two Boar hunters, who claimed the reward. The Police confirmed the bodies were of Jeanette May and her friend.

Both women's high heeled boots were in good condition, so the police suspected that they might have been carried to their final destination. They were taken back to Rome and there was a report that Jeanette's neck had strangulation marks on it. Their watches had stopped, giving the time of the 'murder'. No more information has come to light till present...I am working on it.

AN ASIDE

Some months before Eddie died, there was a big drama at Andre Bernard. A murder.

Every morning at about 8.30 am, Dawson (my boyfriend at the time) and I would drive through the park in our white Alfa. We always went through the same gate by the Albert memorial.

Later in that particular morning, I was in the workroom at Harriet in Margaret Street when my PA came and whispered in my ear that the murder squad were in reception and wanted to see me! I thought it was a joke; it wasn't. Apparently, Andre, one of the directors of Andre Bernard, had been murdered in the exact place a few minutes after we had driven past! They showed me an identikit picture of a man, which looked exactly like Eddie, and asked if I knew anyone fitting the description. I didn't hesitate. I said 'NO.' There was no way Eddie could have killed anyone; he was not like that, and he admired Andre as he had given him the chance to get out of the East End.

The murder has never been solved but some of the papers thought it was a 'hit job,' maybe by the Mafia in Paris where Andre had run up considerable gambling debts. He also owed money to some man in London, and rumour had it that this man had paid a hit man £5000 to shoot Andre. I feel it must have been someone he knew as he had stopped his red TR at the roadside, opened the door and switched his engine off. He was shot twice in the head and died on the pavement. Andre was gay, a big gambler and a kind gentle person.

We will never know the true reason. Eddie was heartbroken.

Chapter 6 part 4

Ski-ing in Courcheval - phew!

Some friends of mine, Gordon and Pat, asked if I would like to go skiing with them. I had just designed my first 'après ski' collection, and I had bought some ski pants from France. I had never skied but was eager to try.

Courcheval was magical; thick snow and chic people everywhere. I got kitted out, but the weight of the skis made my right knee click out of place, so my skiing was really over before it began. I tried a bit on the nursery slopes, but I was scared it would click again. One evening everyone decided to go to bed early, and Pat and I thought we would go to the bar for a glass of Glühwein or something! The bar was empty, and we sat talking to the barman. Just as we thought we would go to bed, two men came in. One stocky young man and one of the most beautiful men I had ever seen. 'Wow,' I said under my breath. They came over and asked us if we would like to join them for a drink. Without hesitation we said 'yes'. We discussed snow, the weather tomorrow and then what each one of us worked at, you know the usual thing. I realised that the good looking one was moving closer to me as he spoke whilst his friend made a sort of lean towards Pat. It was then that I could have summed my life up had I have known the future. Pat's man was 'son of Ciba', the giant pharmaceutical company; he was rich, very rich. My wonderful delicious man was his ski instructor. That was the difference between Pat and me; she had a nose for money, and I fell for looks, my downfall you will see.

Well let's just say we danced until 3am; the music was lovely, and I remember it clearly – 'I wish you love' by Gloria Lynne. I still play it now, and it reminds me of my holiday love affair. I didn't get to ski at all, but I was pretty happy. We both fell 'in love.' His name was Peter and he lived in Zermatt. He still lives and works in Zermatt. I know because I looked him up online, and he is still so handsome. When I left to go back to London, he said he would come to be with me after the ski season had finished. He phoned every night and we had some steamy phone calls.

Unfortunately for him, when I got back, work came first. Harriet was busy. I had the Press wanting to borrow clothes for Vogue and Harpers. I had photo shoots I needed to be on, and, to be honest, I sort of forgot him! When he finally came over to surprise me, I was surprised! Jean was with me that day, and I managed to say under my breath, 'book him into an hotel' and she did. I broke his heart, I'm afraid. He got over it, but, apparently, still holds a grudge. I don't blame him for I was heartless.

Out of the blue, an actor called Peter Burton started to take me out for an odd meal; that was if he could stop me working long enough. He was good company and a good actor. Everyone liked him, including me although not in that way; we were 'just good friends'. One evening we had been to the theatre, and he had dropped me back to my flat. He opened the boot of his car and brought out a bunch of slightly crushed red roses. He said in his best RADA voice, 'Well my darling, it had to be red roses one day didn't it'. He had fallen in love with me. I was not ready for that, and it didn't fit into my plans. I said, 'Thank you' and 'Good night'. I was still feeling guilty about poor Peter from Zermatt!

A few months later, I was taken into hospital with terrible stomach pains. My doctor thought I was pregnant, but it turned out to be polyps in my uterus. They operated and all was well. The surgeon came to see me afterwards and said that he was unsure as to whether I would be able to have children. They advised me to try as soon as possible. Like anything else in life, if someone says you can't have this or that, you want it. I had never even thought of having a baby as I was having too good a time and work was so demanding.

Me and Simon

I still saw Peter from time to time at his flat in Chiswick; sometimes we went out to have a Wimpy, or I would go to his place for beef burger and crinkle chips, his staple diet! Peter was still so much in love with me, but I managed to make him understand that I had my girlfriends and work commitment. He didn't like it but as long as I saw him most nights, he was satisfied, and it suited me. We made love from time to time, but I always went

home, never stayed the whole night. Again, I was tormented by the fact that there were two men in my life. Although in theory Paolo and I were just 'good friends!' A friend of Peter's suggested we should go away from London for a few days and said we could use her little cottage in the grounds of Hardwick Hall. I had a cat called Simon; I always called him my first born and would never leave him. So, we took Simon on holiday with us; he hated it (see the picture!)

Chapter 6 part 5

Harriet and the Lesbians trousers!

Everything was going really well at Harriet. We had a good team, and everyone enjoyed working there. Never a dull moment. One day I had a call from Gavin Robinson. He was doing well with his model agency, and we rarely saw each other as we were both so busy. 'Darling, what are you doing tonight?' he said in a mysterious voice. 'Well, working on the new collection, why?' He said he had been asked to a big fashion party and thought I ought to be seen there. He wouldn't take no for an answer, and, to be honest, I didn't put up much of a fight. I needed to get out occasionally, I suppose. An evening with Gavin was always worthwhile. He insisted that I wore trousers; when I asked why, he said 'Wait, it's a surprise!'. A surprise it was!

Dolphin square

He picked me up, and we drove to Dolphin Square, the expensive flats down by the river. I think even then it had a bit of a reputation, but I didn't think much about it at the time. Gavin knocked on the door, and, as he did so, he turned to me and said, 'You are broad minded, aren't you?'. Before I could answer the door flew open. There were several 'darlings' and big hugs and more 'darlings'. I was introduced and was duly hugged. I sort of felt uncomfortable but thought no more about it. Gavin popped a drink into my hand and almost immediately someone tapped me on the shoulder and asked me to dance, 'Well, maybe when I have finished my drink'. He looked me squarely in the face and said, 'But darling, surely you can do two things at once!'. He grabbed me and twirled me around the room, glass and all. We danced for a little while he seemed to be squeezing me tighter and tighter. I saw Gavin over my shoulder and gave him a 'help' look, but he and his friend just laughed. The music stopped, and before this strange man grabbed me again, I did a sort of double twirl and headed for the loo. I had escaped. Only when I got to the loo did it dawn on me. This was a lesbian party! Gavin had done it again. I must have been dancing with one of the few men there. NO, I realise, he was a she! I am sort of broad minded, but then I am also a bit of a prude, secretly. I went back to Gavin and asked him to thank the host and left.

The next morning the papers were full of pictures of semi naked men and women dancing in the fountain in the front of the flats. Phew! Glad I missed that. About mid-day, Gavin called to say he was sorry; he thought I would enjoy a night out. He then added that he told everyone that I was a dress designer and that Harriet made the best trousers in town and had handed out my cards to everyone at the party. The very next day the 'girls' started to come up the stairs. They wanted trousers, Harriet trousers. Gavin had done a good job!

I wasn't about to start measuring inside leg measurements, so I handed it over to my mother and Sister Mercedes. They were very matter of fact - my mother did the measuring and Sister Mercedes took down the details, their names, addresses and then asked for a £5 deposit. It always amused me if I was around as Mercedes often made the sign of the cross as she walked back to her workroom! The stream of 'girls' went on all day. How on earth were we going to cope, but cope we did. It was the start of a new money earner for Harriet. There was a hairdresser called Joseph in Hampstead, who called one day to make an appointment to meet me to discuss working together. He had heard about our trousers and came to see me. He placed a big order, and that was our very first wholesale order. Of course, Joseph became very well-known, and it was nice to be in at the beginning of his success.

My life was confined to the little boutique at the top of the stairs. I was not complaining, but I did realise I was missing things by just dedicating my life to my work. Peter was also getting fed up with me always being tired. He came over to the flat or I went to him for supper. We sometimes went out to Daquise, a Polish restaurant in South Kensington. That was very adventurous as far as Peter was concerned, but not for me of course. One evening during supper, Peter asked if it would be a good idea if he took me away for a few days so I could rest. We decided to go to the cottage at Hardwick Hall again. So, a few days later, having left lists for everyone, we left for our mini break. I couldn't leave Simon, my ginger Tom, behind so he was bundled into a cardboard box, grumbling of course, and off we went. We had a lovely time; we just walked and sat in front of the fire and read sometimes. We actually enjoyed each other's company for the first time for months.

Back to work and trying to catch up after my break was not easy, but I did feel better, and I was in a better place with Peter. I decided to try a little harder with our relationship. Sadly, after three weeks, we had drifted back into the old ways. Crinkle chips and burgers!

My agent phoned and told me that I had been booked for a week of shows in Bournemouth, at Bobbies. I was excited as it meant that I could get to see my Auntie Vi and Auntie Barbara in Boscombe. So, although we were really busy at the Boutique, I accepted. Also, I could do with the money! The money was always a worry, and it seemed sad that everyone worked so hard, but there was never any money in the bank!

We met all the mannequins at Waterloo station, lots of hugs and giggles, lots of flashing cameras as usual. I loved getting back to work with my lovely friends, I had missed them. I realised that I had been working like a zombie, and a few days away behaving badly would do me the world of good. The 'behaving badly' started that night; we had had rather a lot of wine at supper. Then we had an 8pm rehearsal which went smoothly, and Michael and his partner Bill were relieved. By the time we got to bed, we were so wound up that we couldn't sleep; someone suggested we had a bed race up the corridor as the beds had wheels. Well, it was fantastic, so liberating. However, we made so much noise the other guests complained, and the manager had to come and calm us down!

The show went well, I think, but there was a lot of waiting around, boring. So, Jean and I decided to jazz it up a bit and blacked our teeth out. When we slid down the catwalk towards the compare, who in this case was Nola Rose, we did a spin and smiled at her. Of course, she burst into laughter, but the audience couldn't see us; very childish but great fun! In another performance we wrapped Shirley Osborne in two toilet rolls, and she missed her turn, more laughter. It was wonderful to be so relaxed with my friends. I realised how much I had missed.

A few weeks later my life took a turn, a big turn, a very big turn. I was pregnant! So, my lovely gynaecologist, Mr David Roberts, who had told me after the operation to remove my polyps that it was very unlikely that I could conceive, was wrong.

For a moment, I panicked; then I cried, then I laughed, then I called my mother, then Jean and then Chrissie. I decided for the moment not to tell Peter; I needed to get this sorted in my head.

Chapter 6 part 6

A Baby - and a Mouse

One morning when I was opening up the boutique, I felt my first 'kick'…With all the excitement around Harriet, I had forgotten that I was pregnant, silly me. Wasn't life just wonderful.

My doctor, lovely Dr Roberts, gave me a big lecture at our next appointment. He was nervous about the long hours that I was keeping, but when I explained that I was a workaholic, he could see there was little he could do to stop me. He insisted that I went to see Betty Parsons, who was going to teach me the art of giving birth! She was a delight. She answered all our questions and addressed all our worries. She had a wonderful format, something I still use now. She taught the Queen of England to deliver the next King of England, Prince Charles, so I suspect I was in the right hands!

Jean decided she was going to be in charge, always bossy. I must say, I was relieved as I was beginning to feel rather nervous. Trying to work and staying calm was difficult, but I would manage I was sure. Jean, who was living next door, was always on hand. She decided that we should practice everything. After supper one evening, we would do a practice run. We practised the puffing and panting that Betty taught us; well, it was more giggles than puff. She would clear the kitchen table, make me get in the right position, more giggles. I did try to point out that by the time we had done all this, it would be quicker to go St Georges Hospital, which was ten minutes away!

Dr Roberts was quite cross with me as he soon realised I was drinking, smoking and generally working too hard. He arranged for me to have a scan and then crossed his arms and said, 'Well, I am not happy for you to go on like this. I want you to come in on Tuesday, no arguments. In fact, I almost feel like saying you should stay in now, but I know you have to organise everything. So, have a restful weekend and then I want you at the hospital at 10 am on Tuesday 20th April. Understood?' I didn't dare argue and knew he was right.

Then panic set in. I knew this was going to be the most important event of my life, and I was ready; well, as ready as anyone would be having a baby on their own. I had the support of my team, Peter, my mother, Paolo and my dearest friend Jean. How difficult could it be!

Remembering what Betty Parsons had taught me, take your OWN nightie, take a couple of lemons and some damp flannel, I checked once again everything was in the suitcase. Here we go. Jean drove me to the hospital, but at the last moment, we decided that we should have some breakfast, so we went to the Royal Garden Hotel and ordered a big 'fry up' - our 'last meal' before motherhood. Only when the meal arrived did I remember that in about half an hour's time, I would have to have an enema! So, I sat and watched Jean eat both breakfasts, hoping that if I hadn't had anything to eat, they would not have to give me an enema. I was wrong!

At the hospital, Jean settled me into bed. We chatted most of the day, girls' names, boys' names, which school to send him or her to? I had almost forgotten why we were there. They decided to do more tests on me, so Jean gave me a big hug and left! Then the nurses took over, taking my temperature and blood pressure. When, at last, I was alone, I got out of bed and looked at the clock by the park. I stayed up watching the clock until it was 12 midnight. I knew that this was the day I was having a baby. In the morning, more nurses and more temperature taking, along with non-stop blood pressure pads being put on. There seemed to be a problem. Apparently, my temperature was erratic. I knew what the problem was but didn't want to tell anyone as I was so embarrassed. The problem was that they kept sending young good-looking student doctors to check on me. They would lift my nightie and put a little horn on my big belly to listen to the baby's heartbeat. Every time they did that, my temperature went up. (Come on, they were all rather dishy!) At about 11 am, Dr Roberts made his decision. I had to have a Caesarean. I tried to explain that I was all prepared to have my baby naturally, but he just said that my baby couldn't breathe in there, so he needed to operate now! That was it. I called Peter and Jean. I was taken at great speed up to the top floor for the operation. As I drifted off to sleep, I vaguely remember wondering where my own nighty was, and the lemon...

My baby was born on 21st April by Caesarean in St Georges in Hyde Park, now a hotel called The Lanesborough. When I came around, I could hear guns firing, the 21-gun salute for the Queen's birthday. I was quite sure it was for me, and no one could convince me differently. (Every year Sarah, my daughter, and I go to stand in the doorway of the Lanesborough hotel with the doormen and drink a glass of bubbles together. We listen to the 21-gun salute for this was a special day for the Queen and my Sarah.)

Peter, Jean and my mother were with me when I saw my little girl for the first time. I knew she was something special; we named her Sarah. I stayed in the hospital for 3 days and managed to feed her. I was so proud; everything was going to be alright after all.

Peter took us home in Tikie, the red TR, and Jean and my mother followed slowly behind. A sort of royal parade, I thought.

I must admit that once I got home, I started to panic. I felt there were so many germs around, and everyone smoked as well. I bought lots of Milton and 4 face masks and made everyone wear them. If you wanted to pick her up, you had to wash your hands in Milton. Maybe all new mums do this, who knows. It did seem that I had a truly wonderful baby; I'm sure all mums say that, but mine never cried at night. She gurgled and smiled and kicked her legs in the air with gay abandon; she was special from the start. Jean and I used to take her out in her huge Blue Cross pram, and everyone looked into the pram as we walked around the Round Pond in Kensington Gardens. I think they thought we were royal or something!

Everything was perfect, and we soon fell into a perfect pattern. I would feed Sarah at about 7 in the morning and get her ready for the day before I shower and get myself ready. At 9 am my mother would arrive, and I would go to work over the road. Smooth operation, yes! I popped back every feed time and we all had a cuddle. Jean would sometimes come in to check everything was OK and play with her goddaughter. We were such a happy little group. Peter was always around somewhere or other. He still had his room in Chiswick, and he was still doing his City and Guilds motor mechanic's course.

Out of the blue, Mouse turned up with his new wife Carola. She seemed very nice, and I thought Mouse was very calm. I gathered he was still meditating, but that was what he wanted. I suppose it was under control. They 'cooed' over Sarah and left.

I tried to call them over the next few weeks, but they never answered the phone. I presumed they were sort of on their 'honeymoon' and didn't want to be disturbed. Tom lived in the same house, 19 Calthorpe Street, and when I spoke to him, he would just say every morning there was a rubbish bag outside with several opened baked bean tins and the odd empty bottle of wine. So, we left them alone.

About three weeks later I had a call from Tom. He was in a terrible state. He asked to speak to Peter, but he wasn't there, so he told me the news. Mouse had got up early in the morning, walked down the road to Farringdon tube station and thrown himself in front of a silver tube train! I couldn't take it in, and it still makes me feel sick every time I think of it. My darling Mouse dead. He was such a calm and special person. What he had done was not the sort of action he would have taken unless driven to it. Tom needed Peter to go with him to identify the body, or what was left of it. When Peter came in, he was too upset to drive, so I made him some tea and waited until he stopped shaking. I decided to stay at home with Sarah. There was nothing I could do, but I wanted to scream. Marcus, Marcus my darling friend Mouse!

Peter went to the mortuary with Tom and then they went back to be with Carola. Peter phoned to say she was in such a state of shock that he thought he had better stay next door with Tom to help her organize the funeral and things. I suggested she could come to the flat, but he said she wanted to be near all Marcus's things.

AN ASIDE

So, I mourned alone and tried to work out what could have happened. I have always had a feeling that something like this might happen, and now I began to think through all those little tell-tale signs that I had obviously missed. What an idiot I was. I might have been able to stop it if I had addressed the problem sooner. Marcus disappearing to Finland. Marcus meeting a girl and marrying her so quickly. Marcus staying in his room with his new bride and living on tins of baked beans, not very Mouse like! Then I think, only think mind you, that I have solved the puzzle. A few months before, Mouse came to tea with me and was very anxious about a man coming up to him and saying, 'I'm glad!' I laughed it off and said, 'Well, perhaps he was mad like you,' but it did cross my mind then that the man had actually said, 'I am gay'.

Much later, long after Marcus's death, it was suggested that Carola might have been a prostitute in Finland. I thought nothing of it at the time, but now I am wondering if it could perhaps have been a little true; it would explain Marcus's behaviour. You see if Marcus decided to 'prove' himself, he would have asked Carola to marry him, he was such a gentleman. Had Marcus picked her up, married her and tried to prove he was not gay? I won't say any more now, as when I speak to Carola, soon I hope, I am going to ask her to tell me the truth. I can't let my dear friend kill himself in such a dreadful way and not find out the reason for his actions. I need to know if, in a way, it was my fault. Could I have done anything to stop it. I know how much he loved me, but he also knew there was no hope of anything happening between us. Why hadn't he called me?

I went to Marcus's funeral in Highgate and put my arms around Carola. We didn't say anything, what was there to say! I loved Marcus 'Mouse' beyond words. He was my first friend to die, and would I ever know the reason? Peter was there beside Carola, but we didn't speak. Tom held my hand tightly. I cried for my dear friend that night. I was alone with my baby. I was lost...

What I didn't know that dreadful day, was that Carola and Peter, only days later, started having an affair. A few weeks later Peter just stopped coming to stay with us. He came to see Sarah when I was at work. My mother would let him in and when I got back from a hard day at Harriet, I would know he had been there as his very very sweet black coffee would still be there, unfinished, together with an ashtray filled with 'Senior Service dog ends'.

Thinking back now, I didn't mind too much about Peter just disappearing from our lives. I needed time to mend my broken heart, and Harriet was so demanding. I had a wonderful little girl to come home to, and, of course, my first born, my Ginger Tom Simon! So, I just carried on! Life just went on.

Chapter 7 part 1

...a Few Days Away

I think trying to be a mother, mourning my dearest friend's death and the odd situation between Carola and Peter had taken its toll on me. I had to stop breastfeeding Sarah as it wasn't giving her enough nourishment, and Dr Robert's thought it best that I changed over to Cow and Gate. It was disappointing to stop after such a short time, but I knew he was right, and I had done my best.

Everything was working like clockwork; my mother saved the day, and Jean and Tom were great godparents. Harriet was starting to make a small profit at last.

Customers wanted to see me and me only, and I felt torn apart. I wanted to be with Sarah, but the business needed me. As that was our only source of income, I needed to spend time making it grow. One evening, when I was speaking to Paolo in Frankfurt, he asked if I would like to come to stay with him and some friends in Santa Margaretta for a few days. 'It would do you good,' he said, and he was right as I was feeling very fragile.

So, again, with my mother's help, I packed, made umpteen lists for her and for everyone at Harriet, kissed Sarah and cried. She gurgled and I cried again.

Picture of Paolo's blue Sports car

Paulo was at Milano airport waiting for me. He looked even bigger than usual, and his arms engulfed me. I was safe. He had a brand new royal blue sports car and we drove off towards the coast. 'Let me tell you darling that I bought this new car with you in mind as I know how much you like sports cars. And I chose this blue as it's your favourite colour'.

It was the sort of thing he would do. Always thinking of me and about me. It was just what I needed at this difficult time in my life. He was right. I needed a break, and I also needed to look back and work out my next step with the business and to think about Sarah's future.

When we reached Santa Margherita Ligure, we dropped my bag with the Concierge and went to meet Paolo's friends from Y&R, Eve Marie and Ed. They were lovely people. We had supper and too much wine and then Paolo asked if I would like to go to Il Cavo, which was an outdoor night club. I was tired but I didn't want the night to end. So, we all crammed into his car and sped along the sea road to the club...we sang 'Quando, quando, quando' at the top of our voices. I relaxed for the first time in a year.

Paolo bought me a red belt as a present. I still have it now although my waistline is slightly larger than it was then!

We ordered more drinks, and the music wafted over the sea. When Procal Harlum was playing, he swept me up in his arms and I sank into his body like a cuddly cushion. I had my hand on his neck, he had a big neck, a nice neck I remember very clearly. As I peeped over his shoulder, I could see the pinkish moon shining on the sea. I knew then that moment would stay with me forever

Me on the beach outside the Lido Hotel

and ever, and it has. When times were hard, and they were, I closed my eyes and that scene reappeared. If Procal Harlum plays 'Whiter shade of pale' on the radio, again that moment comes flashing back. How lucky I am to have that moment all to myself! It was late and I was very tired. We made plans with Eve Marie and Ed to meet the next day at the Marina. We had been lent a Riva speed boat by Diana Crespi, one of Paolo's very rich friends. Ed said he would book a table for lunch at the little fish restaurant in a cove, which can only be reached if you have a boat. So excited!

We drove back along the coast road, and Paolo was singing softly. For once, I loved him singing, maybe it was the drink! When we arrived at the Lido hotel, I realised that we were most probably going to share a room and a bed! For a moment, I think we were both a little awkward, but only for a moment. We kissed and we made love, on the balcony actually. It was wonderful, and it was the first time in all our years of being in love that we had managed it.

We fell back into bed and I realised I was crying. I looked up at Paolo and he too was crying.

That moment we had both realised what had just happened. Yes, we had made love, but we also realised that it was because we were no longer in love in that way. I cuddled up to him, and he just smiled, and we fell asleep. In the morning, we didn't speak, but I know we were in a way relieved our desperate love had turned into a deep, deep friendship, one that lasted for another 35 years and ended only when Paolo died of a heart attack.

AN ASIDE

Paolo and I never mentioned THAT night. We didn't need to; it was our secret. I worked hard and so did he. We continued to see each other whenever work permitted. We were both successful in our chosen careers. I remember once that Harriet had a few money problems. It was a big hiccup, and I needed £5000 to get the company out of a hole. I called Paolo to ask his advice, and he insisted he would give me the money although I told him that I didn't need his help. He knew I did, and he was cross. He said that I was cutting off my nose to spite my face, a stupid saying but in Italian it's even more stupid. (I'm not sure that was what he said, but I think, when translated, the meaning was similar.) Anyway, it was before you could transfer money easily between countries, so Paolo said a Mr Tucker would contact me and hand over the money in secret.

Harriet grew into a large wholesale business, selling dresses around the world. I had a new man in my life called Dawson, who became my sales Director. One day Dawson and I were in a meeting when my secretary put a call through to me. It was Paolo. He sounded excited but nervous. He told me he had met someone, and he wanted to marry her. For a second my heart seemed to stop, but I recovered quickly. 'Darling, how wonderful. What's her name? When can I meet her?' Paolo sounded relived and said, 'can we come this weekend?'.

'Yes, of course. I will throw an engagement party for you.' Well that was it. I was excited for him, and I did throw a lovely party for them at the Artist Asoffe. Her name was Christine, and she was pretty and thin! I didn't think we would ever be great friends, but we could manage something, I was sure. Paolo looked happy.

They were married in Melun, just outside Paris. I was not there as a few days before the wedding, I was rushed into hospital with a twisted gut. Well, that's different, I suppose.

The first time that I saw them as a married couple was in Paris. Dawson and I had dinner with them at the Orangery. We chatted, but without much feeling, if you know what I mean. We ordered our meal. Christine ordered Dover Sole and insisted it must not be cooked in butter. It was, and when Paolo suggested that it was not important, she picked up the whole Dover Sole and dropped it on his head. The butter ran down Paolo's face. We all smiled and tried to say something appropriate. I was lost for words. I couldn't look at Paolo. We managed to get through the meal with a few pleasantries somehow, then Dawson and I fled.

The next morning, I sat in our hotel and wrote Paolo a letter. It was a mistake, I suppose, but he was my friend, and I loved him, and I was embarrassed for him. I wrote from my heart. I said that he must remember all the wonderful times we had had together, all the laughter we had shared. I asked him to remember happier times.

Paolo left the letter in his pocket and Christine found it. She forbade Paolo to ever meet me again. Silly woman. Our friendship was stronger than that. We continued to meet for many years after that awful episode. No one would ever stop us seeing each other.

Several years later, I received a call from Paolo's assistant. Paolo had had a stroke. He was OK, but his speech was affected. His clients insisted that they wanted to deal with him somehow and the agency set up a loudspeaker system. I called the office and was put through to my darling. I heard 'clip clop, clip clop', then laughter, that was my darling. We had a strange conversation. I told him what I was doing; he laughed and then said, 'clip clop'. That was it, my last conversation. He died a week later of a massive heart attack. His secretary

Obituaries

WORLD   U.S.   N.Y. / REGION   BUSINESS   TECHNOLOGY   SCIENCE   HEALTH   SPORTS   OPINION

Paolo Ajroldi, Advertising Executive, 57

Published: April 24, 1990

Paolo Ajroldi, an international advertising executive, died of a heart attack Friday at his home in Chantilly, France. He was 57 years old.

Mr. Ajroldi was a partner in T.B.W.A., an international advertising company he helped found in 1970 with William Tragos, Claude Bonnage and Uli Wiesendanger, three associates from Young & Rubicam.

He is survived by his wife, Christine of Paris and Chantilly; and a brother, Luca of Milan.

Here is Paolo's obituary from New York Times

at T.B.W.A. was so upset that she forgot to tell me, so I missed his funeral. Well that was it.

No more Paolo and Wendy. Never to see him again was too much to bear, but of course, I have my memories and those nobody can take away. So, life continued in a different way. He was always in my thoughts somewhere or other. I just wish he had been around to cheer me on!

Chapter 7 part 2

The Importance of being Harriet

My life seemed to be settling into a pattern, a hectic pattern, but I think I was in control. I'm not sure I could have managed without my mother. Every day, from the moment I opened my eyes until I finally fell exhausted into bed, was filled with Harriet. The business totally devoured me, as did the customers; they had to see me, nobody else would do!

In between being Harriet, I was also a 'mummy'. My routine was the same 7 days a week: wake at 7, quick cuddle for Simon, my ginger Tom, check Sarah was awake and ready to be fed. She was always awake, but she never screamed or made a fuss; she only smiled and gurgled. That was our special time together, tucked up in bed and having her first feed of the day. I always hummed a little tune to her as I fed her, and she would look up at me with absolute trust with those beautiful eyes. It was our moment away from the hustle and bustle of the day ahead. Our time together. So precious. Then it was my turn; a quick shower, a cup of tea and some toast. Check my 'to do' list.

My mother always arrived at the flat at 9am. Whatever the weather, she was there for us. I picked out Sarah's outfit for the day and fled the flat to become Harriet. Leaving behind my lovely daughter was very hard, but we had to have money and I was the only provider. Peter rarely appeared and never offered any money for his daughter's keep, nor mine. He used to come to the flat in the afternoon to have his strong black coffee and smoke his Senior Service cigarettes. My mother never mentioned that he had been there, but I knew he had paid a visit because of the dog ends and the dirty coffee cup. It was odd really, but I was too busy to have an argument face to face, so I didn't say anything. I presumed he was still living in Chiswick, and I presumed he was still taking his City and Guilds mechanics exams.

Meanwhile, my mother was in her element. She adored Sarah, and every day she would parade her granddaughter up and down Kensington High Street, then continue on to the Round Pond in Kensington Gardens. I had bought a very expensive Blue Cross pram, the sort of pram that the royal children were seen in. I really think my mother believed Sarah was royal!

Exactly at 9.15 I would open the boutique doors, open the post, generally bills, check there was plenty of milk and coffee ready for the first customer. Check the diary, open up a page in the cash book ready for the day's takings, check inside the Grandfather clock where we kept a tin box for the takings, making sure there was plenty of change. Then on the dot of 9.30 Harriet was open for business.

This was the time also that my outworkers would bring in their finished garments or the unfinished ones ready for the first fitting. I always paid them the moment they handed me an invoice, and that was the start of my problems. I paid everyone promptly, but my customers were rich, very rich, and they rarely paid before 60 days, sometimes longer. So, I did always have a bit of a cash flow problem. We were so busy it never dawned on me that I should control the money situation. Plus, it was very embarrassing to ask 'Lady Whatnot' to pay when she collected her daughter's three ball gowns. If I did, she would say, 'Of course Harriet. Send in the invoice. We are off to Cowes tomorrow, but I will make sure you get paid as soon as we get back'. That meant at least three weeks again!

I designed new styles every week, which really worked as regular customers loved to come in, have a coffee and look at that week's latest creation. Over half of them bought the latest designs as it became the thing to do, and they could boast that Harriet had designed for them exclusively. I did, in fact, attend many of the balls and parties that the clients were going to. I had to be careful not to outshine them! Also, we had to keep a note of which client was going to which ball in case two people arrived in the same dress. That would be unforgivable. Every week new designs appeared on the rails, the crazier the better. Word got around pretty quickly back in the 60s. We were hungry for any new ideas; the wackier ideas happened over night and disappeared by the next day sometimes. We had been living in a pretty dull world after the war, especially in terms of music. That is until my hero Elvis Presley came on the scene. Then there was Lonnie Donegan and then the music took off with Bill Haley. That was the start of the crazy 60s; forget burning our bras, who wore a bra anyway!

The trend those days, clothes wise, was to work all week to earn your living, then go to the latest boutique and spend all your wages on an outfit for Saturday night. The dresses didn't have to last long because they would be replaced the next weekend. Thus, shops like Biba, Wallis shops, Miss Selfridge, River Island and Bus Stop thrived.

Harriet was a different market. We aimed at the debutante market, the seventeen year olds who had wealthy parents and ones who 'did the season'.

They would go to all the balls in London and the tea parties and, finally, the Coming Out Ball in Berkley Square. Then they would be presented to the Queen, after which they had 'come out!' Slightly different meaning nowadays. So, early in the year, mothers would bring their daughters to Harriet to buy their wardrobe for the Season. This was when we made big money as they would order 2 or 3 suits, 3 or 4 cocktail dresses, several afternoon frocks and at least 3 ball gowns. Harriet was the favourite as we knew how to talk to the mothers, and all the debutantes wanted to look like me. So, we won hands down. We all worked through the night sometimes, but nobody cared. We all worked so hard, and being busy meant we were on the road to success, and success meant money in the bank!

I had, in the end, to get a regular assistant to help me. Her name was Aileen, and she was an angel. She never minded how hard she worked although Harriet was not her business, but I think she was lonely. So, she adopted Harriet, the boutique. Perfect for me and the business.

this is the dress I designed this for lovely Julie Christie..she won the Oscar for 'Darling'

I think one of the most exciting things about being a dress designer in the 60s was that unbelievable things happened out of the blue. So, there I was sitting behind the desk, in front of the Grandfather clock. I heard steps and prepared to meet the possible new client. There at the top of the stairs was Julie Christie, closely followed by Warren Beatty!

Working with Julie was a dream; she was fun and gorgeous, a joy to design for, and such a lovely person. She had been nominated for an Oscar for the film Darling, so, she had to look like a winner, even if she lost! I designed a gold lame shirt dress. She did win that Oscar, and she did look absolutely wonderful. I was so proud of myself. But there was a downside. Sister Mercedes, my lovely sample machinist, had made Julie's wonderful gold outfit and did not notice that the gold leaf on the fabric had covered her habit. Father Joseph noticed the gold as she went into evening prayers. After prayers she was disciplined and the next morning, I received a call from the Father saying that Sister Mercedes would not be coming to work at Harriet anymore. I was upset to say the least. It was unfair on Mercedes as she wouldn't do such a thing on purpose and very unfair on me. He made it clear that he had spoken and that was the end of the matter. Julie heard about the drama and insisted on phoning the Convent. She tried to change the Father's decision, but she failed. It was the first sad thing that happened at Harriet, but not the last.

Shortly after the upset of the Sister Mercedes drama, we, of course, had to find another machinist, pretty difficult. So, the only thing to do was to ask my outworkers to spend some days in the boutique. That would have to do until I found a replacement.

This is the chicken and the Harriet top with new sleeves!

We just had to hope that we wouldn't get too busy. But then all hell let loose; we seemed to have queues down the stairs and around the corner!

We even had the three Beverley sisters asking us to recreate their image!

Then one day, up the stairs came Fanny Craddock with her grunting husband. She was very demanding but great fun. I designed several tops for her. She never bothered with bottoms as she was always shot from her waist up on her TV programmes. Unfortunately, almost every show the stitches started to break; she was so active when cooking. On one show she was preparing a buttered chicken, and it slipped out of her hands. She bent to pick it up and came back on screen with one sleeve hanging on like grim death, patted the chicken and said directly to the camera, 'don't worry. No one will ever notice...'. She ignored the gaping hole in her sleeve and continued as if nothing had happened. The director decided to cut that piece, so she and I both saved face. Johnny, Fanny's husband, generally stayed cool whilst Fanny flapped about. They made a lovely pair, and I was very fond of them. I heard that they threw great parties and although Fanny tried to get me to come, I always made the excuse about catching up with work. If I took time off, it would be to be with my precious daughter.

Chapter 7 part 3

Wallis saves the day – head hunted

I was beginning to think I was fighting a losing battle. I couldn't keep up with the bills and pay the wages. However hard we all worked, and however many customers we crammed into the boutique, the bills never let up. My head was spinning all day and at night, in the dark and quiet, but I still couldn't find the answer to my problems. One and one used to make two but now it seemed 1 x 1 = 300. Deep down I knew what the problem was; my Commerce Master at Business College, Mr Whelen, had told us about 'cash flow' troubles. I had to act now.

So, I had a large red note put at the bottom of our invoices. PAYMENT MUST BE RECEIVED WITHIN 14 DAYS OR 10% WILL BE ADDED TO INVOICE.

There, let's see if all my lovely smart customers will start paying promptly and save the day. I made another decision too. I would hire a part-time bookkeeper to keep a check on slow payers; it would be easier for a third party to ask for payment as I had made friends with all my clients, a mistake, I know, but that's me.

Mrs. Leda Woodward was the name of our new member of the team. She was 74 years old, Russian and very proper. She chain smoked like we all did, and the cigarette never seem to leave her lips. We loved her the moment we met her. She had been working in a bank in St Petersburg, so quite a climb down for her, but she was so loved by everyone that I think she thought of us as her children. Each morning she would give me a list of late payers, and the paying in book, then a suggestion of outstanding invoices that were due by us. The figures spoke for themselves. We were getting deeper in debt. Poor Mrs Woodward, she looked worn out with worry. One particular morning, I saw her standing outside her little office, and I could see she had been crying. I know it sounds silly now, but I couldn't think what else to do. I took the bills that I should be paying, tore them up and ate them! Gone mad maybe, more like a nervous breakdown really, but we both burst into laughter then we felt better.

Sometimes miracles do happen. I know because I had little bouts of good luck every now and again. They always came when I had almost thrown the towel in. This one came in the form of a call from a friend of mine, John Bates, who was a very talented window dresser and a friend of Gavin Robinson. John was working with Wallis Shops now and had been in a meeting with Jeffry Wallis and his brother Harald Wallis. Apparently, sales were slumping a bit, and it was decided that Wallis needed some sparkle, someone young and full of ideas to get Wallis on track. John suggested that I was the right person to turn the business around. They agreed, and even Lady Claire Rendlesham agreed. Claire was friends with Yves St Laurent, and she worked with Vogue; she had incredible contacts. When John phoned me, he suggested a meeting. I said I was pretty busy, but I would manage a short meeting to see the layout and to listen to their proposition.

Shortly after John put the phone down, I had another call from Jimmy Hamilton, the head of all sales and very popular with the Wallis Brothers. He suggested we met next Monday at 11 am at their head office in Brewery Lane. I did realise that if I did take on any extra work, I would not be able to see so much of Sarah and that made me sad. I was so enjoying my baby. Well, perhaps it won't be for long, just until I get Harriet on its feet, I remember thinking. The meeting with Jimmy Hamilton, he had designed the famous CHELSEA BOOT, went well. Jimmy and John Bates were friends going way back when they worked at Bata in Oslo.I trusted both of them. Jimmy explained the job they were offering me. It was an easy job, the sort of thing I could have done with my eyes closed. Mainly pointing the designers in the right direction. I would be in charge of creating a new image; easy, I thought. I asked how much leeway I would have, and the answer was, 'It will
be your baby completely. Do whatever it takes, just make it buzz again. There are 149 shops dotted around the country and the main flagship shop is in Marble Arch'.

I met the designers who were in that day, Michael Faye and Sylvie. They both worked on the coat and jacket section. The head of that department was Jeffry Wallis whilst Harold Wallis worked on the dress section. Finally, I met Jeffry. I liked him. I could tell he was a hard worker and a big worrier…if he didn't kill me off, nothing would! We discussed money. He suggested £3000 a year for 3 days a week. I explained that my daughter and Harriet came first, and he didn't seem to mind. We shook hands and that was that.

I received a letter a few days confirming my post as design controller of all 149 shops. The last sentence worried me but also excited me. Miss Lewis you will be expected to take your team to Paris 3 times a year to produce PICK OF PARIS. (What the hell was that, I thought…).

As I drove back to the boutique, I had time to digest what I had let myself into. I called John when I got back and plied him with lots of questions. The conversation lasted an hour. John was a special friend, and I knew he wouldn't let me get involved with anything that was not absolutely above board. That night I went to sleep buzzing with ideas.

I had a staff meeting the next day, and we made plans for my absence. It was only 3 days a week, which left 3 days for customers to see me. It was going to be tricky, but it was worth a try. I realised that I needed to design and plan to spend time with my daughter. However, Sarah was only a baby, and as long as I was always there when she woke up and when it was her bath time, I could relax and pray that I had the stamina to make it work. The extra money would save Harriet, and I hoped that something good would come out of the experience.

My first morning at Wallis arrived, and, as I was driving across London, I just wondered why I had to push myself so hard. But I knew the answer, of course. I was trying to prove that I was superhuman! For my mother maybe? The first morning was mainly just getting to organise my office, meeting my team and signing for the management toilet key! Jeffry sent over a message asking me to join him for lunch. We spent the whole meal throwing our ideas around the table. I was captivated by Jeffry's ideas; he had obviously spent time working things out. You could tell by talking to him that he was totally dedicated to Wallis, but his ideas were slightly behind the times. I was pleased about that as now I could see how I could help. I suggested we set up a meeting with the senior pattern cutter, Mr Brandon, to discuss changing the block, thus creating a more up to date shape for Wallis.

The next part of the day was the most important part. I was introduced to the WALL...the bloody wall. It didn't seem so bad when I was first confronted with it. It was just a cork wall with prices down one side. When we stood in front of the wall, Jeffry turned into a sort of weasel; he just said to me, 'Wendy, you and I will work on the wall every day. Any design put on to the wall must be the best shape, best value and sell in the shops as from day one'.

That wall became a menace. Jeffry would put two chairs in front of it, and we would sit there for hours. The designs were shown to me, and I would say which price range they came into, and they were pinned beside the selling price. At the end of each day, Jeffry would ask me for the 10th time if I was positive that they were in the right order. In the end, if Jeffry disagreed with any of my choices, he would move the sketches around and so on. By the time I left, I was exhausted and completely muddled; I felt destroyed. He made me late home for Sarah every time as well!

I remember that after the first week I was a nervous wreck. I cried all the way to Wallis the next week and cried all the way home in the evenings.

Michael Faye was a sweet gay designer and very talented. I liked his simple lines and when Jeffry took his designs down, I managed to sneak them back! Michael told me all the gossip, and we became good friends.

One morning Jeffry sent me a memo saying that JOHN BATES, the designer from Jean Varon, had agreed to design 10 coats or suits for Wallis every month, but it had to be on the QT. His name must never be mentioned, so I gathered he was doing this without permission. Michael and I decided to call him simply 'God'. On the first of every month the designs were left in an envelope near the wall; we never saw him. The designs were brilliant; some had too many seams, thus making them in the high end. After two months, the wall began to sparkle, and I was proud with the change. Harold and his designers often came to look at the wall, and it was good to get some feedback as Jeffry did tend to make a statement and walk away.

Michael warned me that any minute now the subject of 'Pick of Paris' would crop up. Apparently, we were to fly to Paris with the designers and would be allowed into some of the shows. Jeffry usually bought 2 or 3 designs at Chanel, perhaps 2 from Yves St Laurent and a couple from the Courreges show. We had to take explicit notes of all the collection and then I would choose which garments I wanted to see close up.

When the day came, I was really excited. We all met at Heathrow, and Jeffry and I went into First Class while the other part of the team went into 'cattle class'. We stayed at the Georges V, a beautiful hotel. We decided on an early night as the next day we had 3 shows to go to, Chanel, Yves St Laurent and Courreges. About midnight, I heard scratching at the door, a mouse I thought but it went on and got louder and louder. I went to the door and whispered through the door, 'Who is that?'. 'It's Jeffry. Open the door. I want to talk about tomorrow!' I had been in the business for long enough to know when someone was lying. 'Sorry Jeffry, I have taken a sleeping pill and need to go back to bed. Night night.' Silence.

The following morning, we all met in the foyer. I smiled at Jeffry and he smiled back. Phew! That was that hopefully. The first show was Chanel. The salon was

filled to the brim. We were lucky that we
had front row tickets, and I was so excited.
The lights went down, and the salon was
silent. As the first Chanel suit came through
the curtain, I looked up and saw Coco
Chanel sitting at the top of the stairs. She
was tiny, and she sat there wringing her
hands. It was obviously as important to
her as it was to her audience. I will always
remember that moment. Back to work,
I had my notebook ready; the idea was
to describe the outfit Number 13. Fabric,
weave, colour, trimming, buttons and
length of jacket and skirt. You had to do a
quick sketch without anyone noticing as it

was forbidden to sketch, and, obviously, one could not take pictures. Although
50% of the garments were Chanel suits, that was what she was famous for, each
one was slightly different, very confusing when working in a hurry.

Jeffry asked me to choose 3 garments from the collection. I conferred with the
designers and gave Jeffry the three numbers. We were ushered into a cubicle;
there were 4 of us, so it was a bit of a squeeze. The 3 garments were brought to
the cubicle and the head vendees simply said, 'un heure sil'vu plait'. Wallis had
had to pay £1000 for the honour.

For one hour, we sketched and snipped tiny bits of fabric from the hems; we
had to take all the details possible so that the workroom could make an exact
replica for 'Pick of Paris' week back in London. They had to produce exact
replicas over the weekend and then John Bates (display manager) would create
a beautiful window display. Jeffry was so anxious it was difficult to concentrate;
then he whispered in my ear, 'Rip off a button'. I was horrified and whispered
back to him, 'No!'. He looked as if he had been shot in the back. 'Now,' he said
in a loud voice. 'NO,' I said and walked out of the cubicle. Later we did not
speak. I suspected no one had ever refused to do what he wished, but to me
the garments were works of art, and I would not be responsible for damaging
them.

The next show was Yves St Laurent; brilliant, so dramatic, very black, his
favourite colour for that particular season. We chose our designs, which was
very difficult as the collection was amazing, day wear, sportswear and evening

dresses. I remember the choice we made for the evening, a black Grosgrain fabric and an exact copy of a man's evening jacket worn with a long pencil skirt with a slit in the front. It was a knockout and turned out to be one of Wallis's best all time sellers as well as Yves trademark for a couple of seasons. After the show, we were invited to a small gathering in the showroom; mainly press and a few French actresses such as Jean Moreau and Simone Signiory, with her gorgeous husband Yves Montand. Plenty of British press there. I knew a few, and they knew me, which did help my image. Jeffry noted everything I did, and he was quite puffed up with pride by the time we left. Bridget Keenen waved

at me across the room, and Ernestine Carter came and chatted to me. She loved Harriet evening dresses. Great! Then I didn't feel so guilty about being away from my two babies, Sarah and Harriet.

The last show we had to go to was Courreges, very young clothes, very Wallis. We went through the same ritual, but when we had finished, I had to disappear for a while to digest the collection. It was so amazing, with the white leather cut out boots and simple cut out dresses. It was just simple but amazing. I felt tears welling up in my eyes, so I went outside and looked down at my feet at the curb side. I was in floods of tears, still don't understand why, but I was so emotionally moved. At one point I felt an arm around me. It was Jeffry, and he too had tears in his eyes. He felt the same as me, and we bonded at that moment. We never mentioned it again, but I noticed that Jeffry made things happen for Harriet. Both departments, suits, coats and dresses all made appointments to come to the boutique, and they all placed orders for Wallis shops. I was always grateful to Jeffry.

During the weekend, pattern cutters and sample machinists worked their socks off. They had to create an exact replica of all the garments we had chosen in Paris. The atmosphere was very tense, so I decided to stay around for part of the weekend as I felt responsible for the outcome. I went home to have a bath and spend time with my lovely daughter. My mother stayed the night, so I was able to go to the Marble Arch Flagship store to check the windows were in order. I hadn't realised that one of my friends was the manageress; we used to work together when we were mannequins. Her name was Penny Gillard, and she was very well respected by the Wallis company. It was great to catch up with her. The press started to arrive followed by Jeffry and Harold. At 8am the garments arrived from the factory. By now the windows looked spectacular and soon the models were clothed in their new finery. John and I had a coffee and you could see how tired he was but also excited. Exactly at 9am, the curtains opened to show 'PICK OF PARIS'. The whole scene took my breath away; I had been in Paris and seen the real garments, and these looked identical. The press, as always, were astounded at the outcome, and they gave wonderful revues. The rails were nearly empty by 4pm! What a day, what a success; it was wonderful to be part of it.

AN ASIDE

Lady Claire Rendelsham used to pop into Wallis from time to time; she seemed very at home. The designers used to pull faces behind her back. She seemed bossy, but I could do bossy too! Sometimes, she worked at Vogue in Hanover Square and sometimes at Wallis. I think Jeffry liked to have a 'Lady,' floating around as it added class to the place.

One day I had a memo from Claire, asking to meet her in the canteen for coffee at 11am. We met and I was not at ease with her. In fact, I didn't like her, but I was out to get as much as possible out of anyone that I met when away from Harriet. She wanted me to go to Paris with her to check on any new trends happening in Paris. We had to do this from time to time so that Wallis was always a step ahead of all the other stores in London. I agreed to go with her the following week. 'I will arrange all with accounts. There is a plane that gets to Orly at 8 am.' 'Blimey, I thought...a bit early for me!'

A few days later we met at the check-in counter. We had no luggage as we were only going for the day. Claire arrived in a full-length mink coat, of course. I wore

Yves St
Laurent logo

my mink tie! The one I bought from Avery Row, THE place to buy them if you couldn't yet afford the full mink! The plane arrived on time, and we were immediately shown to a small building and when we entered, we were in total blackness! There was a small light in the corner of the room but that was all. We were offered a coffee and seated.

I gathered we were meeting Yves St Laurent. It was a mystery, but Claire obviously didn't want to share the moment with me. With a great flurry, Yves entered the room, kissed Claire on both cheeks and shook my hand.

They then proceeded to talk very fast in French. I caught some of the words, but the more heated Yves got, the faster he talked. I just nodded as if I understood, like one does! Well I think from the little I could gather, Yves and Claire were going into business together, opening up SOLDES shops (sale.) My French was not very good, and the room was almost pitch black and I started to fall asleep.

The meeting went on for 2 hours.

Well that was it. I had to go to sleep. Claire kept on digging her elbow in my side, but I had missed my chance to talk and they were obviously disgusted by my behaviour!

I can't believe that I fell asleep during the most prestigious meeting of my life!

WHO would believe me!

Chapter 7 part 4

Wallis Taking Me Over - so I run like mad!

I knew Wallis was taking over my life. I felt I was being sucked in by the company. Jeffry always managed to turn up late for our meetings. So, there I was at night sitting in front of the bloody WALL. 'Are you sure that that's the coat we have been waiting for? Is this the million-dollar seller we've been hoping for; can you be sure!' Jeffry never stopped asking people advice, so I began to wonder why he bothered to ask me at all. I had been having good publicity for Harriet recently and it needed following up. There was a marvellous article about three top influential women. Millicent Martin, Wendy Lewis at Harriet and Madam Gareige…blimey!! Talking about the influence we had over people from our points of views, their make-up, the kind of restaurants we ate at after work, etc. We were becoming celebrates and people wanted to have our sort of life; no idea why, as my life consisted of working until midnight going to bed with a hot chocolate and a sandwich, if I was lucky! Then out of the blue someone came up the stairs at Harriet carrying lots of garments. He was very good looking. He just grinned at me and said in a wonderful voice, 'Hello, my name is Dawson Baker and I work for Roger Nelson. As I was passing by, I thought I should pop in and show you some of Roger's latest top selling suits and coats. Do you have a moment for me to show you?'. I was about to say that I only saw people with appointments, but he was very good looking, so I just nodded!

Roger Nelson was a very important designer. His collection was young, cut beautifully and, although quite expensive, filled the gap between stuffy collections, such as Wetheral and Dereta. I could see a good market for Harriet here as the mothers always asked for suits and coats for the Winter season. I couldn't resist buying 6 to test the market. Then I waited to see how well they sold. I offered Dawson a coffee, and we chatted about trade in the UK and the States. Rogers' biggest market was mainly in New York, and it made me think about, perhaps, trying to sell there. But, of course, I was struggling and couldn't start thinking about new markets. The 6 garments sold by the end of the week. So, I put an advert in the Evening Standard for a pattern cutter for coats and suits with experience in the 'top end' market. That was when I was lucky enough to meet and employ Mr Fagan! He never smiled, and he was always grumpy, but he had magic fingers. Soon, Harriet became THE boutique to buy

Winter and Spring suits by Roger Nelson, as well as Harriet.

That day Dawson stayed for another coffee. As he was leaving, he turned and said, 'Would you like to have supper one evening?'. I gave him my home number.

He called the next day and suggested dinner at Artist l'Assoife that evening. He would pick me up at 8. We had a nice dinner and chatted about everything and nothing. Later, we went to Dolly's, one of the clubs in fashion at the time. By 12 am I was tired and bored! Dawson turned out to be the most boring man I had ever gone out with; he only talked about Roger Nelson or his wife Christine who was having an affair with some black leader somewhere or other. By 12.30 I stayed in the loo trying to think of a way of getting home without upsetting him too much. We drove home in silence. He was a gentleman and walked me to the door. Waiting inside was my Simon, the ginger Tom. 'Don't tell me you like cats!' Dawson glared at my darling cat. 'Yes!' I said, 'thank you for a lovely evening. Good night'.

Thank goodness that was the end of that friendship.

The boutique was busy now, and I was beginning to I think that I couldn't carry on this double life with Harriet versus Wallis for much longer. It seemed that the harder I worked, the deeper in debt we became. It didn't make sense. I decided that I would give it a few more months then hand my notice in to Wallis. I had made my decision.

Sarah and I had wonderful weekends together; she was beginning to walk and said the odd word like 'bee be', her best white little lamb, and 'si' for Simon. There was a slight problem. She became really overweight caused by the Cow and Gate formula she was on, we had to put her on a diet! Jean and I used to take her for pram rides around the round pond in the 'Royal carriage'. It was lovely to be a mother and to have such a perfect baby daughter. Sarah always smiled; she was such a happy little bundle of fun. Peter rarely came around at the weekends, which was a relief really. He was very demanding, and when I managed the odd day off, I wanted to see Sarah and Jean and relax.

Dr Bramwell called one evening and told me he would like me to attend a special Gala Ball in aid of the Jewish Boys club or something. Mr and Mrs Taft were organising it. They worked tirelessly on these functions and needed all the support they could get. Obviously, I said I would go. He added that Silvia and Dennis Naar, friends of his, would collect me at 7pm and take me there. That meeting was the start of a new part of my life.

There were things developing around Harriet, which I thought might come to something, but I dare not think about it too much as I didn't have a 2nd plan. The Naars were very nice, very Jewish and were in the 'rag trade'. We chatted most of the evening as I was on their table, along with Avril and Denis Norden, the script writer and general funny, funny man. I had a nice evening with nice people. Denis Norden and I both loved dancing, especially the Quickstep, so at every opportunity, he whisked me away to dance. That too was the start of a lovely relationship.

A few days later, I was in Littlestone's, the Jewish Solicitor that Silvia and Denis Naar used for all their business transactions! They had made me an offer I couldn't refuse. Their dress business at 65 Grosvenor Street, W1 was failing. They had always been in the business, and their family had always been in the business, but now there was new young 'swinging' crowd of designers. So, the Naars were completely out of their depth. They had approached me a few days after we had met up. They had looked into my background, asked Dr Bramwell and others if I was honest and hard working. 'Yes,' the answer came back from various banks and landlords, I was worth investing in, so Harriet was saved. The shares were divided 50%/50%. Later this was a problem, but I wouldn't have gone in with them if they had offered me less. So be it…

AN ASIDE

Long live Harriet wholesale Ltd…better to have 50% of something than 100% of nothing, I hope!

Chapter 7 part 5

Harriet Boutique closes - Harriet Wholesale Ltd opens

Now, it was time to tell the loyal staff at Harriet, not a job I relished. They had all become my friends and had stuck by me through thick and thin. Life moves on, I said to myself, but my tears streamed down my face uncontrollably. Of course, the girls had guessed something was up and were ready, but it was not easy. Aileen was devastated. Harriet had become her whole life. I know she was hoping she was coming with me when I reopened as Harriet Wholesale, but she was not the right image I wanted for the new venture. Poor Mrs Woodward was so relieved that I had found backers, and she said that she would always keep an eye out for Harriet. However, she was ready to retire; in fact, she died a few weeks later. I think she was happy to go. She had a beautiful Russian funeral with an open coffin. As I looked down on her dear face, I could almost imagine her winking at me! Mrs Finston, my favourite outworker, was going to continue to do 'specials' for some of my old clientele. She needed the money and loved Harriet almost as much as I did. All my outworkers remained friends, but they had other work, so I knew they would not starve.

As I closed the door for the last time at my little boutique, I think I closed a bit of me inside. I wish I was back there even with all the problems; it was, after all, my baby.

That week we moved briefly into 65 Grosvenor Street, just off Bond Street, where Silvia Naar had her Couture showroom. It was to be only a temporary move until Mr Naar found some premises for Harriet. It was a bit uncomfortable as their staff felt they were being squeezed out. Happily, Mr Naar found the perfect building for Harriet at Highlight House, the corner of Great Portland Street and Margaret Street, perfect position, bang in the middle of the proper 'rag trade'.

Now Harriet was a proper business, a business I hoped would grow and provide for my little daughter, my mother and I...

Well they say when one door closes, another opens. So, fingers crossed …here we go!

Chapter 8 part 1

Harriet going for the big time - building our team

The move from Kensington and Grosvenor Street to Margaret Street went without a hitch. Mind you, we didn't have that much equipment, no stock to speak of, and staff wise there was just Carol, who was the Naars sample machinist, and then me, Harriet! So, the first two weeks were hectic. Not only was I designing the Spring/Summer collection for the new company, but I also had to advertise for new staff and meet the would-be candidates. I needed a pattern cutter, two more machinists, a stock keeper, a secretary, a bookkeeper and a cleaner. I put adverts in Drapers Weekly, and the Evening Standard, as usual. The phone rang nonstop, and by the end of the first week, I had an almost full team.

Highlight House on the corner of Gt Portland Street and Margaret Street.

Two more machinists, Mrs. Orris, Mrs Web (she smoked non-stop and coughed over the ironing board all day!). A stock keeper, Mick, who was a strong character and turned out to be wonderful. She counted every button and every buckle coming into stock and guarded everything as if her life depended on it. She had a built-in look 'don't mix with me kid!'. Perfect.

Then we hired lovely Phyliss, who was a bookkeeper and generally kept an eye on everyone for me. I found out later that she also reported to my partner on a daily basis, which upset me a bit at first; mainly, I suppose, because I had always had Harriet under my control, and I didn't want anyone interfering!

We kept the existing cleaner on, Silvia; she was lovely and 'mothered' me from day one. She made sure I ate and brought me mugs of tea and coffee throughout the day, which was exactly what I needed.

Now, my main problem was a pattern cutter. I had finished the collection, just twenty garments, five in each section: five sportswear, five day dresses, five suits and finally five evening dresses. I was pleased with it, I remember. But, of course, I still couldn't get going without a damn pattern cutter, sadly Violette couldn't join us in the new venture. I had designed the whole collection with a theme. It was the best thing to do as then the buyers could make the windows look interesting, and the window dressers could go to town with a story line, which made their life more interesting. So, for my first Harriet wholesale collection, the theme was RUSSIAN. It would be easy to wear and very colourful. I patted myself on the back, but without the pattern cutter we were stuck. The position had to be held by someone who had a lot of experience and felt they could work in the new style of the 60s. The cut was very different then from the shapes like THE NEW LOOK, in the late 50s and early 60s. Now we had an entirely new look, the SACK DRESS. I asked Mary Sinclair, one of my pattern cutters who worked on and off for me at the boutique, to do some freelance work for me whilst I was looking for a permanent person. She said she was too busy, as by now Foale and Tuffin were beginning to grow, and she was snowed under with work from them. Still, she agreed to help out until I found a new person, so she did the patterns for the first five day dresses, Tolstoy, Ivana, Zara, Trotsky and Alexandra. When they were machined and pressed, I hung them up in the showroom and had a mini showing to see what everyone thought of the start of the collection. It went down well, and Mary and I were pleased with the result. Almost after that the phone rang, and someone called Niamh said she was interested in working with me at Harriet. We met the next day, and I engaged her in the afternoon. And the very next day she started work. Niamh worked for many years with me, and we became great friends too.

At last we could get going. Niamh and I went into a huddle and worked on the block. This is the basic shape of the fashion house, and it was based on an old block I had from Polly Peck when I was their mannequin. We used the block from the trousers I designed for Joseph. I called some of my fabric contacts and they came and showed me their collections. I went to M. Klein to buy some buttons, then on to McCulloch and Wallis, where I ordered the new Harriet labels. The fabrics had arrived, so now we were in full swing. The noise of the Singer sewing machines clattered all around the workroom.

In my office I could switch off, but I didn't want to, really, as it was the start of my big empire! By this time, I was smoking 100 cigarettes a day, mostly left in ashtrays around the building hardly smoked!

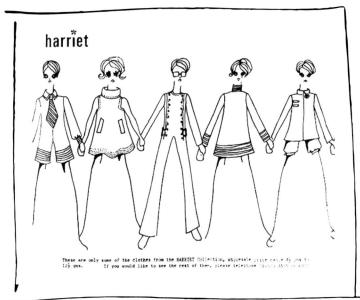

harriet

These are only some of the clothes from the HARRIET Collection, wholesale price range 4½ gns to 12½ gns. If you would like to see the rest of them, please telephone 01-xxx 4575 or xxxx

five day dresses from the Russian collection

My plan now was to contact all the press that I knew to tell them that Harriet was back in town, a new trend was about to start, so it was very exciting. I splashed out and found two secondhand chandeliers for the new showroom. The blinds were parchment with green trim on the hem. It looked fresh and unusual.

I had decided to have just 2 showroom mannequins when buyers came in. Having a big show doesn't always pay off, and I would rather sit one to one in the showroom. Then when I had some bookings, I was going to speak to the Danish centre around the corner who made lovely open Danish sandwiches. All very exciting. I lit up the first of my ciggies at 9am and telephoned my press contacts, the most prestigious first...I had to have a ciggie with each call to give me courage! Well, my list of acceptances was very impressive. The press knew that there was a new look about to explode on the streets of London, and they wanted to be in on it but were not sure where to start. I do great phone!

Then it was time to call the major stores, many of them knew of me and had stocked Harriet before, so it wasn't a hard sell. Harrods Way In and Harrods Younger set first, yes from both of them, Wallis, yes, Simpsons, Liberties, Miss Selfridge, Galleries Layette, all said 'yes' and wished me luck and were really excited. By the end of the first day, I had twelve buyers booked in, spread over week one.

The date for the press show was September 12th. The catering was organised.

We decided to send Harriet invitations to both press and buyers to remind them of their booking. We were committed; how scary that was. I wondered where

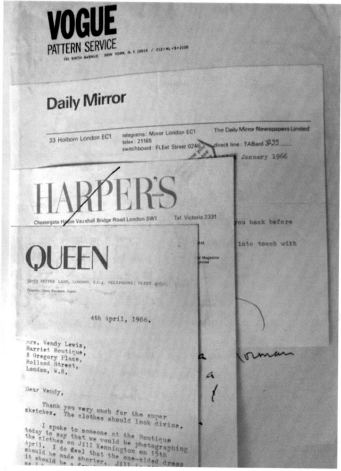

a few major press
acceptance letters

I got all this energy from, where had that little boring child with pig tails go to, I wondered? By the end of that week, all the samples were ready. I opened a bottle of Champagne, and the team all celebrated... we knew we had it in the hat... But, of course, it depended on the buyers, whether they liked the 'look' and whether the price was right. Harriet was luckier than most new wholesale business' starting up as the name was quite well known then and had a good following.

Mary Sinclair, my temporary pattern cutter when I started, kept in touch, and we worked together when I had a crisis. Mary generally wore sunglasses before they were cool. I would call her and make an appointment to meet up with my latest designs, generally about 5 designs. When the date was fixed, she would always add 'come to the front door'. We would run through the designs and work out where the darts should be and the length of the skirt, etc. Her big pattern table lifted up to one side, the pins slipped through the centre crack, and that is where she slept. About the same time, I was sleeping under my cutting table in Kensington too. After we had finished our meeting, Mary would say, 'Go out through the back door please'. One day I left my handbag behind and I went back to Mary's to pick it up. Mary's secret was up; she was working for us all. Sally and Marian of Foale and Tuffin...they had obviously come in the front door as I had left. Poor Mary! It was an embarrassing moment for her, but it didn't matter to us as she never discussed the other designers' clothes with me. Mary looked as if she had had a stroke; her face was purple!

Chapter 8 part 2

Ready Steady Go...a possible Sales director?

The collection was finished by the end of the week. We were all utterly exhausted, so I told everyone to go home on Friday at lunchtime. They had all worked so hard and were very grateful. Anyway, I needed some time to myself to run through things, to check everything was ready for the big weeks ahead. I had made the decision to show the collection to the press first and then to the buyers as that way I could judge the press reaction. The press would book garments to be photographed and put their sticker on the ones they had chosen. So, when the buyers started their buying, they would almost certainly buy the chosen styles; they would back up the press. You scratch my back and I will scratch yours...

I needed a big cuddle from my baby, and all I could think of when I got home was that cuddle, a deep bubble bath and then bed!

I arrived early at the showroom on Monday, and, whilst I felt excited, I did seem to be smoking five cigarettes at once! I had collected fresh flowers for the showroom on my way in, and the showroom looked spectacular. Niamh arrived first. She hadn't slept a wink, and I think we both could have done with a whiskey to steady our nerves. The two mannequins arrived and were putting on their faces. I had decided not to use Jean and Chrissie this time as I felt it would be uncomfortable for me, don't ask me why.

I looked at the press list...

The first appointment was with Brigid Keenan - The Sunday Times at 10am

Then Vogue - June Ogalvie

Harper's Bazaar - Ernestine Carter

Queen - Lady Clare Rendlesham (we worked together at Wallis)

Honey - Gillian Cooke

Daily Sketch - Jean Rooke

Sunday Express - Veronica Papworth. I was always her favourite so had to keep her a special place.

Daily Express - Deirdre McSharry

The Evening Standard - Barbara Griggs

Daily Express - Jill Butterfield

The Daily Mirror - Marje Proops (agony aunt) was not the fashion editor, but she always liked to keep up to date with everything, and I liked her. She always said what she thought.

Evening News - Penny Graham would come when she had time, but she was very keen on everything I ever designed. So, I made sure she was in on all the new designs.

The newspapers were always more difficult to pin down as they worked close to their printing day and more on the spur of the moment.

By the end of the day on Tuesday, I was on my knees, but the response from the press had been amazing. I think everyone enjoyed themselves. We spoilt them; we presented huge wooden trays of Danish sandwiches and pink Champagne with Russian Truffles.

The first day for the buyers was a week later, the important ones first, the ones I could rely on like Harrods and Simpsons. Harrods Way In, Miss Helen Keyes, was first to see the collection, and I could see her delight as the mannequins swirled around the room. She ordered 200 assorted garments, which was good for a collection of only 20 pieces. Of course, Helen was a friend, but I had to show her the collection first because you couldn't have two fashion departments selling the same items within the store. So, Helen chose for her Way In in the morning, and Liz from Younger Set on the first floor of Harrods came in later in the day.

You always had to be so diplomatic with the larger stores as if you put a foot wrong or perhaps a buyer changed her loyalty, you could lose huge amounts of revenue. So 'tread lightly' was my motto.

I had one embarrassing moment when Claire Stubbs, from Simpsons, came to see the collection. She was always chatty, and we were totally relaxed with each other. I turned to the rails to show her one of the dresses and I farted, not a little 'peep' but a fully-fledged one! I stared at the rail for a moment then turned. My face was bright red, but I continued with my selling points about the dress I held in my hand. I know it's just one of those things, but I clearly remember it 50 years later. Claire remained a lady as always!

After each order, I would go into the back office with the orders to tote them up. We had a huge adding machine which made a sort of hiccup every time we entered a figure, I grew to love this machine for as Harriet grew, the machine hiccupped most of the day. At the end of our first week, most of the garments had reserve tags on. So, it would follow that if the press gave us the seal of approval, the clever buyers would follow their lead. That way there would be plenty of exposure in the magazines and papers. The following week was just as busy, and it was obvious I needed a salesperson. We had plenty of other staff, but someone in the showroom and out on the road was what would be needed, I was sure. Another advert was needed, I thought!

Out of the blue, on the Friday of that week, Dawson Baker turned up at Harriet showroom. He was cheerful and chatty, and he brought a bottle of Champagne from Roger and himself to congratulate Harriet for moving into the big time. We chatted, and I rather gathered that Roger had sent him to find out if I had any 'open to buy' for Wallis shops. By this time, I must say I was quite important in the rag trade. The time I spent with Wallis had been well worth it. I was definitely in the limelight and respected by some. I told Dawson that I would put a word in the right direction with Silvie, who I thought would be a better bet than me as now I was just a supplier to Wallis.

Dawson called to tell me he had shown Roger Nelson's collection to Wallis and they had placed a big order. He finished the conversation with, 'Would you like to have dinner with me one evening?'. I had forgotten how boring he was the first time, so I heard myself say 'yes'.

Dawson called later that week and asked if I would like to go to a party and meet Roger Nelson, then we could eat later. I met him at Palisades, a new boutique that was throwing an opening party. I met Roger, a nice guy but not a lot to say. Nevertheless, it was good to get away from Harriet for a while. We stayed for a couple of hours and then Dawson suggested we should go and eat. We went back to L'Artist Assoife where we had gone before. Dawson seemed to know the owner Stella very well, so we got special treatment. I had had a couple of drinks, so I was very relaxed, and Dawson seemed to be more relaxed this time too. We talked and talked the night away, and we just fell in love in between courses!

Chapter 8 part 3

Press and Buyers' enthusiastic - off we go!

After our evening together, I decided that Dawson would be perfect for our sales director. Forget that he was already working for Roger Nelson. In my mind it was a done deal; well, perhaps I should suggest it to Dawson and see if he would like to join Harriet. Once he showed interest, I knew the battle could be won. I knew he was attracted to me and in those days, I had more confidence. I called Dawson at his office the next day, strike whilst the iron is hot, and asked him if he would meet me at my showroom in Margaret Street as I had something to discuss with him. He agreed. I asked Niamh to be there too for support as she was much tougher than me. So, if my powers failed, she could jump in! The meeting went well, and Dawson seemed interested when I suggested that we would like him to join the team as Sales Director. I explained that he would be in charge of the showroom, and he must look for good agents for France, Germany, Denmark and Sweden. We would provide him with a car and expenses account. He said nothing except, 'Where is the toilet?'. He smiled and left the room. Niamh looked at me, and I could see she had the same thoughts, his briefcase. I dashed over to it and open it up. I was looking for his Friday payslip, and there it was; his salary was £3000 per year.

I closed the brief case and sat down. Dawson came in and smiled. He said nothing. I was a bit perplexed at his behaviour. I asked if he needed time to consider the position. 'No, I have considered working with you for some time now. I decided to take any position you offered me, pending on salary and prospects! I was one jump ahead of you, so tell me what salary you are proposing and what else goes with the position, and I will give you an answer today'.

I looked over to Niamh and she winked at me. '£3500 per year,' I said in a high pitched voice. 'Done!' Dawson sat down and lit a cigarette; he had a triumphal smile on his face, and I realised I had been 'played'.

Niamh left, and Dawson and I had several matters to discuss. So, I made us a coffee and began to calm down. Dawson went to his briefcase and pulled out a wodge of A4 sheets, I looked through them and was amazed at the plan he had put forward. He had already spoken to Roger Nelson's agents, with Roger's permission. They were interested in representing the Harriet line, so they would come over to meet me should our deal go through. 'You have been busy!' I said. 'Well, I have been keeping my eye on you and your company, and I realise that I am in a rut with Roger. There seems to be no plan for the future, so I need to look ahead and I decided you were my future'. I was amazed. I had never had a conversation like that; for some reason my face was bright red and my heart was fluttering away; strange, I thought.

Dawson was watching me, I knew he was. I thought perhaps I should say good night, then I thought, I don't want to! 'Are you hungry?' he said. 'No!' I said. Without hesitation Dawson moved very close to me and almost whispered, 'Good. Then we can skip supper and make love instead. You realise that is going to happen sooner or later, and it's best to get on the right foot to start with!' We made love on the new Sisal carpet in the showroom, christening it, I thought. I can tell you that Sisal scratches like mad, and I don't recommend it!

The next day I realised I hadn't introduced Dawson to my partner Dennis Naar, so I fixed up a meeting the next day. All was well. Denis approved of my choice as Dawson was hot property, sales wise, as well as being good looking, polite and well educated. So now we had a sales director and I had a new lover, I thought! I felt guilty that night, and I felt I was letting Sarah down. But I understood that that was bound to happen sooner or later. I was only 32 years old, so I decided not to feel guilty. A few days later, Dawson called to say that he could start next week, but his secretary, Jackie, was devastated that he was leaving and had decided to leave as well. He told me that Jackie was excellent at all the paperwork associated with shipping abroad and was friends with most of the press, so she would be invaluable to Harriet. I said I would get back to him. Dennis was a little worried as he wanted to see some results from sales taken by Dawson, and I suggested we waited until we saw the orders before committing to another wage; he agreed. Jackie decided to leave anyway but three weeks after Dawson started, the orders were so promising that we decided to hire her without passing it by Dennis. We were all one big happy family… well, not for long!

This was the team. A few extra faces but I will tell you about them later

1. Yolanda -machinist
2. Tony - packer
3. Mick - stock keeper
4. Niamh - pattern cutter
5. Mrs Orris - head machinist
6. Dennis Naar - partner
7. Phylis - accounts

8. Daisy - machinist
9. Gonzalas - presser
10. Jacquie - P.A. and Press

then on floor left to right
11. Steve - packer
12. Me
13. Dawson - sales Director

Chapter 8 part 4

A sales director thank goodness -a   white Alfa Romeo

Harriet goes into wholesale business...

to do this we needed a good collection, not too gimmicky but a certain something to catch the eye of the press - we also need the buyer to spend money on a new name - easy!

our first order...

picture of me with sales director Dawson and Niamh my wonderful pattern cutter

the buyers...

* 21 Shop ...Vanessa Denza
* Way In......Helen Keyes
* Fifth Avenue...Shula
* Simpsons....Claire Stubbs
* McDonalds...Linda Lang
* Harrods younger set ..Liz Brown
* Bazaar (Mary Quant) ..Annabel Taylor

Why don't you act like a girl for a change?

COURTELLE
harriet

MARY QUANT
WITH COMPLIMENTS

BAZAAR

our first best seller...

on our way... ⟶

Dawson and I worked wonderfully as a team. We were both good looking and full of life, so buyers and press came, placed their orders and stayed to hear all the gossip. Dawson loved gossip. I always laughed at him, saying he behaved like a woman. The young buyers would place their orders, Dawson would flirt with them, and the order would increase!

Dennis realised that Dawson was going to be an asset as far as Harriet was concerned. He also agreed that we should hire Jacquie as my Press girl and P.A. We had, of course, already done that, but we thought it would be good to let him think he had made the decision! She fitted in with everyone. I must say that the strain we all worked under was extraordinary, but we never fell out. We backed off if there was going to be an explosion, and we respected each other. I know now that that was my happiest time in the 'rag trade'.

One day, I was working in my studio when I heard someone 3 floors down in the street honking their horn continuously...'bloody idiot,' I shouted out of the window. Then I saw Dawson standing by a beautiful white Alfa Romeo! He unravelled a large piece of paper which said: 'LOVE YOU BABY'; this is for you from me!! Oh, that bloody man always found a way to make me love him more. We were very happy. We talked only about Harriet, but it was very exciting. We were the only couple in the rag trade that wasn't Jewish, but they accepted us and although we always got the holidays wrong and didn't go to

Synagogue, we were always welcome. On the 2nd floor of Highlight house, there was a lovely man running a 'garment' business. He had so many tricks up his sleeve. He suggested to Dawson that he should try sleeping with the buyer if the collection was not very good. It seemed to work for him, but, luckily, we didn't have to go to those lengths, for my collections were always well received. Bob still, every so often, would call Dawson and say, 'Just sending the buyer from so and so up to you. I've got her in a good mood so you can take over!'. I don't think Dawson had to carry on the good work, but who knows! Bob had a wonderful wife, a large happy lady called Irma. She was such a kind person, and I wondered if she knew what he was like at work.

Every day the showroom was full, but the orders weren't that big. I knew they were testing us. Obviously, Harrods and Simpsons knew how easy Harriet dresses sold, but I did understand that to some buyers we were new to their market and naturally they had to be cautious.

One story always makes me laugh even years later. Miss Selfridge opened up; it was a new concept. They were trying to copy the success of Way In and 21 Shop. They took on a very young girl to be the buyer for the first Miss Selfridge. Dawson would greet her, give her a welcome kiss on the cheek, signal Silvia to make a coffee for the buyer and then the door would close. We knew she had a large 'open to buy,' so she was pretty important. I waited outside the door to hear what was happening, but it was very quiet; then the door swung open and Dawson threw a skirt at one of the machinists. 'Miss so and so's zip is broken in her skirt. Can you replace it as fast as possible?'. It was done quickly, and Dawson just put his arm through the doorway and closed the door sharply. We never discussed it. The order was very healthy, so why should I complain! But every season she did the same thing.

Chapter 8 part 5

Adviser to the bankers Arbuthnot - an American problem

I must say I think I planned the new Harriet really well. The team were good, and the press were starting to get excited as the magazines came out. We had a mention in most of the big glossies and, also, in some of the important press like the Times and the Telegraph. One morning, I received a call from the bankers Arbuthnot who were trying to understand the 'swinging 60s fashion industry'. They asked if I would sit in on the meetings with various clients who were asking for money for setting up a business in the industry or clients who were in trouble and needed guidance! What me! 3 out of 100 for maths…well you see it's the way that you look at the problem. The fashion industry is a different kettle of fish from other businesses… there are no rules. Now young entrepreneurs were venturing into the business, a different approach was needed. I was in my element. I have never enjoyed anything so much in my life. They paid me £100 for each meeting, but I would have done it for nothing. One of the companies in trouble was Blaines, but, sadly, their troubles were too great, and they had to go into liquidation. Another was Jaeger, a well established company which needed to tweak their image to keep up with the changing market, and that was very exciting and fulfilling.

Dawson and I were working well together, and it was good to see him at work with the buyers. They all liked him and flirted with him too when they thought I wasn't looking. We were working on a selling plan, and I must say he came up with some good ideas. So far, Harrods, Harvey Nichols, Miss Selfridge, Simpsons, Dickens and Jones, Browns, Fifth Avenue and McDonalds had placed substantial orders. Now we had to round up the smaller shops and groups. Open up new accounts, sort out the agents and tackle Asia, Europe, Australia and USA…we had a long way to go, and it was tough work; we never stopped.

Dawson would often stay late at the end of the day, but I left on time, so I could be with Sarah for her good-night story. He never stayed the night; I had a lot to sort out in that direction, and it needed careful handling.

One morning we received a call from an Israeli woman from a boutique called BIBA, not 'the' Biba but someone copying the name. They were here in London on a buyer's trip and would like to see the Harriet collection as soon as possible. Dawson made the appointment and the owner of the boutique said she was bringing her own mannequins with her. Well, Dawson nearly collapsed when these 3 very tall busty ladies appeared ready to work and model the designs. The thing is that they had no clothes on and they just floated about from room to room. Nobody knew where to look, and Dawson's face was scarlet. I thought he would explode! We laughed for many years about that.

So, the plan was to tackle the USA first, and this was done through a 'buying House' based in London. Dawson made an appointment with the biggest one, AMC which was run by Big Bill, can't remember his name now, but he was a large gentleman, who wore a huge Stetson. Next, he made an appointment for Bloomindales for the next week. Wow, we hit the jackpot, we thought. BUT a few days later, walking in off the street, came the buyer from Alexanders', a store in New York. I had no idea who they were, and the order was only about 20 pieces, but it was our first American order. We were chuffed.

The next week Bloomingdales came in to place their orders. They loved the collection and made plans to call the press when they got home. Then they suggested that next season they may have a Harriet corner, which would be very exciting. Dawson said that would be wonderful, but the order would have to be sustainably more to have an exclusive corner. Good for you, I thought! As they walked out of the showroom, the buyer turned and said, 'I hope you haven't sold to Alexander's across the road from our store'. Dawson didn't say anything for a moment and then said, 'Good heavens. NO'. Everybody was smiling. The door closed behind them. Then Dawson turned to me and said, 'Now what do we do?' We had sold to Alexander's the week before, and they were delivered yesterday. Of course, we didn't know any better!

We looked at each other, and we obviously had the same thought. Dawson booked 2 cheap flights to New York for the following day.

My mother said she would stay and look after Sarah, thank goodness, and so all was set.

We arrived at Alexander's straight from Kennedy airport, complete with a pair of scissors and immediately performed a double act...I found the Harriet clothes and grabbed 3 of them to try on, in the cubicle I carefully cut out the Harriet label, then handed them to the sales assistant saying I need a different size and then duly cut those labels out as well. Within half an hour, I had taken the labels out of all 20 garments, and no one was any the wiser...whew! We did laugh a lot about that for many years. Whilst we were in New York we, met up with Macy's and Saks of 5th Avenue just to have a chat and make sure when their buyers were ready to buy, they would come to see us in London.

Chapter 8 part 6

Moving to Barnes - we lived on Pepsi cola

All seemed good at Harriet; the orders were healthy, the adding machine sang happy tunes nearly all day and going to work in the morning was something to look forward to. I had a policy with my staff that if they woke up in the morning and couldn't face coming to work, then they must take the day off. It never happened. Perhaps they knew that they might catch me on 'one of those days', and I might sack them!

Dawson and I were still working very hard, and we made a good team. The Harriet team liked him, but it soon became clear that Dennis and Silvia Naar didn't. I think Phyllis knew, but I didn't like to put her on a spot. I had a feeling that Dawson showed them no respect. He took his orders from me, only me, and Dennis liked to come into the showroom when Dawson had an important client and just sit there, making stupid remarks that made the buyer uncomfortable. He always introduced himself as Mr Harriet! Ugh!

Dawson had started to come over for tea to the flat, and we would go out for a walk with Sarah to the Round pond, in Kensington Gardens. We would go to a café in Kensington High Street. One day we were queuing up to get in, and Sarah was in Dawson's arms when she bent down and scooped all the cream off a big iced cake and covered him and herself in cream. We took a look at each other and fled down the street giggling like naughty kids.

I decided that I should buy a house as paying rent was silly. Although it meant a journey in the morning, it seemed to make sense. London was so busy and there were so many robberies. The one that Sarah and Melina were involved in was the deciding factor. She was over playing with Chrissie's daughter, Melina, and they were in the square of Iverna gardens when they saw 2 men with masks rush out of the Tara hotel and jump into a car. Apparently, the police had had a tip off, and the four burly policemen had waited in their Land Rover. As the thieves fled into the square, the police made chase but had to turn sharply around the corner to make chase. The Land Rover rolled over and landed with its wheels in the air, the thieves escaped. Sarah and Melina, both about 5 years old then, were called as witnesses. That was the end as far as I was concerned. We moved to the country, well Barnes.

A friend of Niamh's had a house for sale in Rectory Road, Barnes. We went to see it, and it was perfect and a stone's throw from the pretty Barnes Common. Jean came too and agreed it was for the best. The price was £10,000 (now those houses are about £1.5 million.) Skipton Building Society offered me a mortgage, so with my savings of £2000 and the £8000 mortgage, we were off. We had so much fun rushing up and down to Habitat and going to the sale rooms. We didn't have much money for furniture but to this day I still have most of the stuff.…. I'm a terrible hoarder and never throw anything away. Sarah is worse than me though, perhaps that was my influence.

I managed to get Sarah into the local school called Putney Park. She was very happy there and made many friends. Our first Christmas there was lovely. My mother and stepfather came over, and we ate too much but as Christmas goes, it was quite fun. My mother didn't like Dawson, of course. She was still hoping I was going to marry Peter! Sarah had a bicycle from Father Christmas, so Dawson used to take her up to Barnes Common at the end of our road. It was wonderful to watch them; we really were a happy little family, Dawson Sarah, Simon and me.

We decided that it was time for Dawson to move into the house in Barnes; nothing was said, it seemed natural. I did tell Peter that that was what I wanted. I said I needed someone to be more of a father to Sarah, but he didn't offer to move in, so it just happened. Life just changed, and I think it was the right thing to do at the time. Except, one night there was a bang on the door, and when I went to open it with Dawson just behind me, there was Peter blind drunk holding a baby in his arms and another child standing by his side. All he said was something like I've got a family too. I didn't say anything, I never guessed that was why he was never around. I never even guessed he had another family. I stood there with my eyes popping out and said 'goodbye', closed the door and then passed out.

The shock was too much for me. I was overworked and tired, I know, but it was such a shock. I remember it as if it was yesterday. Dawson made me a cup of tea, and I sat and shook for a while. Then I called my mother. She told me that he was living in a room in Chiswick with my friend Carola, Mouse's wife, and the two children, but Marcus had left her a huge amount of money, so they were buying a big house nearby. She knew all the time. She said she didn't know what to do. I suppose it must have been difficult for her, but it still hurt.

Thank goodness Sarah was with her girlfriend up the road. I would have to work out how to tell her. I suppose I was a coward and, because we were such a happy little family, I didn't say anything. Would be easier to tell her when she was older. I must say Peter never forgot a card for Christmas and her birthday. He left it with my mother, but after that awful night we didn't see him anymore. A few years later, I had money problems again and couldn't manage Sarah's school fees, so Jean suggested I write to Peter. I did get a letter back simply saying, 'I can't pay the fees as I have three children of my own to pay for!'. I'm sure Carola could have released some of Mouse's money; he would have wanted that, I know. I never asked for anything ever again. I also never told Sarah; I saw no point as it would have hurt her unnecessarily.

My mother was always waiting at the house for Sarah when Les, the bus driver from Putney Park School, dropped her off. Except one day when sarah said to Les, 'I'm going to tea with my new friend Lucy'. Lucy nodded, so Les dropped them both off at Beverley Road and thought no more about it. Of course, Sarah and Lucy had made their own arrangements without Lucy's mother knowing anything about it. That would have been OK except for the fact that Sarah had no idea what her address was. Marian, Lucy's mother, called the school and sorted the whole problem out. Les got a ticking off, but all ended well. Very well, in fact, as Lucy and Sarah are still friends now, and Marian is one of my dearest friends today. When I was working on the new Spring/Summer collection and the Missy collection for America, I had a call from one of my favourite fabric reps. His name was Bill Velutini; he was very large, gay and a

very good cook. So we always spent extra time after I had chosen my fabrics swapping pasta recipes.

This particular time, he had a fabric that he said was not for sale. It was a sample for Pepsi Cola for window dressing or something. I loved it and persuaded him to let me sample it. It caused a riot.

It was the first time names appeared on fabrics. I made a sports collection, and Bill said he had to see if Pepsi Cola were OK with that. He kept saying 'Copyright' and was very nervous he would get the sack. I told him to ask the Pepsi press department to come to see the show and have tea with Harriet. They came, and they were over the moon as I was providing them with unlimited publicity since every magazine photographed the clothes.

The Managing Director was at the show, and he said at the end that we would receive a crate of Pepsi Cola every week as a way of saying thank you. He then made us promise when we went on a sales trip that we would go to the main Pepsi Cola factory to have our pictures taken. We did go, and they made such a fuss of us…also the collection was our best seller for a whole year. Happy days. But we did have many many crates of Pepsi Cola and in the end, we couldn't give it away!

Pic of me and sarah in pepsi trousers

I had been working so hard that I decided we all need a holiday, not easy with a business like Harriet, you have to make lots of lists. Lists for Niamh to start the next collection, Mick to order fabrics for next season, cheques all signed for Phyllis and so forth. I was exhausted when we did finally get away. We went to Amalfi and stayed in a lovely hotel on the beach, called the Miramar. We had such a lovely time; we laughed from morning to evening. Sarah made friends with Tara, Joan Collins' daughter. There was a drama on the 2nd day as Tara was swimming and went out of her depth. Sarah had just passed her life saving test in the Brownies, so she jumped in to save her. It was very dramatic, and I was very proud. I turned towards Joan, but she hadn't noticed. Tara rushed to her mother crying and Joan pushed her away saying, 'Go away. Look what you have done on my new top. It's soaking wet!'. Poor Tara! She looked very hurt. I gave Joan one of my 'cold stares!' She chose to ignore it. It was difficult as I spent the rest of the holiday on my sunbed beside her.

That night, we let Sarah stay up to dinner with the 'grown-ups.' Her prize for saving Tara. I remember the band played 'Raindrops keep falling on your head'. Sarah danced on Dawson's feet. We really had a lovely holiday, and I vowed I would do it more often.

Chapter 9 part 1

Harrods fashion show - the bed department!

Helen Keyes, the buyer for Way In, telephoned to make sure we had got our invitation to their annual fashion show. Apparently, they had not had many replies and were getting worried. I decided to ask the workroom to make me a stunning outfit as I knew there would be plenty of press there. I chose an apricot silk jersey fabric, and Mrs Orris ran up a simple shift, on the cross, so it fell beautifully. Just simple, but I must say I did look stunning. I scrapped my hair back into a French knot. When you look good, it gives you confidence, and I knew that was what I needed. Dawson looked great too; he had one of the 'Harriet's man' collection that I had been working on in secret.

Dawson in one of jackets from the Harriet's first men's collection with Jean who was wearing 'Charlotte', a green velvet dress.

When we arrived at Harrods, they had laid on Valet parking, and we were directed to a special V.I.P lift, which shot up to the private theatre. We were a little late, so people were already seated. I knew most of the manufacturers there and waved. A couple of press from Vogue and Tatler took some pictures of us. Then the show began. We were very privileged to be at this private show; it was an honour bestowed by the management. Our Harriet dresses were second on, and we got a lot of applause which made me so proud, as you can imagine. The show only lasted three quarters of an hour. Then we had Champagne. I hate Champagne, so Dawson and I wandered around the store. We walked to the bed department, and I was looking at sheets as we did need some. Meanwhile, Dawson had other ideas and just bent down and scooped me up into his arms! We made love on a £2000 bed with a fur throw over us. Well, I must say, that was special!

I met Alistair Cowan, another designer. We had lots of things in common and were the only two Gentiles in the rag trade, which always made us feel a bit awkward, not part of the 'Jewish brigade'.

Sarah was allowed to stay up until we got home as it was the weekend, and we had promised to bring back a Pizza. So, it was family time tonight. We often played a 'piggy' game which was fashionable in the 70s. The log fire was alight, and I remember thinking how happy I was and what a lovely little family I had.

Secretly I had been designing a men's collection, I wasn't sure if it would be a commercial success but time would tell.

A couple of weeks later we were asked to the opening of the Playboy club in Park Lane. Dawson wore the same jacket that he wore to Harrods and was stopped by Rod Stewart who wanted to order one.

So, perhaps, 'Harriet's Man' is worth a go, but not this season as I had so much on my plate. I did include the odd style from my Men's collection whilst trying to see if it was a good market to go into. I concluded that at the moment, there was not a big enough market to sink money into it, maybe later. Meanwhile, the press were really on my case. Jacqui was doing a good job. She was relentless and sent garments by taxis from one side of London to the other.

Harriet became well-known for our pretty delicate evening dresses, so although I had designed them for the 'debs' that crammed into my little boutique a few months ago, now they were seen everywhere.

Male!

THE SUNDAY EXPRESS LONDON DECEMBER 17, 1967

VERONICA PAPWORTH

Those so-dressy

Female!

Every debutante in the country owned at least one of these dresses

DRAWINGS BY
VERONICA PAPWORTH

Chapter 9 part 2

Finding sales agents - blue movies!

Dawson was trying to find agents abroad, now we had tackled America. So, we decided to try Germany, Denmark and Sweden. I could do France as I had so many contacts there with the help of Gill Hass and Claire Rendlesham. I decided to wait for Dawson to sort the agents out; then I would head for Paris, maybe with Chrissie, and pick up my contacts.

The Drapers' Weekly turned out to be a God send. A German agent who represented Polly Peck and Louis Caring called and said he was in London and would like to see the Harriet collection. He thought it would complement his existing collections as the German public wanted Boutique clothes. Word had spread. His name was Herr Marx, and he was charming, but didn't have much of a sense of humour!

Then the next day somebody called Kai Willison came to the showroom to check us out. What a lovely man; we became great friends. He covered Denmark and Sweden as well as Iceland. Dawson and Kai were a wonderful team and they were always up to tricks. We made plans to manufacture a set of samples for him and then go to Copenhagen to pay a visit to start the ball rolling. Dawson and I flew there a couple of weeks later and had a great time. What a lovely place Copenhagen is and delightful people. The press came to meet us, and they set up various articles to introduce us to the Danish market. We stayed at Kai's lovely house in the woods and learnt about his magical life in Denmark; I was envious. On our second night, Kai said he had booked seats at the Venus club, which sounded exciting, we thought. Well, it was, but not in the way I had expected. Kai and Dawson were like naughty boys sniggering. We arrived at the big heavy studded door and realised we were in a sex theatre. No wonder they were happy. Me, well, I just went with the flow!

We sat down at a table right in the front row, 'so we could get a good view,' Kai said. Great, just what I needed. The show was good, very professional; there was one rather large lady that they called Venus. She had everything big, I mean big, and she strutted about the stage virtually naked and pointed to people. When she pointed, she came down off the stage and put the poor person or persons through a very vulgar routine. It was funny really, but not if you were the person being picked on. Dawson had shrunk beside me, hoping that she would not see him. That was what she wanted, poor Dawson. This large lady plopped herself on his lap, her body stretched all over him, and he seemed so tiny under her. She turned to look at me and I gave her one of my Wendy looks. 'Don't bug with me baby,' I thought, but said nothing. Venus, at

'Sebastian'

Debs' favourite ball gowns

BOOMING BOUTIQUE

recognition at last

Another best seller

Chrissie in my favourite dress 'Charlotte'

that point, swivelled around to torture the couple behind us. Both Dawson and I sat there very still not wanting her to come back to us; we looked like we had turned to stone! We had to sit through various sex scenes and then, at last, we could go home. Dawson was never the same again!

Sales proved to be strong in Denmark, and Kai wanted to start approaching the press in Sweden, ready for his visit. He asked if I would come for 2 or 3 days to meet the press and set up a fashion show. Reluctantly, I went, but I hated going away as it meant I missed being with Sarah at bedtime, and I missed reading to her.

Kai was a perfect gentleman, except at night when he kept tapping on my door and singing! I kept the door firmly closed.

We went to Gothenburg, Oslo and Bergan. Lovely, so fresh and so clean. They were thrilled to meet me, and the trip was a success.

Before we left for the airport to go back to London, Kai asked if I needed to buy anything. I bought a Swedish rag doll for Sarah and a silk scarf for my mother. It was Dawson's birthday shortly so I asked Kai what I should buy. He suggested a blue movie. He came into the shop with me and I just pointed at one of the tapes; I didn't care which one I bought as I was sure Dawson would like it.

Kai and I talked about the blue movie business in London. There were shops in Soho that sold various sex videos and sexy nighties etc., but otherwise the market was wide open then. A couple of weeks later, Kai came to London to see the new Summer collection. He came into the showroom dragging an enormous suitcase; he unlocked the suitcase and said, 'there' in Danish, I think! The contents didn't surprise me; there were about 60 Blue movies...Dawson's face lit up, and I left the showroom, closing the door behind me.

Kai and Dawson went into the blue movie business. Kai would bring them over, and Dawson would sell them to his biggest client National Carparks. Every evening when we finished work, we would call the garage, and one of the boys would come and pick us up in the Alfa. They were eager to do anything for Dawson as they wanted to be part of the Blue Movie business! There was a constant stream of customers wanting to buy the movies. So, it seemed that Dawson had a brilliant new business, as a sideline!

Chapter 9 part 3

Ibiza - Dawson Sarah and me - then Colombe d'Or

Oh! We loved Ibiza in the 70s. It wasn't like it is now with clubs, drink, drugs and generally bad behaviour! Well, actually, it was some of that but based mainly on drink, drink and Hierbas We seemed just to drink in those days; we were not into drugs of any kind. I'm sure they were there, but we were too busy drinking and smoking.

The idea was to book a long weekend with our travel agent, leaving at 4pm on a Friday and returning 9pm on Sunday night, the cost £19. We always stayed at the Felicia Hotel in Santa Eulalia. As we were there at least once a month, we soon became friends with the owners, Pepe and his wife. Just down the road was our favourite drinking club run by lovely Sandy, called 'Sandy's Bar'. We spent many a night there. I didn't always remember going back to the hotel. We all drank such a lot in those days; we mixed drinks, and every night we would always finish with a bottle of Sambuca! Dawson always chatted up Sandy with his 'gay' impressions. Poor Sandy fell for it and for Dawson! In fact, he was so good, I did begin to wonder if Dawson was just a little bit gay himself???

There were so many fun-loving people there, always over the top, like Terry Thomas, the comedian with the gap in his front teeth. He had his Rolls Royce painted with the same tropical print as his shirt. He was friends with some odd characters like Gordon Frazer, a bit part actor who always wore a bowler hat around the pool. Most of his friends were pretty seedy people, so we started drifting away.

We took Sarah to Ibiza when she was about 7 and discovered a pretty hotel/restaurant called 'The Wild Asparagus'. It was calm and away from all the crowds. It was surrounded by fields of daisies, miles and miles of pretty white daisies, heaven.

We relaxed there, and the three of us were so happy. I spent a lot of time regretting that I was missing Sarah growing up, but these little 'breaks' helped to make up for our lost mother/daughter moments. Nobody knew of our secret hide-away as it was before the damn mobile telephone. So, we could just disappear and relax.

Then one year, we had heard about the Colombe d'Or in St Paul de Vence in the South of France. There we lost our hearts and went there year after year. It was there that Sarah learnt to swim, she also learnt to play 'Scrabble' in French, with Simone Signoret, Yves Montand's lovely curvy wife. Yves was a marvellous boule player, and Dawson played with him a couple of times but lost. Life at the hotel was special. We tried not to tell anyone about this secret place, which was discovered by the advertising agents like Y&R and CPV. Lunch there was special, and, in fact, when we went back there about 20 years later, the menu was still the same, always a lovely experience. First course was hors'devre…10 little bowls of lark's tongue pate, prawns, humous, large saucisson chopped on a board, Quale's eggs, caviar followed by lamb with Lyonnaise potatoes, grilled tomatoes and green beans, then Raspberry souffles.

The swimming pool was green not blue; I remember it like it was yesterday.

We would lie on the sunbeds and gently tan. We all wore huge sunglasses,

Colombe d'Or in St. Paul De Vence

mainly because it was the latest trend but also it allowed one to see all the film stars that were either around the pool or in the open restaurant. I met James Baldwin there, interesting man. Paul Newman came in one day to ask to see the rooms, but Madam Roux looked at him and said firmly 'NO.' Madam Roux ran the place with a rod of iron. The family had had the hotel for many years and when she died, the whole town was at her funeral, and everyone was crying.

Colombe d'Or became famous first of all as it was where Picasso would eat; when he had no money, he would give Madam Roux a painting. The same with Matisse and several others. They are still there today; the restaurant walls are covered in priceless paintings. Nobody would dream of stealing them as they are so well known that they would have to stay in hiding forever.

When Simone Signoret was not filming, she would stay in their hotel. She always stayed in the first suite by the pool near the big parrot. She would eat alone or with my daughter and then go for her siesta, which was generally shared with one of her lovers. At about 5pm, she would come out and stand by the edge of the pool wrapped in a huge towel. She would throw her arms theatrically in the air and say 'c'est manificant!' then, gracefully, she would let the towel fall to the floor and simply slid into the pool. It was a daily occurrence, and we wouldn't have missed it for the world!

The Colombe d'Or pool where Sarah learnt to swim

Our favourite place to eat on earth

Chapter 9 part 4

Chrissie and I in Paris again - Grapevine

One day after our usual liquid lunch, Chrissie and I decided to go back to Paris again. This time was going to be different as now I was in the proper 'fashion industry,' and I had had several letters and calls from boutiques in Paris, asking me to come and show them my collection. I was very excited. Chrissie was to come as my mannequin, and she agreed to no fee but all expenses, so cheap labour! Remember, to us in Great Britain, Paris was still important. We did all secretly think the French led the way as far as fashion went. However, the 60s and 70s were pretty amazing, and you could tell that the French thought of our fashions as the next craze, and like all other countries they wanted to climb on board. There was no good denying the mini had arrived, and London was slowly creeping up the ladder. Paris didn't like it, but, obviously, they didn't want to lose their position in the world of fashion. I spent the week before we left calling all the top shops and making appointments.

We flew this time. We had 2 suitcases filled with samples and a list of all the top shops. They were not calling themselves boutiques yet. So, armed with a map of the Metro, an order pad and plenty of pens, we set off to conquer Paris. Gudule was our first appointment. This was a very trendy shop, and they clapped Chrissie every time she twirled. We got a nice order for 30 dresses and 20 trousers. Little did they know the trousers were based on Dior's pattern anyway!

Next stop was Dorethee Bis, very important contact. I was a bit doubtful that the buyer would like my collection, but, worry not, she did and placed an order for 120 dresses and the whole of the beachwear collection. Blimey, I was drunk with success. That's what we needed after that order, a large Bacardi and Coke; yes, that did the trick! The buyer, from Dorothee Bis, Madam Esprite, thought we should get in touch with a friend of hers, another designer, called Ted Lapidus. I had, of course, heard of him; he was always in Elle magazine, and he reminded me of Roger Nelson as a designer. Soft tailoring, always with a matching hat; all his designs were utterly lovely. She kindly called him, and he said we should come to lunch at his new apartment tomorrow. Afterwards, there was a show in his showroom, so we could come to see his latest work. It was like a dream come true for me, and it turned out to be very lucrative too.

I thought that was enough for one day, and both of us were pretty tired, having left UK at 6am. We had still to find a hotel, and we were, as usual, hungry. Let me explain about model girls and ex models eating habits; both of us were very very skinny, but we had the appetite of an elephant, or is it a horse? We were also very costly to keep too as only the best would be good enough for us.

We decided to go to the Left Bank, Rive Gauche, where we knew there were some little inexpensive hotels; no brothels this time! Luckily, we found the sweetest hotel in Rue de Buci, called l'Hotel de Buci.

It was dark as French hotels often are, but cosy and smelt of stale Gauloises cigarettes. Having had a quick nap and unpacked, we decided to wander around our area and get our bearings. It's lovely around that part of Paris, the real Paris I always think. We strolled along Rue de Sevres and window shopped. Why is it that wherever you walk in Paris, the women always looked so beautifully clothed? Perhaps because French women spend lots of money on a basic suit or coat with simple well-cut lines whilst English women buy cheap clothes and add expensive jewellery!

We popped into a little Bistro and had a Steak Frites, followed by a Crème Caramel...ah just right. And now for bed, an early night for once.

The next day we had 2 more appointments and then, of course, we were having lunch with Ted Lapidus. Both buyers were very complimentary about the collection, although they were not brave enough to jump in. They decided to buy a little of certain styles and then would increase the order should they sell. Fair enough, and, actually, both shops called to increase their orders before the first was delivered. The fact that Elle magazine had done a lovely article about Harriet helped! I was so happy. Everything I had worked so hard for was paying off. I found a phone box and called my mother to check on Sarah and then called Niamh to check all was okay. I told her about the orders and asked her to tell Mick and the workroom. I promised next time she would come with me. Dear Niamh. She was such a lovely person. The whole team was like my family, and this was such a happy time for me.

It was 12, and we set off for our lunch appointment with Teddy, that's what everyone called him.

The address we had been given was 22 Boulevard St. Michel, so we decided to go via the Metro and when we got off at Cluny Metro. We were overwhelmed by the beauty of the houses and the whole area, which was close to the Luxembourg gardens, so peaceful.

We arrived exactly at 1pm. We rang the bell, and a good looking young man, about 35 I guessed, open the door with his arms outstretched to welcome us, 'Welcome to my new home. You are one of my first visitors. Come in and meet the rest of us. I am Teddy, by the way'. Then he stopped and the expression on his face changed dramatically. 'My meubles have not arrived in time for our lunch, so now we are having a picnic. Come in, come in but excuse no meubles!' Chrissie and I held back the laughter, but both of us fell in love with this crazy man.

When we entered the room 3 people 'rose' from the floor and greeted us, yes indeed we were having a picnic, but what a spread: a huge pot of caviar, Parma ham, smoked salmon, fresh baguettes and a big basket of strawberries. We sat on huge red velvet cushions and were given a glass of very tasty white wine. This was the life.

One of the men, I remember clearly, was an architect; his name was Paul Mermont. He wasn't very good looking, but he had a kind smile, and I could see at once that Chrissie was interested. In fact, they talked non-stop throughout the meal. I sat beside Ted Lapidus and we talked about fashion in Paris and in London, the only two places that existed as far as we were both concerned. I had brought some press cutting with me, and he was so excited to listen to the story of the creation of 'Arriet,' and to meet 'Arriet in person. Meanwhile, Chrissie and Paul Mermont had gone over to the huge window and they were deep in conversation. Paul looked as if he had fallen in love with Chrissie; he was all misty eyed, obviously a fast worker! We joined them, and Paul started to explain what his big project was. He had been asked to build a tunnel and a small city under the Seine! Whew, no wonder he was so excited. Well, I'm not sure if it was Chrissie or the under-water city that made him throw his arms in the air nonstop.

Teddy called again about his 'meubles' and was in a state of total exhaustion. Then there was a call, from the showroom I gathered, and he said, 'We must leave now. The customers are arriving for the fashion show. Come 'Arriet, you sit with me in the front, and Paul and Chrissie can go on looking into each other's eyes in the back of the car!'.

When we arrived, there were already about 100 people silently waiting, and a piano tinkled in the background. We were ushered to the front row by Teddy and then he disappeared. I noticed Chrissie and Paul were holding hands by now. I nudged her, and she just winked at me.

Here Chrissie is wearing one of Teddy Lapidus copies made by Harriet.

The show was exactly as I expected; well-cut coats and suits with a whimsical look about them. I can't explain, but having met him, I knew what I meant. Teddy came on stage and took a bow. We clapped so loud he knew it was us, so he did a theatrical bow just for us. What an experience; I knew I would never be able to compete with someone like him. He had, of course, been formally trained whilst I made it up as I went along! I was still proud of what I had achieved and felt that my look was more for the young street people whilst Teddy's clothes were for his young wealthy clientele.

He let me choose a couple of styles to take into the cabine and to copy them; he said it was a present. He also said he would come to London to see my show and expected his two styles to be in the show. Well, he did come to London, and the copies were also in the show, and I could see how proud he was. 'Hey 'Arriet, they look better than my originals.' And I think they did as my interpretation was different but the same, if you know what I mean!

On the plane back to London, we decided that it would be a wonderful idea to do a monthly REPORT MAGAZINE, reporting on all the clothes in the shops each season in New York, Paris and London. That meant we got to travel to these cities at least twice a year, which we did.

AN ASIDE

I often wonder if Paul Mermont ever did build the city under the Seine...never found out, but I suspect it never happened!

Grapevine was my first fashion report magazine…and the last!

215

70's...bigger shapes...oversized manly jackets - feminine blouses...full waisted trousers... scull caps...bags worn across the body...lace up shoes...stiletto heels for on the town

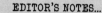 excerpts from Wendy's fashion report 1978

EVERYTHING IS OVERSIZED..........

BIG COTTON SHIRT 17.90
COTTON WAISTCOAT 9.50

Both from FIORUCCI
Cotton HINDI trousers
from SHERIDAN
BARNET at ELLE

hair ...plaits (like Heidi)...small knots... and of course the eternal 'FRIZZ.' belts...double some worn bandolier style across the body. bags... hunting bags as last season... mainly in tweed.

EDITOR'S NOTES...

Autumn '78 promises to be a very interesting season if the main story from Paris and London is to be followed...a wealth of oversized manly jackets coats and suits...teamed with pretty feminine blouses with intricate detailing. The baggy blazer (tipped for success last season) is now an ESSENTIAL! With long lines and even longer revers...low buttoning and narrow hips... works for day or evening.

COATS tend to be on the same lines...but most of them have pleats...tucks or top stitching. What's new in JACKETS? Watch out for the PARKA (sporty) and the cropped SPENCER jacket (dressy) to be brought to life again. An abundance of natural tweeds...leather.

To wear with jackets trousers are firmly back...with fullness on the waist and narrow at the ankle...often with soft folds around the calf...tucks - pleats and neatly belted in.

DRESSES very much around in soft tweeds or checks of all sizes...but worn with either a GILET or waistcoat over the top. Wear as much as three layers in different sizes...pile it on! Plenty of KNITS still around...oversized ...lacy and sparkly. Clever mixes around instead of CLASSIC mohair.

LEATHER and SUEDE makes a big comeback ...seen in nearly all collections...expensive but worth it.

For evenings it is pure HOLLYWOOD...garish glitter ...imitation jewels...sequins...beads... satin lounging pyjamas... Hats...small knitted skull caps...berets...1940's trilby's...and fishing hats to go with the tweed fabrics Shoes...sporty and laced up...low heeled...suede boots that crinkle at the ankle...stiletto's for the evening.

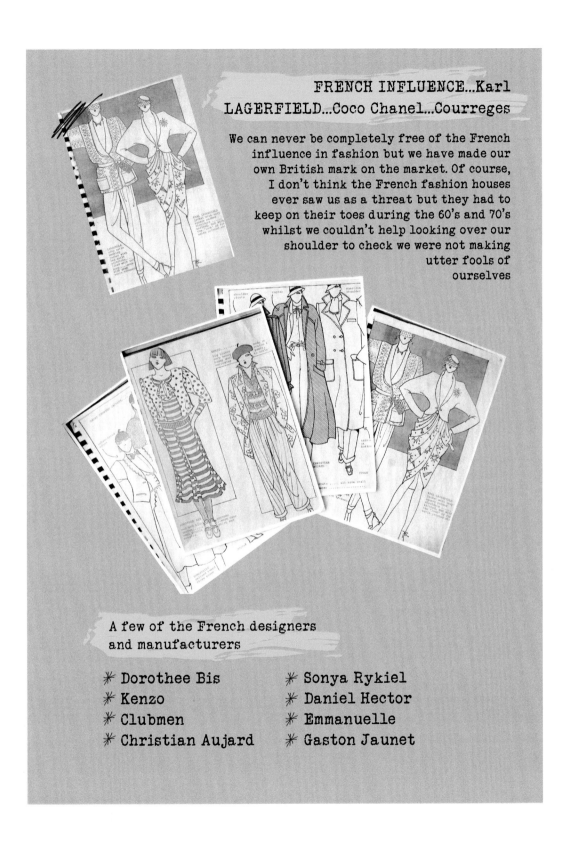

FRENCH INFLUENCE...Karl LAGERFIELD...Coco Chanel...Courreges

We can never be completely free of the French influence in fashion but we have made our own British mark on the market. Of course, I don't think the French fashion houses ever saw us as a threat but they had to keep on their toes during the 60's and 70's whilst we couldn't help looking over our shoulder to check we were not making utter fools of ourselves

A few of the French designers and manufacturers

* Dorothee Bis
* Kenzo
* Clubmen
* Christian Aujard

* Sonya Rykiel
* Daniel Hector
* Emmanuelle
* Gaston Jaunet

Chapter 9 part 5

Opening new boutique in Bond Street

We came back from Paris buzzing; I proudly presented the orders to Dawson, and he was impressed. I had a list of garments for Jacquie to send over for photography, so the trip had been worthwhile. Also, I was more relaxed as Chrissie and I always had fun. Generally, we got into some kind of trouble, but this time was mainly work. Oh! And Paul falling in love with Chrissie is worth a mention!

There was a mound of post on my desk but no bills as Phyllis had removed them; not my problem, thank goodness. Don't have to eat them now!!

Amongst the post was a letter from Bernard at Andre Bernard, the chain of hairdressers. They would like to suggest that Harriet open a little boutique in a corner of their Bond Street salon. I had suggested this to him a few months ago, and it had taken time for all the directors to agree. I was really over the moon about this. I had done my sums and we would make a profit within 6 months. The company was very generous and had asked for a low rent, so we couldn't lose. Andre Bernard had a good setup, and all I needed was a salesgirl and stock. We were to meet at the solicitors and sign up to the idea as soon as possible. What fun. I phoned Eddie to thank him for I knew he was behind this. Must send him a bottle of Whisky. When everything was signed and sealed, I went with Jean to the salon with lots of props, and together we created a beautiful boutique. Sadly, I don't have any photos of that little venture. We put an advert up in reception in case any of the customers would like a job. Within the week, we had found the ideal person. Alice was her name, and she was enthusiastic, pretty, well dressed and full of fun. A press party and ask all the names on Andre Bernard customer list, so that meant about 500 people, Bond Street buzzed that night, for one night only.

Invitation for open of new Harriet's

I didn't get to the Boutique unless I was having my hair done, so, really, I think it became a bit neglected, and Alice seemed to spend her time gossiping and having her hair done. The only exciting bit for me was the fact that the press loved a 'rags to riches' story, so we got lots and lots of valuable exposure. We were in every magazine almost every week, from Vogue and Harpers to She and Flair.

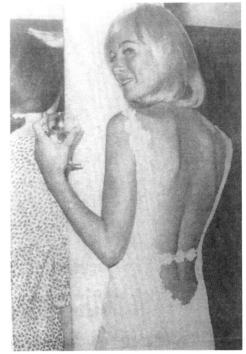

Merrill at opening of Bond Street Harriet.....

John French was asked by Vogue to take a picture of me for some reason or other. He was one of the most famous photographers in the UK, so I was very honoured.

AN ASIDE

There was another advantage to having the Boutique within the Salon. I had a key to the premises and that meant that I could 'pinch' unlimited amounts of free shampoos and hair spray, silly really, as by now I could afford these things. BUT it still gave me a thrill as it reminded me of my school days when we used to take sweets from Woolworth's open sweet counters!

PICTURES BY JOHN FRENCH
WENDY LEWIS wears her design for Harriet — the long skirt in red, white and blue flowered cotton (price 6½ gns.) is worn with a long sleeved ruffled blouse (also 6½ gns.)

Me in daisy skirt

Harriet makes the grade

By Harriet, this Navy dress, with flowers on front and back in fabulous colours! Approximate price 14 gns.

(SEE OVER)

April, 1964

different gimmicks

for top fashion houses, I also, by the way, write children's stories.

"A year ago I was chosen as one of the models to take part in the Fashion Group show which went to Paris and caused such a great success and then we took the same show to Zurich. As far as I was concerned I had reached my goal in fashion modelling.

"Just to complicate matters even more, I decided to open a boutique, mainly with model girls in mind. We have tried to make "Harriet" a little bit different from other boutiques—no gimmicks. We have a ready-to-wear collection which I designed myself and I design specially for introduced clients. I am a terrible bully and I never let anyone walk out in something I think unsuitable. At the moment I work a seven day week and often through the night as well."

This cheeky beach dress sells at approximately 9½ gns. It has a calico petticoat underneath it.

Designs from Harriet's 'daisy Collection'

220

Chapter 9 part 6

Jean and Stephen - working in Korea

Jean and Stephen bought a house near us in Putney, so they were never far away. They were by now such an important part in our lives.

Because I was always working, it was handy that Jean was always just a shout away. She and my mother got on really well, so I knew whilst I was working, everything at home was under control. Jean and I spent so much time together and a lot of time laughing and playing tricks on each other. So, life at home was always fun. One evening when Dawson and I were having supper with Jean and Stephen we got talking about the fact that none of us had ever smoked 'pot,' so it was up to me to ask Niamh, my wonderful pattern cutter, if she knew where we could get some. She was the only person we could think of that might know where to get some. She said leave it to her, and she will fix it up for me. I thought no more about it until one day Niamh whispered to me, 'It's all arranged. Your 'dealer' will be in touch'...panic, what was I getting myself into! Sure enough, at about 5, when Dawson and I were ready to leave, my studio phone rang. The voice was muffled, and whoever it was said, 'Meet me in 10 minutes on the corner of Margaret Street and Great Portland Street'. This reminded me of a 30s detective film, and I felt like a total fool but also couldn't help enjoying the secrecy. I wish I had a Balaclava or something, but I would go and meet him. Dawson offered to go in my place but no, I wouldn't 'chicken out' now. The 'passover' was smooth. Neither of us spoke and I didn't look up, then we swiftly went our own ways.

Now that we had the 'stuff', the next thing to do was to smoke it! We made a date with Jean and Stephen. We were all nervous, but there were four of us, so we felt we would be safe. That evening, Jean and Stephen came over. We put some music on. I remember it so clearly, 'Bridge Over Troubled Water' by Simon and Garfunkel. We all sat on the floor, even us senior hippies sat on the floor then. We were trying to get the setting right, ready for our first 'smoke.' Ready go...Dawson was first, Steven next, actually, he said he had done it before, but I doubt it by the look on his face, then Jean and then she passed it to me. We sat there waiting for something to happen, nothing, so we went around again, then again. I began to get the giggles as I imagined how funny we must all look sitting on the floor in a circle bolt upright and puffing at our 'joint'.

That was it really, I continued to find everything funny and Jean joined in, so both of us were falling about uncontrollably laughing. Stephen was sitting bolt upright with his 'Look at me. I'm very handsome and desirable' look on his face. Dawson had disappeared. I stopped laughing for a moment and went to the fridge. I was starving. I looked for Jean and found her cuddling the record player and singing to it. All of a sudden, Dawson appeared at the top of the stairs. He was completely naked. Slowly he walked down the stairs, then stopped and put his arms in the air.

'I am clean, I am free,' he said, and then lay on the sofa and went to sleep. Well, I'm not sure what all the fuss is about, but at least we had done it, and it was fun. Forty years later, I still have the remains of the joint, I'm keeping it for a rainy day, maybe?

I remember going into work the next day, and Niamh came up to me and said, 'Did you smoke it?'. She looked worried. 'Yes, of course we did, why?' Apparently, the man who sold it to us had sold us the wrong one, Opium instead of 'grass'. Well, we survived, that's all that matters!

I did actually smoke some Opium a couple of months later, although at the time I had no idea that I had.

Jimmy Hamilton, from Wallis shops, and Ronnie Scofield, a sort of friend of his, had decided that they should go into business on the QT. Ronnie had been dealing with the Korean company for a while, selling fur coats and jackets. Jimmy suggested that the designs were behind the times and that Harriet should design a collection for them. They put the offer to me, and I jumped at it. I love a challenge, and I would only be away for 10 days, so Harriet could manage without me, and Sarah was very happy at her new school. I phoned Marian in Barnes to see whether Sarah could stay with Lucy, Sarah's new best friend, over the weekend, so that my mother could have a break. Now everyone was happy, I gave myself permission to go away.

Niamh and I checked all was OK with the new collection, which we would show in 3 weeks' time. The fabrics were ordered, Mick as usual was on the ball, and Niamh could get on with grading, so I was free to go.

It didn't take me long to design 10 leather jackets and coats. I decided to leave the fur designs until I got there as I had no idea how to go about it. How difficult could it be?

Chrissie, Ronnie and I met up at Heathrow and we chatted most of the way. Exhausting, but that is Chrissie; she never stops talking, often rubbish but every so often, you could have an in-depth conversation. But I wouldn't change her, she was unique!

At Seoul airport, a car was waiting. We didn't have to go through customs. I liked that. It meant that the man we were going to work for was rich and powerful. UJ was his name, and we never knew his real name. He was quiet and very good looking; his English was perfect. He had arranged for food to be laid out in our suite as he presumed we would be tired; he was right.

The next morning, the limo picked us all up, and we went to the factory. A huge grey block with hundreds of rather small windows, very depressing. In fact, the journey to the factory was pretty depressing, everything seemed to be grey and dull. Glad I don't have to live here; there was a 10pm curfew as well, so lots of early nights, I suspect.

I met the pattern cutter and the machinists and realised none of them spoke English; this was going to be difficult. But I had done the designs, so, surely, they could work from them. I was not used to working in leather, so it was new to me. Not sure I understood what seam allowances to allow when working in leather, but I was quick to learn.

There was a sound in the factory that took some getting used to; it was clicking. I think it came from the 20 or so machinists all working in a rhythm; it was either the metal instrument they tapped the leather with, or the noise came from their mouths. You soon forgot it, but I, too, seem to work to the same rhythm…perhaps I should introduce it to Harriet machinists; it may speed them up a bit! There were 5 floors in the factory, and each floor had its own coloured overalls, red on top floor, blue on the next and so on.

As I was working one day, the clicking stopped for a few moments and out of the corner of my eye, I saw a flash of red falling past my window. Within seconds the clicking started again. I asked what had just happened, and I was told that one of the girls on the red floor had jumped out of the window. 'Don't worry it happens most days.' How desperate they must be to jump; it was strange too that nobody showed any interest.

A few days later all 10 samples had been made. Chrissie walked up and down the factory floor to show off the new styles to all the machinists, and they happily clapped their own work. As I suspected, the fur collection just needed a few alterations, a reshape of the block and a few unusual tweets here and there. At the last moment, I produced a crazy fur and leather jacket. It was sensational, and we all knew this was the star of the show; even I liked it!

The owner, UJ, was given a private showing, and he looked impressed and clapped continuously. So, everyone was happy.

That evening we were told that UJ had arranged for the company to take over a Geisha house for Chrissie and me. Ronnie was going somewhere else; he looked pretty happy, so I suspected it was also a Geisha house but for men only. We didn't understand why this had been arranged, but the moment we got out of our taxi, we were escorted by 4 beautiful girls. They had pure white faces, so you hoped they were pretty. They had arranged a 'beefy' man to play drums, my favourite; it was very hypnotic. We sat at a long table laden with exotic food. I sat at one end with my Geisha, and Chrissie at the other beside her little Geisha. Chrissie was nearly 6 foot tall, so it did look very funny. Chrissie was munching away, but every time I went towards the food, my Geisha shook her head and said, 'no no!'. I looked towards Chrissie, and she mouthed 'open your legs!' I went hungry that night!

The next evening, we were eating in the main restaurant, chatting away about the day and looking forward to going home in a few days' time. Then a good looking man stopped at our table. He was American and looked a bit worse for wear, one too many Bourbons, I thought. He said rather quietly, 'Do you know what today is?'. He sat down, drew a deep breath and said, 'It's July 4th, which is independence day!'. Of course, that was why there were so many American flags around. The man introduced himself and said he was going to give a party and wanted us to come. We agreed and arranged to go to his suite at 8. I didn't feel very enthusiastic as he was already pretty drunk, but poor man, he was away from his family and friends and it was after all Independence Day. When we rang the bell, he came to the door. He looked much better and had obviously had a rest and perhaps a shower. 'Welcome ladies.' He handed us a drink. I noticed a giant turkey on the trolley and enough food to feed an army.

We sat down, and he told us about his ranch and his family back home. He obviously missed them all, and I felt sorry for him. We were still drinking and chatting a couple of hours later. Obviously, there was not going to be a party. Our host, whose name I can't remember, offered us food and more drink and we continued to chat. Then he said would we smoke a little pot with him. I wasn't keen but having done it before, I thought I would. Chrissie had always smoked, and she was easily persuaded. Just like many things in life in those days, it seemed the natural thing to do, hardly worth making a fuss. Something didn't seem right, but I continued to puff and handed it to Chrissie. I stood up saying, 'I'm not feeling good. I think I need to go to my room'. I stumbled out of the apartment and keeping the wall close to me to steady me, I got to my room, no keys. So, I set off down the corridor, and I can still feel the strange feeling. The desk seemed to be tiny and miles away, and the receptionists were laughing at me. They gave me a key and helped me back to my room. Alone in the room, I went straight to the enormous window, which was from the ceiling to the floor. I put my hands above my head with the palms on the glass. I felt I had to smash my way out and jump. Something stopped me, and I stumbled to the phone and I called Chrissie, who in turn called Ronnie. Moments later, Ronnie was banging on the door and somehow, I managed to open it, but by now I could hardly stand. My whole body was shaking. The next thing I remember was being plunged into cold water in the bath. I had no clothes on! Then I passed out.

Don't ask me what happened then. I think I know but I'm not sure...a mystery. My drink had either been spiked or I had smoked Opium again!

The next morning, looking around the room I realised what a terrible state I must have been in, but now I had to get ready for today as the three of us were going to Tokyo for a day trip, as one does!

We were going to choose snake skins for a new collection. Ronnie looked rough, but Chrissie was her usual chirpy self. It was only a short journey from Seoul to Tokyo and then we had to catch the Bullet train. Before we joined the train, we managed to buy some sandwiches from an amazing shop. There was a large shop window, and they had filled the whole window with crustless sandwiches squashed up to the glass, I wish I had taken a picture but that was long before the iPhone.

Chrissie and I sat in our seats and opened up our sandwiches. But after one bite, a guard came up to us and shouted something in Japanese. Before the train took off, we were dragged off the train and the guard pointed to a sign on the platform...EATING ON TRAIN NOT ALLOWED...they confiscated our sandwiches, sadly.

The snake skins were beautiful, but I didn't feel like using them. It seemed so sad, and I was convinced that the jackets were better to be made in leather that I had designed them for, so the journey was a waste of time.

We stayed in a huge hotel called the Imperial hotel and did some sightseeing.

That night we were taken to a beautiful expensive restaurant, like those kind, and experienced real Japanese food. Very different from the ones you get in the UK.

I had 'mucus' from a bird, actually slime I think, then thin slithers of milk fed cow, lots of sticky rice and prawns cooked various ways. Nice evening, but I'm pleased to be going home in two days' time. It had been an experience but not at all pleasurable.

I am British after all! A month later I presented the leather and fur collection at a high-profile fashion show at the Carlton Hotel in Knightsbridge. I dressed the stage with huge china Leopards from Casa Pupo that no longer exists but is sadly missed. The Korean top brass were there, and they were very impressed. UJ, the president of the company, looked very pleased with himself and came and bowed several times in front of me.

Everyone very happy, I think.

Chapter 9 part 7

Best Sellers - Helmut Newton - Cecil Beaton

I seem to have been away for ages. Sarah was so excited to have her mummy back; she threw her arms about me and gave me a special hug. I felt warm all over and vowed that next time I went away Sarah would come with me; she was now of the age when she was changing almost daily and I wasn't prepared to miss any more.

Dawson was full of news. Apparently, the showroom had been very busy, and as I went through the orders, I was amazed. I congratulated him; he had done a great job. Bonwitt Teller from USA and Georges in Australia had been in and placed good sized orders. We seem to have achieved more than I could have dreamt of. Hard work had paid off after all.

Jacquie had been busy too, and she put together all the requests she had received from the magazines.

So, I spent the first week back from Korea in the studio with Helmut Newton and below is the article...

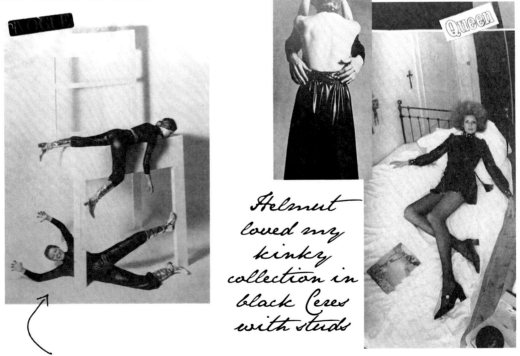

Helmut loved my kinky collection in black (eres with studs

My friend Bernie Wan at Vogue was asked to make an enormous chair, 3 times bigger than the models.

Various photographs of some of Harriet's best sellers...

hand printed collection sold worldwide, best sellers.

Shetland wool collection

Why don't you act like a girl for a change?

Haven't you noticed? Mannish suits have left us. In their place, cardigan suits like this one. Elegant in a fascinating zig-zagged Courtelle raschel. It's low-cut with wide flared trousers. Wear it with the belt becomingly low—and act the lady. Cardigan suit by Harriet. Brown/white only. Style Dagmar. About 15gns.

COURTELLE
harriet

RASCHEL JERSEY STYLED BY

London Way In, Knightsbridge; Colants Boutique, Royal Parade, Blackheath; Bath Image, Northumberland Place; Coventry Victoria Mitchell, 35 City Arcade;

Best Seller

petticoat

New collection of beachwear

THROWAWAY FASHION

THE GUARDIAN
Tuesday November 12 1968

queen

Navy chenille blazer £15.60, with pink white and navy striped waist-coat £5.10, and trousers with striped patches, £10.30. Pink Tricel shirt, £6.80. All by Harriet. Blue suede boots, £8 by Bata. Plastic eagle brooch.

A magical shoot with Cecil Beaton in his beautiful house in Pelham Place London...

QUEEN

Liberties asked me to design a collection around their charming fabrics this is just one from the collection.

My friend Bernie Wan at Vogue was asked to make an enormous chair, 3 times bigger than the models.

Recently, I went to the funeral of my dearest friend John Bates. Everyone from my time with Wallis was there and many from Vogue, including Bernie Wan. We laughed about the huge chair (page 227), and I asked where it was now… 'In my front room,' Bernie said. 'I became very attached to it and couldn't bear to throw it away!' We both laughed, but I understood.

AN ASIDE

After so much publicity, and the memorable day I spent with Cecil Beaton on the Liberties shoot, I felt on top of the world. Tired of course, but that didn't matter. I had achieved what I set out to achieve, and I think even my mother was surprised by my success. At the beginning, I didn't think I had a hope in hell of making a success of the boutique. What with having little money and no experience. I made it up as I went along, and it worked! This is when I realised that although I didn't have a huge amount of artistic talent, I was determined to turn my dreams into reality…and I have!

Chapter 10 part 1

Things are getting difficult - Dawson leaves

It seems when I was away in Korea, tensions started to rise. Dawson asked Dennis not to come into the showroom as he told long boring 'funny' jokes. It seemed mean as poor Dennis had nothing to do now; he thought he was helping. It's a difficult situation made worse because Dennis and Silvia didn't like Dawson from the beginning.

Dawson and I were great together. We managed to keep our sense of humour and were never lost for words as we worked together. There was always some gossip or problem that needed to be discussed. If I worked late, Dawson would stay to drive me home; bit by bit he was becoming my chauffeur. Sales started to slip, and he would disappear for a couple of hours a day here and there, no explanation; he was just not around. I also noticed that Phyllis was keeping an eye on everything. Recently, I overheard a conversation between her and Dennis. He was worrying that things were not adding up and were getting out of hand. So, he asked her to check sales and stock. Of course, he should have spoken to me, not my staff, but Dennis knew I would stand up for Dawson. I was used to checking stock every evening and, generally, had no worries. But I did have to admit, something was not right. We had recently taken on a new stockman, Dereck. He was amazing; he looked after the stock as if it was his newly born chicks, so no doubts there. Then my thoughts rested on a new young boy called 'Jon'; he was a packer. He would pack all the orders as Dereck allocated them. 'Jon' was a nice boy, and his father, who was our delivery man, asked us to take him on as he couldn't find a job. Of course, we were always ready to help our team, so 'Jon' started two weeks ago. I had no doubt I would get to the bottom of this. Also, I felt that the team was beginning to break up. I know some of it was because of Dawson as he tended to throw his weight around, and it did tend to put people's backs up.

I noticed that sales figures had fallen drastically. Dawson said that the present collection wasn't as good as usual. Well, that's telling me. Buck your ideas up, Wendy. As a last resort, I went in early one morning to check the stock. All ok, then again about 3 pm when the boxes get taken to the post office. Got it! 'Jon' was packing the stock and addressing the parcels to himself. Then at 3pm he would take everything to the post office. Clever, but surely when customers complained that they had not received their order, he would be caught! I doubt he had thought that one through!

Out of the blue, Dawson told me that he had been offered a Job at Reldon, a huge successful business. He had been headhunted. They wanted him to open a new company called ACT 111. The money was better, and I could see he wanted to take the challenge. So, we agreed that he should leave, but not until I found his replacement. Word gets around quickly in the rag trade and within a few days I had several applicants. I decided to hire Philip Brisbois, a nice guy, with a good sense of humour. He had been working for Louis Caring, who were a well-established company and known for their separates. Philip was excited about the new trends happening in London, and he wanted to be part of it. So, Harriet was ideal. He should be perfect.

So that was it. We had a new Sales Director, but we had lost the sparkle that Dawson brought to the company. We threw him a big party and wished him well.

My heart sank, but deep down I knew it had to happen.

Chapter 10 part 2

Dawson - Parkfields - Move to big house with a ballroom!

Thinking back now, the change was the best thing that could have happened to both of us. When Dawson left Harriet, the Alfa was sold, but Act 111 replaced it with a BMW series 7, nice. We also had more money to spend, and I must admit, the tension in our relationship had disappeared. It's funny that at the time I didn't notice it, but now it's gone, I could feel my shoulders dropping and my frown lifting. It wasn't much of a change as Dawson picked me up after work. At the time, having sold the house inz Barnes, we were living in a pretty cottage in Parkfields in Putney, a tiny little street with flat fronted cottages. We were happy there, but, unfortunately, when I bought it, I failed to notice it was just behind The Arab Boy, a pub in Upper Richmond Road. So, at 6 am the lorries would arrive and THROW boxes of beer and drinks off the lorry and THROW the empties onto the lorry. Our bedroom was at the same level, so obviously we had to get up then. I did try to ask them to put the bottles on the lorry instead of throwing them, but I think they didn't understand English! So, we had to start looking for a new house again. I think Nick Clegg has moved into Parkfields now, so maybe it was best we got out!

When Jean and Stephen broke up, we lost our best friends. We had been so close, and we were heartbroken. We were lucky to meet the Boddington family and our life became wonderful again. They introduced us to friends such as Suzanne and Simon Campbell Jones, who, at the time, worked on Horizon for BBC. They became good friends, and much later when we sold our big house in Putney and no longer threw our famous Christmas carol singing parties, they even threw a party simply to say thank you to us. How kind is that! Our life was now a proper life, with dinner parties, school fetes, school bazaars. My mother was always at home when Sarah came out of school. So, this sort of life became important to me as I realised that Sarah needed a mum that was not always working. Not that I was going to start knitting and making cakes, but I would work more from home. I could design anywhere. So, bit by bit, I started to spend more and more time at home. Niamh would come to the house, and we would get so much done as there were no interruptions.

Dawson seemed to settle into Act 111 and easily made friends. One of them was Terry, a lovely Jewish man who used to play trumpet with Ronnie Scott (as Jean's first husband Les did). Terry had a very pushy wife called Ann. We were

very fond of them both although Ann never did stop being bossy; she meant well. It was just her way.

It was there that Dawson met someone called Jean Van der Steop. She was beautiful, and she was married, but Dawson fell in love with her. There were no thoughts of her leaving David, her husband, nor Dawson leaving me; it was just a statement of facts. We saw them pretty often. I had no idea how Jean and Dawson felt, so it was never difficult. Dawson also had a secretary called Francis. I found out that he was having an affair with her. Again, I had no idea; perhaps I was so wrapped up in my business and my darling daughter to notice anything. Or was I just not interested?

Most weekends, Sarah and I would go shopping; which was great fun as Sarah was now 12 and interested in clothes. On the way back, we always looked in the estate agents' windows. One day we saw THE house; it was Victorian and detached with a big garage. The garden was very impressive; it had a copse with Palm trees and a big pond with croaking frogs!

Both Sarah and I fell in love with it. It was, of course, too expensive, but we were in love with the house, and you know what women are like! Dawson didn't stand a chance. We booked an appointment and went to see it that afternoon. Yes, this is the house that we wanted, no doubt about it.

We went around that night to see the house again with Dawson this time, he didn't say anything as we walked around.. 'He doesn't like it,' I whispered to Sarah. We both tried our hard sell, like frogs, Palm trees, big wine cellar, beautiful studio, log fires, but you could see Dawson wasn't listening, so we shut up! We went into the Music room to talk to the agent. Dawson turned his back to the log fire in silence. He looked at the agent slowly and said, 'We'll have it'. The agent, Sarah, and I just stood looking at him with disbelief. The price was £149,000. Quite a big price in 1980. Oh, happiness we had arrived. We went home to our little cottage and opened a bottle of Champagne, not chilled but who cared!

Dawson had his £75,000 from the sale of his flat in Kensington, and I would have most of the money when I sold the cottage. I was, in fact, £16,000 short, but we agreed that when we sold the house, I would give him back the money. When we sold our wonderful house 10 years later, we sold it for £600,000. It recently sold for 3 million!

We moved into Woodborough Road a few months later. It was sad to leave our tiny cottage, really, as we had been happy there. But now all my hard work had paid off, years and years of money dramas and years and years of uncertainty, all sorted.

lovely stain glass window in my studio!

AN ASIDE

I have 3 regrets in my life so far, loosing Paolo, walking out of Harriet and selling the Woodborough Road house.

Looking back now at our years living in Woodborough Road , I remember happy times but also hell, with dreadful tension, arguments and general untold unhappiness.

236

Chapter 10 part 3

Walking out of Harriet - left my heart behind!

It was strange not working with Dawson anymore, but I suppose it didn't matter that much as I saw him in the morning, when he drove me to work, and again in the evening. Some evenings we would meet and go out for an early supper to our favourite place San Lorenzo's in Beauchamp Place or maybe San Fred's in Fulham Road. As Sarah was quite grown-up now, she could always stay with Lucy or Melina for the night. Life was much easier, I suppose, but I did still have to design 8 main collections a year plus two Missy collections (teenage) for USA. It was something I enjoyed. I had a lot of press calls to give interviews…'What does Harriet eat for breakfast?' and 'What colour does Harriet predict for this Winter?' Silly things like that.

Philip was great, but Dawson's special customers wanted to see me, so I had that extra work to do. Stella, the tea lady, kept crying every time you mentioned Dawson's name, but otherwise things went on as before. Except, Dennis puffed himself up; he could see now that Dawson had gone that it was time for him to start interfering. I walked past Phylis's office one day, and I heard Dennis instructing her to double check everything. This won't work, I thought. I wasn't sure what to do about the situation as, of course, the business was 50%-50%, so it was stalemate. Dennis started bringing his friends into the showroom even if I had customers in and always introduced himself as Mr Harriet. What was I going to do? I spoke to my solicitor who said best to write a letter to him saying that the business was run by myself and if there were problems, we should have a meeting and discuss those problems, possibly with our solicitors if the situation was difficult.

Dennis didn't like that, saying things like, 'I have been in the business many more years than you'. It was pretty impossible, and we started avoiding meeting up. I worked from home on Mondays with Niamh working on the designs. We started at 9am and finished about 8pm, but we always achieved a great amount of work. Of course, the Tuesday when we went in to Harriet, the girls told us that Dennis had bought cakes and sat and talked to everyone, so nobody could get their work done. What a bugger. I was not sure what to do as although I talked tough, I was really as weak as raspberry jelly!

When I told Dawson about this uncomfortable situation, he just laughed it off and said he thought it was Silvia, Denis's wife, causing the problem; Dennis was just a 'yes' man. Maybe he was right.

We decided to go for a long weekend to Nice and have an autumn break, just what I needed. Sarah asked if she could stay in Barnes with Lucy, so that was all decided.

When we arrived at Nice airport, we were met by the chauffeur, sent from the Colombe d'Or in St. Paul de Vence. They knew we were just coming for a short break and were always so kind to us. Admittedly, we were pretty regular visitors, and we always tipped well! We had an early night, and I slept well as it was like coming home. Everyone was pleased to see us, and we loved being spoilt.

Most of the next morning, we just slept around the pool, and after our marvellous lunch, we just sat under the big white umbrellas most of the afternoon, just what I needed. Dawson chatted on and on about his new title, Managing Director, and his new friends. He seemed to be very happy. The next day, I got up early and had a swim. It was wonderful in the warm air, totally deserted, a moment to myself. I sat on the edge of the pool and looked at my knees, odd maybe, but I had started looking and sometimes talking to my knees when I was unhappy as a child. As I gently swished my legs back and forth in the green pool, I realised why my head was in such turmoil. I was absolutely exhausted, deep down exhausted, if you know what I mean. From an early age, with my mother pushing me to be perfect, then Peter training me for marriage, I rarely had a break as I pushed myself hard too.

I made a decision there and then! I would close Harriet. I had achieved all that I had set out to do. Now, I wanted time to myself and time with my daughter. I had no plan; I knew it was over. Looking back now I have never got over that decision to close my Harriet. I miss everything about it, but it was going sour with Dennis and Silvia, and I didn't want that to happen to my 'baby'. I also had to have a life even just for a year...just time to stand and stare.

On the plane going back, I thought that perhaps this was all I was going to achieve, but not bad, really considering; a wonderful daughter, a lovely mother, 3 cats and half a beautiful house in Putney.

The day we got back, I wrote a letter to my solicitor and to Dennis and Silvia. I couldn't bear to say goodbye to my team, so I went there late that night to pick up a few of my personal belongings. Jean came with me, for moral support. I shut all the doors and put a big padlock on the main door. Then as I was about to throw the key down the drain, I remembered that there was a lot of money in the file that had been put there before we went away. So very quietly we had to break back into the building to get the money. I felt so guilty, but I was handing the business lock stock and barrel over to them. I shouldn't feel too bad about pinching a bit of cash, £400 I think it was.

I remember clearly how that money got into the filing cabinet now. When you have overbought a fabric and cannot use it anywhere else or if the factories had returned fabric leftover, one of the ways to sell it was to call up some of the stock businesses that sold cloth in the markets in the East End or maybe in Berwick Street market. One day a Mr M. Klein, who had a shop in Berwick Street I think, came to look at fabric. He was so rude and made me feel like rubbish.

He offered a really low price, and since he said he would buy all the fabrics, I panicked and let him have everything at a rock bottom price. I remember thinking at the time that one day M. Klein would meet me under different circumstances, and I would pay him back!

AN ASIDE

After Harriet had had closed months later and I was out of work, I was asked to a friend's house in Wimpole Street for lunch. I was late, so I had to take a taxi. I told the driver where I wanted to go, and he set off. After a while the driver said to me, 'Do I know you? I know your face. Are you in the 'rag trade?' 'Yes,' I said.

'I was in the rag trade. What's your name?' He looked up at his rear-view mirror, 'My name is M. Klein'.

'Stop the cab now!'. I got out and went to the driving window and said, 'I am Harriet, and a few months ago you came to my showroom and gave me virtually nothing for my fabrics. When I read in the Draper's Weekly you had gone bust, I was thrilled. So, nice to meet you and to see where you have ended up. Now, I am leaving without paying, so don't bother coming after me!'.

Chapter 10 part 4

Party party party - Indian Cotton Board

I cried buckets when Harriet closed down, for I had lost my dear friends as well as my beloved Harriet. Niamh, I hope, will always be a friend, but everybody else just drifted away. Dennis had made sure that they knew I was the 'baddie'. I was the one that just packed up and left. Well, that was it, I suppose. I can never do things by halves. When I gave up smoking 100 cigarettes a day, it took a weekend. When I had become addicted to Valium, during the early days of Harriet's success, it took a week, but giving up Harriet broke my heart, and it's something I regret to this very day.

There was another very sad thing that happened when I closed Harriet. My dear friend Denis Norden, who introduced me to Dennis and Silvia, was so upset at my behaviour that he never spoke to me again. I wish I had insisted telling him what was happening. Maybe he would have forgiven me a little. Denis died a few months ago, so that will never happen now.

Dawson was quite pleased that Harriet was closed, I think. Perhaps he thought I might pay him more attention! He was doing really well at Act 111, and life did seem more relaxed, I must say. I did need to catch up on my friends and spend time with my daughter and my poor mother who never saw me. We always crossed over; she was going as I was coming. So, let's see how I cope with life after work!

Sarah, Lucy and little Melina
The 'hat check girls.'

My team...

Right, the first thing was to have a big opening party in our beautiful new house. Harrods did the catering, naturally. I booked 4 waitresses and our girls were the hat check girls.

We had a DJ and a pianist, and we had the ballroom floor re-polished. The theme was Tarts and Vicars. Sadly, I didn't remember to get anyone to take pictures, so I only have a few snaps...

Me

Dawson

Jean and me

Pat and Michael

The party was the first of many that we had at Woodborough Road. We had parties partly because we loved having a house full, and we were very good hosts, but also because we had begun to drift apart, and it helped to have people around us to stop the tension. Whilst I was recovering from losing my Harriet and trying to be a good mother, Dawson was out and about. He came home every night, but I always knew when he had been unfaithful; women do know generally. He also always bought me a bunch of 'service station' flowers when he had a liaison with another woman...a real give away.

Our parties became THE party to go to. We had Summer Croquet parties, Carol singing parties on Christmas Eve for 40 people. I was in my element, perhaps I should become a party planner!

Here is a picture of me in our beautiful garden… Croquet every weekend with

our neighbours… Life was quite different now, and I think with a bit of practice, I could become quite good at it! Maybe I might also die of boredom, who knows?

I'm so happy, long may it last!

Next step.. punk!

Anyone for Croquet?

Quite out of the blue, I had a phone call from the Cotton Board. They wanted me to design a collection in Indian cotton for the Indian Government! Odd, I thought at the time, but once they explained, I said 'yes'. Apparently, the only fabric the Indians were interested in weaving was MADRAS; they were not prepared to try anything else. However, as far as the Cotton Board was concerned, their statistics showed that the world had moved from Madras cotton. So, Indian fabrics were being left behind, and the fabric industry was in trouble.

I had no idea how to change the habits of a country the size of India. When I discussed it with various people in the industry, they felt that designers and specifiers expected to have Madras from India, so why rock the boat. The Cotton Board had analysed the sales and had come to the conclusion that they had to change their way of thinking or there would be no fabric industry left in India, so it was up to me...and I do like a challenge.

Unfortunately, there was no budget for a model or even a pattern cutter; difficult for a start as I had no idea as to their sizing or the shape of the average Indian woman. I went around at least 20 cotton companies and chose fabrics that I felt should be exposed, and, surprising as it was, there was plenty to choose from. It seemed that Indians chose to hang back on new ideas. They tend to just work with brilliant colours and, although these are wonderful, there has to be more to offer the buyers. So, I was looking forwards to getting them to change the habits of a lifetime.

I cried all the way to the airport; leaving Sarah was getting more and more difficult. She needed me, and I felt as if I was letting her down. Also, I had thought I was finished with the 'rag trade,' but obviously not!

On the plane, I wrote to Sarah, Dawson, my mother and Ann and Terry, they still have the letter now. I wanted them to share my adventure. The journey was long, and I was travelling 'cattle class,' so I was very tired and a bit grumpy as they only had vegetarian food and fruit juice on my Air India flight. When we went through customs, my troubles started. Somehow it seems, my passport had been dropped on the floor in Schiphol airport, where we had to break our journey to take on new passengers. They called Amsterdam and explained that the guards who searched me must have failed to notice my passport on the floor. What a state they all got into. The Dutch didn't have a flight going to Bombay for another two days, and the immigration team hadn't come across a drama like this before. So, after a lot of whispering in corners, they came up with the idea that they should draw a circle around me in chalk, until they found a solution. So, for the first 3 hours I was in custody! I began to feel faint and needed to go to the loo. Best thing to do in this situation is to cry, which I did and then I shouted, 'Get me a phone. I have to speak to my friend the Queen of Great Britain'. Silence and lots of phone calls and then finally they released me. I was to report every day to the Police. So, when my driver came for me, after breakfast, we slowly headed to the Police station, avoiding the giant dips in the road, and carried on to the factory.

We approached the factory, which was an ugly modern block of concrete with small windows. It looked like a prison. Fans hummed away, and papers flew around the workshop. The women were of all ages; some I would say about 10 years old and others as old as 70 or maybe 80. They didn't stop work for a second, and they all machined in unison, first to the left and then the right, stopping only to turn corners, then off again. I set too and waving my arms around I spoke to the pattern cutter; she spoke some English, but it was going to be difficult. I had already designed most of the collection in UK, and the fabrics I had chosen in London had already been delivered, so our first day was very fruitful.

At about 3 o'clock I needed to go to the loo. There was no door as far as I could see, so I asked one of the machinists. She just smiled and nodded her head saying 'No', I think. I started to panic, and at that point, a young girl came into the room. She was my chaperon and spoke perfect English. I told her I was desperate. She laughed and pointed to the huge Nescafé tins on the floor! No way was I going to drop my knickers in the middle of the factory floor! She laughed and said, 'Come with me'. There was a tiny door in the corner of the room, hidden by bails of fabric. 'Stand back', she said and produced a JEYES FLIT GUN; she rushed into the room and sprayed. Flies beetles and bugs flew at us; then she nodded, 'All clear'. There was a hole in the corner of the room for me to stoop over. Maybe the Nescafé tin would have been better!

My chaperon told me on the way back to the President hotel, not the Taj which I had expected, that we had been booked to start a journey across India, visiting the weavers to select fabrics to create this new look for Indian fabrics. We left a few days later for the experience of a lifetime.

We were to catch the train from Bombay main station, travelling first class, what! You have to be joking! I suppose 2nd class was the one where you hang on to the rails and pull yourself in when approaching a tunnel, or on the roof and breathing in when going under a bridge. Old people and children even went to sleep hanging on; it was amazing. My bunk bed was high up, and I left the window open for the beginning of the night; but soon closed it as every time we came to a station, the kids would jump up and tickle my feet saying, 'Biscuits, please, biscuits'. So, no sleep was had!

We arrived at our first stop the next day, Cambatore. It was just a sleepy town in the middle of nowhere, where we were met by a charming elderly man in full majestic attire. He bowed lots of times and moved his head from side to side but never said a word. He was, my advisor they told me, the head man in the area, but couldn't speak only nod! We were staying at his house that night after visiting the weavers and dyers.

woven yarn outside the weavers hut

This was an amazing experience. The weavers sat in a little shed the size of their loom, and silently threw the shuttle back and forth. Outside each hut was a big bath, and each one was filled with either blue or yellow dye; when the cloth was woven, it was pushed into the bath. The women then pushed and prodded the fabric with a big stick. The children played around the baths and you could tell which child belonged to which mother as they had hand marks on them in yellow or blue. Once the fabric was completely soaked, they would pull the length across the grass and lay it down and the occasional fly would be squashed under the fabric. Other times, the length of fabric was thrown across the road, so there was the odd tyre mark visible. We stopped here and there to eat, only in the local places where we sat on benches and there was no menu.

We were asked if we wanted a 'Bombay,' a round tin plate with Dall and Nan on it and perhaps some sort of puréed vegetable. Basically, I think that was the vegetarian dish. The square plate had meat on it, but I decided to become a vegetarian whist there. I also lived on Coca Cola as it had a fixed cap, so nobody could tamper with it.

We arrived at our Mansion house, so they called it; it had green slime running down the front of it, not very inviting, but I was pleased not to be bouncing over big potholes anymore. Just happy to be left on my own. I said I was tired and excused myself; I wasn't hungry just tired and homesick.

I had almost forgotten why I was here. It was such a cultural shock… all I wanted was to go home. Don't get me wrong. The people who drove me around and cooked for me were so kind and so grateful that I was helping them to catch up with the rest of the world.

I was doing well workwise. Plenty of fabrics hidden away, but they didn't understand that these were the true fabric of India. Most of the fabrics were in the table linen ranges, and there were a lot of Damasks. One of the famous ones is the 'Ivy leaf', which nowadays you find, generally in white, on most 'posh' tables as tablecloths or serviettes. I'm sure you have seen it.

We ended up by the sea in Madras. I looked out of my hotel, thank God a hotel with porters and room service and a proper toilet, and saw the sun go down. I saw little mounds of something on the pavement, and on further inspection decided it was piles of poo! During the night, the rain came and washed all the poo away. In the morning I noticed giant black pipes in front of the hotel and realised that there were whole families living in each end of the pipe. The mother was hanging out of the front of the pipe cooking, and behind her, inside the pipe, her children were playing. Others had their legs dangling out, holding a black umbrella to shelter from the rain or the sun, whichever happened to be around at the time.

That day I managed to get a moment to myself and walked down to the sea; nothing special. No children playing, no beach umbrellas. This was a working beach, and everyone was working. In the evening, I ate alone and had an early night. I wrote more letters and that was the end of that day, thank goodness.

The next day we did a tour of the factories. Well, that was an eye opener. Every 3 hours, all the lights went off, and we all packed up and moved to a new unit. The local council permitted factories to work only for 5 hours a day, so most factory owners had several other units so they could operate a full working day by moving from one to another. That day I was working with the machinist and what with the heat and the fleas, I was not coping. My lovely chaperone asked me to come into her office where she said that she had noticed that I had lice in my hair. 'That is why you are itching so much!' That afternoon I had my hair shaved off, that was it. I went back to the factory with a scarf around my head. Then I just sat and howled; in fact, I howled so much and so loudly that everyone stopped sewing. There was a rush of feet and there standing in front of me was an Englishman. He held me tightly and took me back to the hotel, with his arms held out...my saviour...he stayed with me until I stopped sobbing. 'I have to get back to the factory now, but you, young lady, are going to take the day off. I have booked you into the hotel Spa for a couple of hours. Then go back to your room, and I will pick you up and take you to a good International restaurant at 7pm. Is that a deal?' I nodded and as he left, I realised I didn't even know his name!

AN ASIDE

Later when we had supper, he did introduce himself. His name was Tony, and his company was called Tops and Bottoms. I had never heard of them, and I don't think they lasted very long, but he deserved a medal for helping a 'damsel in distress!'. What a star.

I went back to London a few days later, and we never met again. When I arrived back at Heathrow, I remember falling into the arms of a black cab driver and crying all over him! 'I'm home, I'm back, I made it!' Poor guy just held on to me and made shushing noises.

ANOTHER ASIDE

The collection was a success, and the latest fabrics from India were the talk of the town. Whether it paid off, I don't know. I loved and hated India; loved the people but hated the poverty that was everywhere. Glad I took the challenge. I think!

Chapter 10 part 5

Boddingtons' verses Bakers'

Our new friends the Boddingtons were a big happy part of our lives for many years. I met Jane when we lived in Barnes. Dawson, Sarah and I lived in Rectory Road, and Christopher, Jane, Naomi (Nimrod) and Lucia lived in Ranelagh Avenue. Jane and her daughter Lucia went to Balmuir tennis club to learn tennis, so Jane and I sat on different benches gazing with bored expressions on our faces. Then one day, we smiled at each other and went to have a drink at the Arab Boy pub whilst the girls played tennis, and that was it - we have been friends for 40 years. Jane was married to Christopher, rather serious and pompous, who liked to read labels! I love my memories with the Boddingtons. We had wonderful adventures. We went to France and had a lovely picnic in the sand dunes, such nice memoires.

In France, on one of our numerous holidays, we found a respectable Pensione, one that Christopher and I had passed as being suitable, as we were the fussy ones. There was only one problem which we had overlooked - there was only one bath, which had to be shared between the 2 rooms. We were also told by the grumpy landlady that there was water only for one bath! So, we drew lots as to who was going to wash first. I don't know why we found it so funny, but I still giggle when I think of it.

fancy dress in Portugal

We had a villa holiday in Portugal one year, when the girls were about to become adults, so it was the last time we went on a proper family holiday. We had a fancy-dress party on our last night, and a party to remember forever. We also had a dog that barked all night in the next village, so we never got to sleep…but we didn't care.

At weekends, in Barnes, we used to play tennis over the road, and Saturday night was generally party night. They had a lot of really nice friends, and they soon became ours too, so more parties. Christopher was a Liberal and so were most of their friends, we were Conservatives, so we didn't go down that well.

Unfortunately, Christopher left his whole family for his Article Clerk and that was that, men will be men, he left her the house and a black Fiat Panda with an X reg. She was better off without him I think, the girls still see him and expect he is still reading labels!

fancy dress in Barnes

Chapter 11 part 1

Jean's cry for help - Secrets Beauty Salon

It seemed to me that I had sort of retired, and I was expected to stay at home and be a housewife. ME, a housewife! Hanging around was not for me. I had finished cleaning, ironing and general fiddling about by 9am. It seemed a good idea to do some sort of a 'workout', Mr Motivator style which was quite fun. Well, jumping up and down isn't my cup of tea, but it was the trend at the time and, of course, is even more nowadays. Again, how much running on the spot can you do? I did buy a couple of great outfits though, which always helps, I suppose. But deep down, I was missing my team at Harriet, especially Niamh. I didn't contact them as I was still broken, but they had been so much a part of my life that without them, I was a bit lost. NOT FOR LONG!

One morning Jean phoned to ask if she could come over for a coffee as she had something to ask Dawson and me. 'Of course, you are always welcome, and we have lots to catchup on.' I had no idea what Jean was up to, but I knew she was not a very good businesswoman. So, whatever she was coming to talk about would have to be taken with a pinch of salt. No way did I want to get involved with a friend, even my darling Jean, in business.

Yes, that was it. Jean wanted to take a beauty therapist course. She had been working in a salon in Twickenham as a receptionist, and she had been doing the manicures there. Now she was convinced she had found her vocation. Actually, although I had planned to say "NO" to any proposal, this one had potential. She had done all the groundwork and costed equipment, staff, rent, insurance and telephone. Reluctantly, I said I would ask Dawson to see if he might be interested, and he was!

Dawson gave Jean a cheque to cover her course, about £1000, I think. She was so grateful, and she changed completely. It was lovely to see her so fulfilled. Having passed the course, graduating top of the class, she was highly recommended by her tutors. She came over to the house most evenings, filled with plans for the new business. Actually, I knew she would ask me to back her in her beauty salon, but I was hoping she might find the money from elsewhere. She approached Philip Levine, a friend who was a great fan of Jeans'; he offered her £2000 to set up, but that was not enough, so she turned to me.

Obviously, she was my best friend, and I agreed.

We set up a company with shares 50-50%...always a mistake, will I never learn! The first action was to find premises. We had already set our minds to the right area, Barnes. It was filled with young wealthy families and many working, high profile woman.

Perfect, I thought. We found the ideal premises; I think it was a dairy years ago judging by the cream tiles on the wall, now it was Castelnau Tiles, managed by a large French woman called Nicole. I worked the money out, and between us we decided this was the right step; a good location just opposite Olympia Studios, always buzzing. The shop front was already the right style, and we could get 3 cubicles upstairs, a sunbed room and a staff room/make-up lessons. There was a big basement; this was to be Jean's cubicle with a special luxury, very expensive, treatment bed. We had a Sauna put in and a cubicle for slimming, Slendertone and G5! I had no idea what all this equipment was used for, but Jean was in charge, and I just signed the cheques!

We met every day to go through any problems we had, personal and workwise. There was a bench opposite the salon to be, by the bus stop, and that's where we sat to work on the project. Most people now knew that we were opening a salon, and they were very curious. We made friends before we even opened the door. There weren't many salons around in the early 80s, so we realised we had cornered the market in Barnes, Putney and Richmond. The world was our oyster...

Having set up a joint account with the bank, jean put in £5000 and I did the same. We needed a name and it took weeks to find the right one. In fact, we were nearing the opening day, and we still didn't have a name. Dawson and I grabbed a holiday before the salon opened. It was there, staying at Trevor Howard's villa, next to Roger Moore's, that out of the blue I came up with the name SECRETS! So, there it was. The perfect name. The salon became a place where actresses and important rich ladies came, and everything was all done in secret, thus the perfect name.

Martin Cropper designed the hanging sign for us and repeat ones on each window. The name caught on like wildfire...what's this place called Secrets? You could hear people say as they passed by. A friend of mine, Jerry from Photography Place, took photos, and we were nearly there. We needed staff of course....so as usual, I put an advert in the Evening Standard. Three days later we had a full team. I found a company called Club Sport that made beautiful soft Velour track suits, and bought 2 for each therapist and 6 for stock to sell in the salon. We decided to have three day work experience before we opened as we wanted Secrets to be something special. And it was, from the beginning to the end.

Left to right... Irma our lovely cleaning lady. Jean. Anne. Sherry receptionist, next line Jill, me being silly as usual and Debbie... Kim was missing and so was Suzy

This was opening day, July 29th, so excited, so nervous. Jean was in command, and the girls looked beautiful. We were on the right track for sure. We had had several bookings made whilst we were undergoing renovations, and once the price list with our phone number went in the window, bookings started to pour in.

We had our Secrets special client; her name was Isla Blair. She was an actress who lived nearby, and she popped a little note through the letterbox the day before we opened, wishing us luck. Thank you, Isla. It meant a lot to us.

I had offered to work on reception for 4 days a week and Sherry, Jean's sister in law, worked the other two. I didn't have any intention of being involved, but as I had invested a lot of money, I felt I should be there for the time being, learning the trade, so to speak. Ugggg, I hated it; all fat tummies and blackheads, not for me. Jean was amazing; she worked really hard and the clients loved her. The only problem with Jean was that she wouldn't keep to times, so behind the scenes it was a bit chaotic. Jean's answer about time keeping was not exactly helpful. 'My ladies need me.' So, Jean started to float about the place taking a client into her cubicle, listening to all their personal problems, then starting the Aromatherapy. She was brilliant and clients came back every week for the £30 treatment with Jean. The girls, needless to say, were very professional. I still remember their happy smiling faces, so the whole salon was a happy place.

Chapter 11 part 2

A bit of tension - but an enormous success

I must admit those poor girls at Secrets worked their socks off. We were very busy, and their work was so hard at times, but they never complained.

Meanwhile, I was suffering. I was not made to sit behind a desk listening to women discussing their weight, their marriages or their lovers.

The girls teased me at times as they knew that I was not dedicated to the beauty business. One day when we were bursting at the sides with clients and only just able to keep up with the treatments, Anne, the youngest beautician, came to me and said she had a double booking for a facial and an all over tanning session, so she asked me if I could do the tanning session for a lovely actress whose name shall remain a secret. 'You are joking!' There was no way I could do that. I would rather shoot myself, but we were stuck, and Anne was right. I was the only person not working. She showed me how to apply the lotion and pointed me towards the spare cubicle...I can only say that I have never been so embarrassed in my life; she was very beautiful, but that didn't help. I tried not to look, but that was impossible. I had to decide which end to start. Face, I thought then just work downwards. I noticed she had well developed breasts, perhaps I could go around them. No, that won't work, I decided. Just go for it! Till this day, I can still remember that terrible moment. Well, at least it proves I'm not a lesbian, I suppose! She seemed quite pleased with the result. And when I took a look at my work, I was quite surprised, but wait until I get hold of Anne. When I came out of the cubicle, the girls were outside splitting their sides. It was almost impossible to get an appointment at Secrets, especially as Jean always overran her appointments; we were in trouble by mid-morning. Rich and famous came to us, and we had a long waiting list. Jean had her favourites, and she would run an hour over, sometimes. If that person was stressed, Jean took on all their problems. We needed bigger premises. I was eager to open a gymnasium and Pilates studio, but Jean didn't want to expand, and wouldn't even discuss it. We had the opportunity to rent part of Olympia studios across the road, but there was no way I could change Jean's mind; she just switched off and became engulfed in her beloved clients. This was the start of the riff between us. I was all for expanding, and I even considered starting a Secrets Franchise business, but there was no point in trying to discuss anything with Jean as she seemed to have drifted off into a cloud of Aromatherapy oils. We could hardly talk, at times. This became a bit of a problem between us. I started to lose interest as sitting in a chair in a beauty salon, with no possibility of expansion, was not really of any interest to me.

Life at home in Woodborough Road wasn't going very well either. Sarah was growing up and was changing so much. This was bound to happen, I knew. But our little family group was breaking up in front of my eyes. There was no laughter in the house, just bad feelings and continuous arguments. Dawson never let up on nagging Sarah; everything she did annoyed him, so I dreaded coming back from work.

I blame myself for everything, as mothers do, and when Sarah failed to be accepted at her lovely Putney High School as a senior, I had to try every which way to find a school that would take her. Her grades were not high enough for St Paul's, the school I phoned to book a place for her when she was just days old! I had to pretend to her that it was a good break, and every time I met her from school, her first question was, 'Have I been accepted anywhere?'. I made up stories and tried to let her down gently. Unfortunately, many of her friends had got places, so it was beginning to be an impossible situation for both of us. Dawson took no interest, of course. Then I had an idea. When I was in the rag trade, I had a dear friend; he was the fabric salesman who sold me the Pepsi fabric, Bill Velutini. He left the trade shortly after I closed Harriet, and I had heard he had taken a job as an English teacher in one of London's leading schools. I called him one evening at home and asked if he could help me to get Sarah into Godolphin and Latymar. Bill told me that the school was turning from a state school into a private school, so they were not so strict about standards; they just wanted the right sort of girl for the new setup. Apparently, all teachers were given the choice of taking 2 girls they thought had the right background and a certain amount of potential. Bill was gay and he would not be having any children, so the Head teacher gave Bill the same arrangement. Bill stood guarantor for Sarah. I will never forget the happiness on her face that day when I picked her up from Putney High School and told her that she could hold her head up high for she had been accepted at her new 'posh' school Godolphin and Latyimar.

Whether it was the right school for her, I doubt, but it was that, or what?

I loved entertaining at the house, and I must admit, although I rarely saw Jean socially, I did have some wonderful friends. So, although everything was tense at Secrets and also at home, I was in my element and threw parties; anything to make a change for I was not only bored at work but really suffering badly from the tension between Sarah and Dawson. I made myself believe that all was OK, but I knew something was wrong; I just had no idea what it was about. I couldn't put my finger on it, now I realise I was so naive!

Thinking back now, I realise that I was spoiling Sarah. We had lots of money, and I just gave her lumps of money, and I never asked what she spent it on. I wanted her to have everything that I missed, a general mistake made by many mothers. One morning, Sarah had left for school looking immaculate as usual. I was late opening up at Secrets, but I quickly popped into the newsagent to buy some cigarettes. In front of me was a ghastly looking girl with heavy make-up and hair sticking up. As she turned, I was confronted with my darling Sarah! I behaved badly, I realise now. I just dragged her back home down the street and made her wash her face and put her uniform back on. I threw her 'winkle pickers' down to the fishpond. The clothes, by the way, were in a carrier bag in the next door's garden. Apparently, she left every morning looking clean and angelic, then changed behind a bush where she turned into a monster!

Only last week I had complained to the school about some girls not wearing school uniform! It was my 'baby' that let the side down, and it was then that I decided that I needed to be around more often. So, again, I blamed myself.

One person, at that time, I relied on was 'our Mary.' A skinny little person, very Irish. She doted on us. She was our cleaning lady, but we treated her like part of the family. She was quite wise too and kept an eye on us all. She asked if she had to go up to the top of the house. Sarah's little apartment was up there, and she had her bedroom and a darkroom there. The mess and mouldy cups chucked everywhere was more than poor Mary could manage. I would, occasionally, storm upstairs and throw everything away. I would say, 'If you can't clean up your floor, I will throw everything away'. So, more tension! I know that's what teenagers are like, but I got hell from Dawson, and I didn't need more agro.

Chapter 11 part 3

Our Suzy murdered - the stars kept queuing up!

When the therapists were overbooked, or occasionally taken ill, we were always in need of extra staff. So, I decided to take on another therapist and have a part time girl on stand-by.

We had been introduced to a lovely girl called Debbie; she was pretty and fun, a great addition to the Secrets family.

Then we managed to persuade one of the best beauticians around the area to join us as our 'standby-by'. Her name was Suzy Lamplugh, and she was good, very good; she sparkled, and the room lit up when she came into it. The clients liked her as we all did. She was quite feisty and sometimes when I called her with a booking, I could tell I didn't need to ask her to come in as the answer would be NO! She had a strong family, but she was her own boss. I was very fond of her.

Suzy Lamplugh: Appointment

Suzy didn't stay that long, and it was a sad day when she left. Sadder than any of us knew at the time. She was going to be an estate agent and had a job with Winkworth's in Parson's Green.

I wish to this very day that I could have persuaded her to stay safe with us. But Suzy was Suzy and she left. A year later the papers were full of pictures of her. Suzy Lamplugh had disappeared.

She had had a client who called to make an appointment to see a house which he wanted to buy. His name in the diary was Mr Kipper. That was it; we never saw Suzy again; she was murdered. The Police had the man who killed her, but he will not say where her body was. Poor Diana, her mother, and the rest of the family were never allowed to put her to rest properly. Diana has since died, and every few months there are more headlines, 'Suzy's body possibly found'. Then nothing again.

So, Suzy wherever you are, we think of you often, and I still grieve for you.

It was shortly after that I started to put some white wine in a plastic bottle, to take to work, just to help me get through the day. It didn't help, but I'm not very strong about some things, and it began to be a problem as I sipped away at it all day. Then I swapped it for Vodka, just a little, nothing much, I said to myself! Easy to stop, I lied!

We were getting a lot of publicity; word had got around, and there was always something happening at Secrets. We had a call from the press office of the Lord Mayor of London. Apparently, the Mayors wife, Mrs Young, wanted to have an Aromatherapy treatment with Jean every Monday morning, a block booking.

But we couldn't tie her up like that, so we agreed on one every fourteen days. Still, we needed another person to help in that department. All of a sudden, everyone was wanting Aromatherapy, a bit of a problem. If Suzy had stayed, we would have been OK, but poor Suzy was dead!

Vera Lynn started to come in on a regular visit; she was booked with Jean, of course, but she had other treatments with the girls. She was always cheerful, no airs and graces, and we loved her visits. Sadly, she never sang 'I'll be seeing you in all those familiar places!'.

As if we weren't busy enough, out of the blue, Paramount phoned to ask us for help. They were making a new series called TENKO. It was about a Japanese women's prisoner of war camp. They had 8 leading actresses who needed to be brown all over in 8 weeks and then would need 'topping up' weekly after that. What a job! Lots of money of course, but I couldn't block the Sunbed up for those long periods. There was no way we could take that on unless we opened the salon for them on Sundays. So, I volunteered to open every Sunday. Things at home were so bad, that for me it was a break from the tensions there. Sarah always slept, like most teenagers, until eleven o'clock, and Dawson was either in the garden or watching TV. So, I wouldn't be missed. It turned out to be great fun. Each actress needed 12 half hour treatments. It worked out at 6 Sundays, and that was fine for me. At least I could escape from the house. The actresses came in every half hour. They were so chatty, and the salon was filled with gossip and giggles. Ann Bell, Claire Oberman, Stephanie Beauchamp and Stephanie Cole were some of the women. They all knew each other, so it was great for them to catch up with each other.

I would switch on the sauna for myself, so whilst they 'browned' upstairs, I baked and sweated in the basement! The gossip was wonderful to listen to, and it made me really happy on a Sunday. Often, a great friend called Jerry would join me in the sauna with a glass of Rose, so fun was had by all!

AN ASIDE

I recently saw that BBC were repeating Tenko late at night. I watched one episode and was horrified. The actresses were all orange. They didn't look brown, just bright orange, so funny! Ann Bell was one of the girls I remember, but although she was orange, she was still pretty, well pretty orange too!

Chapter 11 part 4

American visit - a laser will make our fortune!

We were on cloud 99. We were crazy busy, making money, but, as far as I was concerned, there was no future.

I had received a letter from my accountant requesting a meeting. He asked me to make an appointment as soon as possible as it was 'year-end'. He also added that unless the figures were inaccurate, we seemed to be making much too much money! I think he was amazed that the turnover was as it was. He had checked and doubled checked the figures before our meeting. When we met his face was aglow. 'My goodness, Wendy. You do put your heart into things. I'm impressed.' I explained the situation between Jean and me and the plans I had for expansion. He agreed this was 'a goer'; this was ripe for turning into a franchise business. He suggested that Jean and I should spend some money on, perhaps, a car for the business. I told him that I was considering buying an American Laser, which was the latest craze in USA, it worked miracles on wrinkles and sagging chins, so they claimed. He urged me to go ahead with buying it and expanding the business that way… if Jean didn't object. 'You need to spend some money and expand somehow as otherwise you will have a hefty tax bill, one that will bring tears to your eyes!'.

He worked away at his calculator and after several minutes of clicking, looked up and said, 'I'm really interested in this project you know; I have a client who is looking for a business with potential. I think this is ripe for him, what do you think?'. There was no way Jean would have entered into any type of business arrangement; she had become a different person somehow. It was a lost opportunity, I know, but it was a waste of time even bringing the subject up. On the other hand, I made a decision at that meeting to fly to New York and look into the Laser claims more closely. I mentioned to Jean that I was going to check it out, and she didn't seem to mind either way. She showed no interest but agreed that the company could buy a laser if the tests all met with our rules and regulations here in the UK.

So, a few weeks later, I came back from New York with the first Laser. The first of many, I said to myself, but not to Jean, slowly does it…The American company had put me through a simple training course; there was nothing to it, even I could understand it. So now I would start the marketing. The local papers and the beauty magazines jumped up and down with excitement; at last something new to start writing about. The only space we had was the tanning cubicle, which was not used that much in the winter; there was nowhere else. I thought that if it was a great success, we would then HAVE to expand. That was my plan anyway. Staff was a problem and with no Suzy to call in, we asked Debbie if she would work full time on the Laser; she was happy to do so.

Well, it was, of course, a huge success from day one. Who wouldn't want to look years younger and not have surgery? I kept the price fairly high as we were so busy anyway and didn't want to have queues of 'ladies' running down the street.

I must say I found it very amusing; some very famous actresses came in and paid for course after course. They seemed very pleased with the results, but they all turned up to their appointments with a scarf or hat pulled down almost to their nose. They didn't want anyone to know that were potentially having a face lift.

Only last week, I heard a radio interview with an actress, one of those that had had the treatment at Secrets years before. When the interviewer asked her if she had ever had any cosmetic surgery, of course, the answer was clearly 'NO' and, of course, it was NOT surgery.

I wish I could mention some of the people that came to have the Laser treatment, but Secrets was the name of the Salon and Secret is what it was!

The salon continued to get busier day by day. The problem was that we were beginning to let people down, and there was little time to chat to the clients as we had to keep moving; one hiccup and we would be late throughout the day - exhausting!

AN ASIDE

The company car that the accountants had advised us to buy to avoid paying too much tax caused some bad feelings as Jean lent it straight away to her new lover and we rarely saw it. Sometimes, he revved up the engine outside when he came to pick Jean up from work, which made me fume. But she was in love with him, and you know what women are like when in love, useless!

Chapter 11 part 5

Leaving Secrets - wonderful San Fred's

Jean and I hardly spoke nowadays. She would get in early to get her Aromatherapy oils all sorted. She would also check that the girls' cubicles were all clean and ready for yet another busy day. We had a lovely cleaner called Irma, who kept everything spick and span, and she was proud to be part of the team.

I turned up about five minutes before we opened, so I didn't have to talk to Jean. I would check all the girls were in and check the appointment book. By 9.30, we were all ready to go.

I would put my bag under the desk. No food, just a plastic bottle of Vodka and tonic. I was definitely beginning to depend on drink. 'I can quit,' I said to myself, but I knew I was kidding myself. In the end, one evening I confessed to my daughter. That might seem strange, but she was at that time the only person I could confide in. She was very grown up and suggested we both go to the AA at the Priory in Roehampton. I 'poo pooded' it at first, but I knew she was right. Everything was getting me down; Secrets was driving me mad and Dawson was not around much and when he was, he was bad tempered. So, my daughter took me to my first AA meeting. I nearly died of embarrassment. Everyone was very kind, but they seemed to accept their drink problems. In contrast, I thought it would just pass soon when I had left Secrets. I did, by now, realise that I had an addictive personality, but does that mean I am automatically an acholic, surely not!

Various people stood up and said their name and then 'I'm an acholic'. That might work for some but not for me; I did go a couple of times again, but I never stood up and admitted that I was an alcoholic because I was not, I was just a nervous wreck who drank a lot!

Over the next weekend, I made up my mind that I wanted to be around my daughter more. I was missing her growing up. In fact, I had missed most of it already. If I was honest, I didn't need the money from Secrets and I definitely didn't need the strange atmosphere there.

I went into the salon on the Saturday evening, wrote a 'goodbye' note to all the girls and one to Jean. I explained to Jean that I had spoken to a friend of ours called Nola Rose. She used to be a mannequin and then she became a compare for the fashion shows Jean and I were in. She needed work, and when I spoke to her, she was delighted to take over from me. So, it worked out for all of us. I suggested to Jean that our solicitor for the company, draw up an agreement for her to buy my 50% from me for £25,000. She could pay me by instalments over the next 5 years. That was very fair, I hope she would realise that.

I went to the shelves and took 2 jars of Clarins Orchidee Bleu cream and some hand cream. Then turned and left, and I didn't look back. It was hard as, of course, it meant the end of a 30 year friendship. But Jean would always be in my heart. I had to meet her once more to sign everything over to Jean. It was sad and difficult, but we didn't look at each other. As she left the room, I just said, 'good luck'. She stayed down in her cubicle for a few years and made lots of new friends. We didn't see each other for a few years, so sad.

I had hoped that life would get better at home, but it didn't. Dawson and Sarah were beginning to argue all the time. I decided that at half term, Sarah and I would go to stay at our favourite country hotel in Lacock. The Sign of the Angel in Lacock was our special place; we loved going there. Sarah would collect the eggs from the chickens in the morning before breakfast, and Maggie, their dog, was always cuddly. We used to go on adventures every day. Then we generally ended up eating at a local pub; we were both relaxed in each other's company. Those days were the

happiest days of my life. Supper was always wonderful when the owner's wife cooked pork with crackling for us. Our friends Pat and Michael lived in Lacock, (Pat used to be married to lovely Gordon), so we often went to eat with them, and they introduced us to the village. We had so many happy memories with them, never to be forgotten.

I remember Sarah and I went to a local animal sanctuary, and Sarah was chased by an Emu or something; he chased her round and round a bush, and it was so funny. I will try to find the picture.

Meanwhile, Dawson was doing really well. Money was pouring in, and we started to go out every Saturday to a restaurant called San Frediano's, San Fred's as we all called it. It was like our club. We knew all the waiters and one of the owners, Franco, was like our best friend; we loved him. I fancied him too! The food was good, and the atmosphere was just perfect. We spent New Year's eve there and birthdays. We always fell out of there about 3pm on a Saturday afternoon, then we went into the nearby shops and spent more money. Being rather drunk, we generally spent a lot! I remember there was a lovely shop the wonderful staff at San Frediano's called Night Owl next door selling sleepwear. And there was the wonderful jewellery shop called Butler Wilson; I have a beautiful necklace from there, one of my prized possessions.

the wonderful staff at San Frediano's

One of the things that we loved about Franco was that he cared for his beloved customers. If, perhaps, a regular customer was eating there with his mistress and, perhaps, their wife came in, he would act at once and get the couple out of the back door. I watched it happen once with a friend of mine; won't tell you who it was, but it was very funny!

It was around this time that we got really friendly with the couple who lived across the road at Number 2 Woodborough Road. They had two little girls, Harriet and Charlotte, and later a boy called Nick. Lucy and Vernon became great friends, and we spent many lovely evenings with them, generally just drinking and chatting. Sometimes, we played Poker with Jerry, and every time any of the kitty fell on the floor, we would leave it for Mary! We only played with pennies. We played Croquet when the sun shone; those days were such happy times.

Vernon was a film director, commercials. He used to do the 'One Cornetto' ads and then the beer one that 'gets to all parts that other beers don't go to?' He was a lovely man, but he died of Leukaemia; very sad as he was so young. He was the only man I ever knew that had a pair of Porsches in the driveway!

my family

Mind you, we had a couple of 7 series BMWs for a couple of days. When Dawson decided to leave ACT 111 to work with his brother, Jim, everything was working well until they fell out, as it seemed that Dawson had pinched his business, yet another bad ending! Whatever happened! I don't know, but, again, the money was coming in, and we seemed to be pretty rich. Dawson called me one day from his office in Marylebone High Street to say that I should go and buy a couple of fur coats and some nice jewellery. Well I'm not into furs, and I only wear costume jewellery, but I phoned my friend Pat, the one in Lacock, and asked her if she would come shopping with me. 'Wonderful, I will make some appointments darling'. She was in her element.

We met a few days later and went to see a Fox coat and a Mink jacket, but I decided that it would be nice if Dawson was there. I took all the details; the cost, only about £25,000. We decided to go on down Bond Street and popped into Cartier. There I bought a lovely Santos watch in steel and gold...I love it to bits.

When Dawson arrived back that evening, he looked exhausted, 'you haven't bought anything yet, have you?' When I told him that I had bought only a watch he looked relieved. Apparently, the Saudis had changed the rules about the amount of sugar that the Tiptree jams were allowed into the country, so he had had to throw the lot overboard. Then he had bought 5 containers of Chickens from the States but when they arrived, their legs were in the air. The Saudis wanted them bent, which was not possible as they were frozen in place. So, again they had to lose them overboard. So, for a moment, we were rich, and then we were not!! Just like old times when I was young.

Well, good for Dawson. He soon got on his feet and did a deal with Britvic and Swizzler's, so again money came flooding in.

San Fred's was such a part of our lives, we had lunch with all our friends there and our whole world seem to involve them. The story of the Italians who owned the various trattorias around London was amazing. Most of them started off, when they arrived in England, as cooks, dishwashers and waiters. Not for long as they filled a void as far as food in London was concerned. So, bit by bit, they started their own restaurants. The story is one of huge success and lots and lots of money.

Alvaro's, Mario and Franco's to name a few. All we wanted to eat in the 60s was Italian. On the next page is a diagram of all the trats that crept into our lives.

At San Frediano's the food was very Italian of course. Dawson always had the same thing every Saturday, Crespolini. Sergio, one of the owners would come from the kitchen clutching a big pottery soup urn with his homemade Bean and Pasta soup. He would come to our table because he knew I loved his special soup and pour some into a bowl, then pour Virgin Olive oil gently onto the soup then sprinkle Parmesan gently over it. Fantastic. I can taste it now! I remember the last time Sergio came with his beloved soup. I remember now because dear Sergio was going

Happy bunny on New Years eve at San Fred's

on holiday. The next day, I read in the newspaper that he and his wife were murdered! Murdered, by mistake, the papers said. They had gone to stay with some friends but on the first night the house was targeted, and everyone in the house was shot dead. A vendetta, the papers said. Rumours started everywhere; the Mafia were responsible. Well, nobody knew, in fact. Sergio and his wife, the papers said, were just in the wrong place at the wrong time, but having witnessed the murders, they had to die too. Other papers said it was just a robbery, who knows.

Dawson's birthday pud at San Fred's

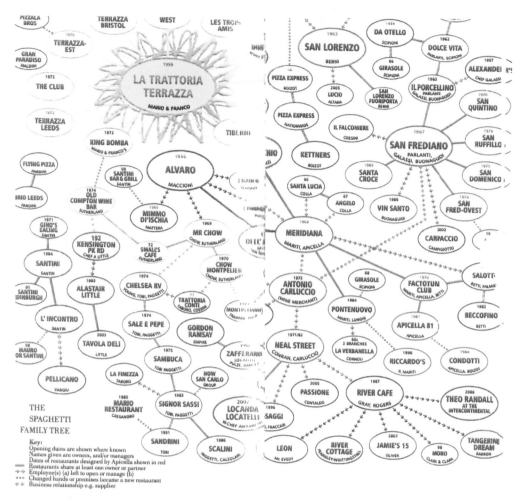

THE
SPAGHETTI
FAMILY TREE

Key:
Opening dates are shown where known
Names given are owners, and/or managers
Dates of restaurants designed by Apicella shown in red
Restaurants share at least one owner or partner
→ → Employee(s) (a) left to open or manage (b)
••• Changed hands or premises became a new restaurant
↓ ↓ Business relationship e.g. supplier

Sarah and Vernon at San Fred's

A few years later, San Fred's closed, and we were devastated. But Franco opened a little restaurant in Hollywood Road nearby called Van Santo. We went a few times as we felt we must support Franco, but the magic had gone.

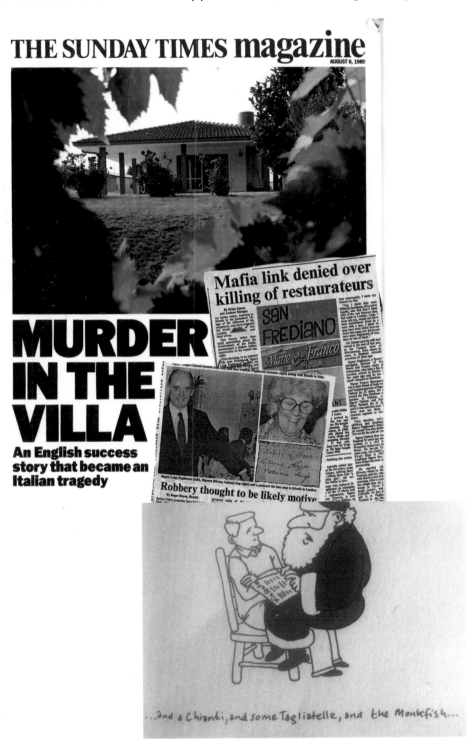

...and a Chianti, and some Tagliatelle, and the Monkfish...

Chapter 11 part 6

Spending time with my Mother - and the six of us

Throughout my life, my mother was there for me. I couldn't have managed to bring up my daughter and work to support the family without her help. I know I didn't see enough of her, but I was always there for her, which is all I could offer at the time. She never wanted for anything.

Chrissie and I had a strange friendship. We had such different personalities. I used to wonder why we were such good friends; it was a matter of who could survive the longest. She was so rude sometimes that I knew she hated me and then so sweet, that I wondered if I was imagining things. But we did have some great times. She was so outspoken that sometimes I would cringe; but everyone expected it from her. She embarrassed me, and I think she did it on purpose, just to see my red face! Chrissie's mother was called Hilda, little rounded Hilda. She and her husband had adopted Chrissie when she was a baby, and seeing them together made me smile as Chrissie was 5'11" and Hilda 5'!

For 3 years we took a holiday together, only a 4 day holiday as there was no way we could manage more than that. For the first holiday we went to Amsterdam.

We managed to persuade our daughters Sarah and Melina to come too, grr... you should have seen the look of horror on their faces, but I think, secretly, they enjoyed the adventure. The boat was a bit rocky, but we decided to drink copious amounts of Brandy to settle our stomachs; whose idea was that I wonder? We booked into our little hotel, then took a boat ride to see the little houses along the canal. Lovely lunch with plenty of wine, mothers getting a bit pickled by then, which was our plan. At one point, Chrissie disappeared. She came back an hour later looking triumphant; she had been chatting up a Dutch biker, which was typical of Chrissie's behaviour, she was such a flirt.

That night we went to a club; the two mothers danced with each other, and it was lovely to see the fun they were having; the girls tried to pretend they were not with us and Chrissie and I continued with the Brandy! A good time was had by all.

Another time we went to Hamburg, another 4 day mini cruise. This was a big drama as the weather forecast warned against any sea travel. I chickened out but Chrissie said, 'Come on, it'll be alright,' and we took a vote and I lost. So, we

went by car to the station to catch the train down to the docks. I didn't know until the end of the holiday that I had driven over poor Hilda's foot, and so she limped around without mentioning it until we arrived back to UK, by which time it was black and blue and twice the size.

We boarded the boat. Looking around, you could see the worry on some people's faces as the boat swayed in the wind. I felt sick before even boarding!

Chrissie had a plan...straight to the bar and ordered 4 Brandies, and 2 Fantas for the girls. Why Brandy, I will never know, but it did seem to stop me from feeling sick. But everyone else was slowly turning green. Chrissie disappeared clutching a fire bucket, never to be seen again; my mother was next and before I took her to her cabin, I told Hilda to hang on to a post on deck. She looked scared, but I promised to come back. After I settled my mother, I went back to collect Hilda, but I couldn't remember which deck I had left her on! I gathered a search party and when we actually found her, she was soaking wet and clinging on to the post where I had left her. Poor Hilda, she still managed a smile before she was sick all over me! The girls had disappeared; who knows what they were up to!

Even though we all went on these mini holidays for our mothers, I think we all enjoyed ourselves; looking at the pictures, you can see our happy faces. The joy our little trips gave them lasted all year, and it gave them both something to look forward to, lovely mums. I miss them both so much.

AN ASIDE

Hilda died before my mother and it was the only time Chrissie, my tough friend, shed a tear in public. I never expected to see that.

Hilda's ashes were in a big jar and served as a door stop for years. Then one day, Chrissie put the big jar on the back seat of her old Citron. She was going to take Hilda to Eastbourne as she had requested before she died. Unfortunately, before they set off, Chrissie went back into the house to collect something, and when she came out the car had been stolen along with poor Hilda's ashes!

Chapter 12 part 1

Becoming an interior designer

Being a lady of leisure didn't suit me at all. Dawson was off to work every morning at 8 and Sarah off to school too. So, the big house was empty, except for the cats, Simon, my ginger Tom, and Gertie the black and white rape victim. Poor Gertie was only six months old when I saw, from my bedroom window, an enormous black cat amble across the lawn and jump on poor unsuspecting Gertie. She had six kittens, Odd Job, Sybil, Humphrey and three unnamed because we gave them away. Odd Job and Sybil were both run over, sadly, and Humphrey was all that was left, lovely Humphrey. He had a habit of scratching the carpet and sofas, so we sent him to a cat psychologist. He put false nails on him and when we recovered from the bill, we took him home where he sat on the carpet and one by one bit the nails off!

When a friend for many years came to lunch one day, I explained why I wasn't coping with doing nothing all day. She found it difficult to understand as she had never worked; she didn't have to as she was married to a wealthy man. She came up with a few ideas, none of which interested me. Then she suggested that I take an interior design course, like she had just completed, and gave me the name of Virginia Stourton from Colour Councillors. In the 1980s interior design was all the rage; everyone wanted to be an interior designer, so I called Virginia the very next day. We met and I took the 3 day 'course,' and was then given my set of boxes. They were colour co-ordinated, and each box was filled with a selection of carpets, fabrics, wallpapers and paint charts. The company sent us leads we could follow up. Day one I had two projects to do and cost. Easy. The first was a Mrs Jones who lived in Kew. She and her husband had just bought the house and wanted everything from furniture to carpet and curtains. I was off and pulled together lots of schemes, so when we met, I had plenty to show them.

Then I came across my first drama. Mrs Jones was having an affair with her son's tennis instructor! So, I had two men putting forward their preferences and by the end of the project, I was exhausted, but I managed to make everyone happy somehow. Mr Jones won in the end as Mrs Jones stayed with him, and the tennis instructor left with his tail between his Plimsoles!

Then the next morning, I jumped in my car armed with my blue boxes to see a Major Klinger who lived in one of those beautiful Georgian houses overlooking the Thames in Chelsea. He was a typical Major with a moustache and one of those 'posh' pretend voices. He took me into the kitchen and asked me to measure for two blinds! I smiled and showed him some fabrics. He chose a blue and white check. I promised to let him have an estimate by the end of the day. The only reason I am telling you this is because that day, day two of being an interior designer, I made a new rule, I would charge £100 per room consultation fee, so I wouldn't just go across London to measure 2 kitchen blinds. Virginia said it wouldn't work, but it did, and I now charge £500 per room, with a minimum of £5000 for my presence! The funny part of this silly story is that 20 years later, I had a call from Major Klinger. He asked if I remembered him and when I answered 'yes,' he asked me to pop over and clean the two blinds! Needless to say, I didn't go!

The Colour Counsellors office in Loughborough phoned daily with various projects, and I followed them up religiously. I was lucky as the few clients I had worked for so far were so happy that they passed my name onto their friends, so I was busy from the very beginning, lucky me.

My turnover began to rise daily, and it wasn't long before I had to register for VAT. Then I knew I was on to a winner.

I flew to Paris to redesign a house and had great fun with a very difficult client. Please don't ever think being an interior designer is easy or fun. It's not. You have to have so much patience, you have to listen to all your clients wants and dislikes, then you also have to hear how their husband doesn't like pink, blue, or green, in fact he doesn't see why they are spending any money of redecorating when it was done 40 years ago! Believe me, I have heard it all.

Then out of the blue up comes a dream project, maybe you don't make much money, but you walk away with a big smile and you are really proud of the whole result. It doesn't happen that often but when it does, it's like the icing on the cake.

I was pretty well established when I received a call from Guinness headquarters, in Portman square. They asked me to come for a meeting with the idea of refurbishing the whole building. Wow, that's more like it. I had £££ signs flashing in my head. The meeting went well, and each of the directors wanted a new scheme for their offices. I made notes and promised to come up with schemes for everything within a week.

The building was a mixture of dark old-fashioned rooms and modern contemporary ones, so I could only presume that was what they wanted. At the top floor lift where the Managing director had his suite of rooms were 2 sheep, Henry Moore's I was told, so obviously money was no problem. The project went well; they seemed to like everything I came up with, so not only did I make a lot of money, but I had a very happy client.

It paid off as about three years later, I had a call from a Mr Saunders, one of the directors. He asked if I was free to work on the new Ealing building they had just completed. Great, I set up a meeting and when I got to Ealing, all the directors were there, some with their wives, who didn't want to be left out of the decisions that their husbands were about to make. The decision had been made that this building was to be totally modern, the paintings were to be commissioned, and I could have chairs and desks made to my design. I had carte blanche, wonderful. I was taken into the finance department and told to come up with a budget, but they gave me a million pound 'open to buy,' as they realised I had to commission several painters and they wanted the best. I had so much fun. I had no idea what I was doing as far as the modern artists were concerned, so I gave them a colour chart for each room and that was all they had. Actually, one of the directors wanted his office to be surrounded by yachts, so yachts he had in plenty.

I must say. I think if I had to work with so many modern paintings around me, I would need a big packet of Aspirin!

The day came for the grand opening of the building, and the Mayor of Ealing was to cut the ribbon. Champagne flowed, and I was flushed with excitement. I was standing with a crowd of admirers and lapping it up when someone came up behind me and whispered in my ear, 'Well done Wendy. Pity 50% of the paintings are upside down!'. I turned and saw one of the artists; he was smiling, and he said, 'Don't worry. It happens all the time'.

So, to this day the paintings at Guinness House in Ealing are mostly upside down, and I never owned up!

Chapter 12 part 2

So, busy and enjoying myself - Dawson in Saudi - rich at last

Being an interior designer suited me. I was free to do as much or as little work as I wanted. I began to drop the difficult clients, the ones that wanted net curtains or who had an Indian rug. My pet hate, an Indian rug. You know that they bought the rug in some far away market, and it ruled their lives from then onwards! They were the sort of clients who wanted to co-ordinate everything to go with the bloody rug, even if it overpowered the room. I always suggest, politely, that they don't really need an interior designer, especially one as expensive as me. All they need is a paint chart to take to their local fabric shop and get some samples of fabrics to match the rug. They were always grateful for my advice and especially took on board the 'expensive' part!

When we sold the Woodborough Road house, we moved into a little cottage in the centre of Putney. The idea was that Dawson and I were going to part. Our relationship was rubbish. He wanted to go to live in France, and I wanted to go to the country with the cats. I thought the country and a dog and ducks would solve all my problems. It didn't, of course, but I couldn't be swayed. We had a miserable time at the cottage. Sarah was going out with a photographer called David at the time, and he moved in with us too. So, we were very snug but not very happy. Sarah had found a flat in Maida Vale, so she would be leaving soon. It was always her wish to be a photographer. Jerry and Frank, who owned Photography place, perhaps put the idea into her head as we were always surrounded by photographers. She taught herself to print and it was not long before she went to an agent to show her work and her career took off. I suppose. David became a little jealous of her success, I think. Anyway, they broke up soon after we all moved in together.

I finally found a house in a little village called Ham, near Marlborough. The Old Malthouse took me ages to renovate, but it was worth it. I made lots of friends there, and I think I was happy there in the end. Dawson stayed in London, but not for long. I suppose we decided that living with somebody was better than living with nobody! We soon had lovely friends around us, and we began to entertain again, which always made us feel needed! Having finally finished the renovations on the Old Malt House, I decided to start to work again. The house was looking good, so now I was ready for a project to earn some money. One day the phone rang, and a rather timid voice asked if I was Wendy Baker. She said she and her husband had just bought a house in Shalbourne, a nearby village. It didn't sound very exciting to me, but I suggested she could come and see me at the end of the day. She seemed to mainly be wanting curtains, so no big project there, I thought.

I offered her a coffee. I tried to look interested but, to be honest, I could tell her taste and mine were miles apart. Still, the workroom needed some work, so I sat and listened. When I asked her if she had any floor plan or pictures of the house, she fumbled around in her big bag and produced a John D Wood brochure. A huge brochure of the most wonderful Jacobean Manor house and outbuildings I had ever seen.

I took a deep breath and asked her if she would like a glass of Champagne!

I went to see the house the next day with her husband in tow. He was lovely, she was not; maybe she was shy or something, but we didn't have anything in common. It didn't matter; I was there to do a good job that was all.

The manor house was wonderful, so I suggested we should take it back to its original state. He said 'yes', she didn't care. She wanted a Smallbone kitchen and Dragons in Walton Street, hand painted bedrooms for the two lovely girls. When I suggested that I could get both the kitchen and the children's bedrooms furniture at half price as the men had workrooms of their own, she said that she wanted everything full price or she wouldn't be able to face her friends and boast!

When I first went into the house, I felt very cramped as in order to see out of the windows, the big windows, we all needed to bend to see out properly. The second time I went there, I took my carpenter with me and asked him to lift some of the floorboards so I could see why the ceilings were so low. When we did this, we found a complete ballroom beneath the floor! Then I heard the real story about the house… Apparently the old lady who lived there for many many years lived there on her own , surrounded by her beloved horses. Her vet, Pip Pocock, in Hungerford, cared for her horses and when she died, she left the manor house to Pip and his wife. Pip's wife hated the house; she was only 5' tall and Pip was 5'2", so they couldn't see out of the windows properly, so, they asked a carpenter to raise all the floors throughout the whole house. Then they put in a new central heating and electrical circuit.

So, when I lowered all the floors and restored the Ballroom, we had one big problem; the radiators throughout the house were halfway up the walls and the light switches were even higher, so we had to have a step ladder to reach the switches to turn on the lights! To do the alterations cost my clients a 'cool' £200,000, enough to bring tears to their eyes.

The carpenter was to build cupboards for her clothes. This was to be done in a whole room, next to the master bedroom. He had a dressing room the other side of the master bedroom. Her cupboards, about 30 of them, all had to have locks on them! Why I wondered at the time!

Towards the end of the work, her husband asked if I could convert one of the barns to house his beautiful ship collection. I don't think she liked that, but he put his foot down and won. He was very happy, and I was very proud of the way it turned out.

Then the girls, about 4 and 5 years old, asked me to decorate their Wendy House in the garden. Perfect. They wanted everything in the main manor house to be made in miniature. What fun! I had never done a Wendy house before, so I decided to call World of Interiors, the upmarket Interiors magazine, and see if they would like to do an article about it, good promotion for me too. So, they agreed to come in two weeks' time. I had ordered replica chandeliers and had already made the 'swags and tail' curtains in miniature. The last thing to do was the hand painted frieze of field mice I had planned to run along the skirting boards. 'I would like my sister to do this,' the owner said one day. 'Of course,' I said. It's always nice if another member of the family joins in. So, I cancelled my artist and handed that part over to the sister. It took her two weeks working day and night to do the frieze. When it was finished, I was asked to come and see it...it was such a shock. She had painted giant rats with Cocoa puff packets on their shoulders everywhere. The rats were bigger than the little girls and the girls looked terrified. I said 'wonderful,' and fled. I called World of Interiors to cancel the shoot, obviously!

That evening I gave them the final invoice and my set of keys and walked away. I was crying. You see, it had been my house for two years, and now I had to walk away. It happens, and it always makes me cry. I heard footsteps behind me, it was the owner. He put his arms around me and said in my ear, 'Thank you, Wendy. You made all our dreams come true!'. That was all I needed, a thank you!

AN ASIDE

I heard a couple of years later that he had left her. All I can say is good riddance!

Chapter 12 part 3

Life in Ham - the 'Salisbury crowd'

Living in the country is not that easy, I soon found out. You have to abide by the rules.

1. Go to church on Sunday mornings.

2. Wear simple clothes, don't try to outshine anyone.

3. Smile all the time. Don't single out anyone in particular, just smile at everyone, as you don't know who they are yet.

4. Ask if you can go on the church flower rota.

5. IF anyone talks to you, just give them your name and a brief account of you and your family, just enough to whet their appetite.

6. Keep all conversations simple, like jam making, cake making and Macramé.

7. Be very interested in church plans like the Bingo, harvest festival and collecting for the local Hospice.

When I went to church on my first Sunday there, I met two women from the village. They bombarded me with questions. It wasn't so good to start with as they just wanted to know all about me and wouldn't let go, rather like a cat with a mouse. In fact, it was dreadful. Why was I on my own? How many children did I have? What did I do for a living? When I finally escaped from the pair, I went right back to the cottage and opened a bottle of red wine and drank all of it!

As it turned out, one of those women became a great friend; Sue and her husband Nigel. They had 3 super children. They really became 'family'. When Dawson came back to live with me, and we became a couple again, only then, it seemed, did the village accept us. They couldn't accept a woman on her own, especially someone as interesting as me.

Most evenings we would walk across Ham green to have a drink or two; with the Hawleys sometimes we had supper too, but generally just drinks, too much of course. But there was nothing else to do, really, gossip and drink! So, this was not good for me as I was still trying to curb my drinking.

They had a Cocker Spaniel called Pepper, and we fell in love with Pepper. One evening having had even more lubrication than usual, Sue phoned the breeder and asked if there was a chance that they had a Spaniel that Pepper could mate with. 'Yes, William would be only too pleased to be of service!' So, the next morning Sue handed me Pepper's lead and an address for the union. That was my first experience of conception. All I had to do was to hold Pepper's bum up in the air and hang on, exhausting! A few months later we had our first puppy, Beatrice was her name. Sue came over one morning with a basket with all the puppies in it. She instructed me to take the puppies to the vet to have their tails docked. Now, apparently, docking was illegal. I found out when I got to the vet and saw the nurse's disapproving face. What a horrid experience; it was not only a bloody experience but very upsetting too. Never again. Thank goodness that it is now illegal.

The Hawleys introduced us to their friends Bill and Bunty in Salisbury, who then introduced us to Rex and Adrianne and Anne and Richmond. Also, part of that group of friends was Rosemary (Peter's sister) and her husband Bernard. So, we joined a large group of friends, and the fun started, drinking, eating and numerous holidays.

We even bought a piece of land in Bargeman and managed to talk Rosemary and Bernard to buy some of the land. They built a house on their land, but we chickened out.

So, for the next few years, we would spend New Year's eve with 'the Salisbury crowd,' as we called them. We mostly went to Cornwall and hired various cottages, lots of log fires, lots of stews and plenty of dumplings. We played games like Charades, did jigsaws and a dice game called 'liar dice'. We went to pubs for lunch most days, generally searching for crab sandwiches, and on our way down to Cornwall, we managed to get a table at Keith Floyd's pub, called Floyd's Inn (sometimes); the food and service were terrible. Keith just drank neat Vodkas all the time but came over and signed one of his books for me and was very chatty. One Christmas we went to a drinks party at the Vicar's house, Dereck and Sonia. They were not your usual run of Vicars and wives. Derek always had a twinkle in his eye, and Sonia often stripped at these gatherings, no idea why, it was just what she did! At one of his parties, we met another couple, the Tweedies; they were good looking and we enjoyed the same things, especially eating. We would travel for miles for a good meal. We clicked the moment we met and became good friends over the years.

When Dawson had his first stroke, he sadly became outspoken, and some of our friends drifted away. So, it didn't end very well, but we did have such happy times, never to be forgotten.

By the time Dawson moved into the cottage, he had closed his business in Marylebone High Street. The company had been so successful, but working with Arabs had its good points and bad ones. You never knew when laws would be changed, so you were always on your toes with your heart in your mouth. He had had enough, so he started to do his 'sofa sit', in other words, he stopped doing anything. He sat on our Kingcome sofas for the next 32 years! Well, actually, he did come up with one good idea, he taught himself to do floor plans on the computer. He called the company FloorPlans Unlimited. So, at last Dawson got off the sofa for a year or two. All the main estate agents used his floorplans service, and we were in the money again.

AN ASIDE

When we decided to move to France. We went to say 'goodbye' to the Tweedies and were amazed to find out that Michael had opened a business, with his brother David. It was called Plans4you, an exact copy of Dawson's business, not a nice thing to do to a friend! Perhaps it would have been nice if he had at least mentioned it to Dawson. Jenny, his wife, was very embarrassed, and Dawson and I were really upset.

Chapter 12 part 4

At last some rewarding projects

As our cottage in Ham, Wiltshire, was only one hour down the M4 to the centre of London, and as there was little work in the country, I decided to try to pick up some work in London, but only high fee projects naturally.

I spent several weeks being seen everywhere. I went most days to Chelsea Harbour at the Design Centre, making sure everyone knew I was back and available. I put an advert in the Temple magazine, hoping to get some work there, lots of lovely Barristers and piles of briefs scattered all over the floor! My plan soon worked, and work came flying in. I had so many projects that I couldn't really cope. But with careful planning, I juggled builders, carpenters and painters. I had a big board in my office with lots of red, green and blue stickers and a good team of workmen.

The first challenge was a great experience. My first Chambers. What fun, what an experience. I had a call from a clerk of one of the biggest sets of Chambers. I loved working at The Temple; everyone was so polite and so grateful. I found on day one that the best way to handle the barristers, mainly men, was to treat them like children. To explain that comment, let me tell you what happened.

I went to the first meeting to see what the job entailed. The Chambers consisted of rooms for eight barristers, two judges and various clerks, all the rooms needing a complete make-over .I suggested that it would make everyone's life easier if I had custom made shelves made to put the briefs on, so they were no longer scattered over the floors. The idea went down well. I told them that it would be very expensive but worthwhile, and they agreed. The estimate for those shelves came to £28,000. I told the clerk I would design all the schemes and come back with them next week. He suggested next Friday, and I agreed. He said he would make sure everyone was present to choose their personalised scheme.

Well it took some time to get so many room schemes ready, but I managed to do some extra ones too, just in case! Thank goodness that I did. The clerks, knowing their barristers better than I did, had a plan. They would arrange a queue with the two judges first, then the barristers and finally the clerks and other staff. A memo was duly sent to each one.

When I arrived, they were already calmly queuing! First judge politely decided on a navy blue speckled carpet and a navy and maroon Damask curtains, easy. Then all the planning went wrong as the second judge also wanted the same scheme and he had brought his wife with him to make sure he made the right choice, fatal. So now there was an argument. I made various suggestions, and finally I had to agree to do their rooms with the same scheme. They were not happy, especially when I said in a jokey way that there were worse things in life. They just glared at me and grunted out of the room!

The rest went down well, but there were a few tense moments, and I understood why the clerks always handled them with kid gloves. They were, in fact, very childlike but charming too. The whole project went well and in the end everyone, even the two judges, were happy, I think. A good learning curve for me. I designed another six sets of Chambers and made a lot of money.

Then one of the barristers came to talk to me; he had decided to take the matter up with the Inland Revenue. His argument was that having to update Chambers with the help of an interior designer was very expensive but necessary, stating that the money should be allowed as an expense and VAT free. Apparently, at that moment they were responsible for the expense themselves. So, he asked me to stand up in court and argue on their behalf. Shock horror, me, not me surely. I felt as if my stammer was about to come back, but as usual I agreed!

It was not frightening, and it was a closed court, so I just opened my mouth and let my belly rumble, nothing unusual there! Anyway, we lost, and the Judge said that with the sort of money the barristers charge, they were quite capable of paying for the alterations themselves. End of! So, although we had lost, I was immediately respected throughout The Inner Temple. More work… The best thing about being an interior designer is that you get to work on beautiful houses and meet interesting people.

My next call came as a surprise. A very well-known interiors designer from America called me one evening. His name was Thomas Jayne. He told me that he had a project in Wilton Place in Knightsbridge for one of the richest families in America, the Merck family. He had just finished their house in Charleston, and they had bought this house in London, but he didn't have any contacts.

So, someone had suggested that he join up with me and together we can do the work. I had heard of Thomas, and I was honoured. Great for me; it confirmed I was accepted by the top interior's world.

We met at the house. Thomas was there, 6'5" tall, and his partner Eric, 5'2", was standing beside him, quite a sight! Once we had walked around the house and had come up with a few ideas, I had generally a good idea what was to be expected by me. The clients, Mr and Mrs Merck, the pharmaceutical family, arrived a little later and they were charming. We got on really well and had several mutual friends in common. Mr Merck, Tony, didn't mind about the plans; all he was interested in was his walk-in man shower. In the end, the only thing that went wrong was, in fact, the shower, sod's law.

The colours chosen were from Farrow and Ball, mainly Downpipe, which is a dark blueish grey for the kitchen, floors and cupboards, very dark. The rest of the house was dark too. This was Thomas's style and they loved it, so I didn't interfere. When it came to the living room, which was dark anyway, Tony Merck explained that they had several Constables arriving, and they wanted it to be cosy; the only lights were to be over the paintings.

Personally, I think I would just fall asleep in such a dark house. I organised all the curtains and spent several days shopping with her; we spent a lot of money. When the last bits were being finished off, there was a terrible crash and we all rushed to see what it was. Tony was there, almost in tears, his shower door had arrived, it was huge and very heavy. The door slipped down the stairs and smashed to bits. Tony just said, 'Well, I will call the Berkley Hotel around the corner and go there every morning for my breakfast and shower'. So, no big drama really, thankfully.

Except when we went back to the hotel, we lost Eric, Thomas's friend; he just went into the hotel opened a door, found a bed and went to sleep. Thomas was beside himself. We both had to go up and down each floor shouting Eric's name. 2 hours later, he appeared bleary eyed. I think Thomas gave him hell when they were alone, but it was nothing to do with me…but quite funny really!

Through that job I had several projects offered to me. I took some of them but, really, I needed a rest. Later in the year, I went to New York to do two loft apartments, which were very rewarding.

When I got back to the country, I was exhausted. I was missing my puppy and even Dawson!

Whilst I was working at that pace, I had to forget friends and family. But somewhere along the line, I met someone called Wendy Cushing. We were at a fair selling our wares, and we were the only two Wendys grafting away, sell,

sell sell. That was our motto. We are both workaholics and, needless to say, we formed a wonderful friendship. She is a very accomplished weaver and has a company that sells passementerie, trimmings to you and me. Pom-poms to go onto curtains and upholstery. She is totally dedicated to her work and talks about pom-poms continuously! It drives me mad, really, and I tease her about it, but she needs people to admire her, just like I do. Wendys give the appearance of being very confident, but, really, they need someone to tell them how good they are most of the time.

We have been on a few trips together, always getting into trouble along the way; we've had fun and we dance and laugh a lot.

Chapter 12 part 5

Some of my interior design projects - more name dropping!

I had a call from Wendy C; she had been working with a man who needed help with a project in Hay's Mews behind the Saudi Embassy in Curzon Street. It was a real 'show off job'; terrible taste, but a sweet team of workers. It took ages to get permission for the works. They had bought three mews houses and were not allowed to change the façade. So, from the front, it looked like mews houses, but then we took away the inside and dug down two more floors for a pool and resting area?? The Sheik had two wives, and they slept in their own rooms either side of his. The décor in each of the wives' rooms had to be identical as the Sheik didn't want them to get jealous! Each bed at the end of the day was sprinkled with rose petals.

The living area had to have several sofas in it as they entertained continuously. Whilst I was on the premises, I was not allowed to use the Sheik's private lift, so I had to walk four flights of stairs several times a visit, with my arms filled with samples. They had assigned a 'minder' to help me and check I wasn't running off with the Saudi diamonds! His name, unusually, was Mohammed. He followed me everywhere and made me copious cups of coffee. We had to drink coffee off the premises if the royal staff were on site, but when they went out to do the shopping, he hid a little glass of coffee in the kitchen, so the other workers didn't see. The last day of the work, he came to me to say how sorry he was that I was leaving. He said, almost in tears, 'I will make you a last glass of coffee and would you like a date?'. Ah, bless him, I thought and said, 'Yes, I would love a date'. He went purple in the face and clapped his hands together in joy. I realised he meant 'a date' not an eating date!

Shortly after the work had finished, the foreman on the project called me to ask if I could do another small one. I was on Paddington Station about to board the train for the country. 'No!' There was silence then he said, 'even if the client was TOM CRUISE?' Hesitation, 'AH YES,' I said walking towards the taxi rank, 'What's his address?'.

It was so funny as he was treated like royalty; I was told not to say anything to anyone. The address must remain a secret and never be revealed. Paramount had rented him an apartment just down a little road opposite Harrods. I had to announce my name, but not say who I was visiting.

A security guard opened the door, looking from side to side. I was 'frisked,' had my picture taken, then told to sit in the waiting area but forbidden to talk to anyone. A woman came down in the lift to take me to his apartment!

I was offered some Kingfisher water and sat down to await HIS arrival. I heard the lift doors below open; then it was action stations, three personal assistants moved towards the lift door, to meet and greet, I suspected. As the lift came gently up, they were on their walkie talkies, whispering into them, saying things like, 'he's at the first floor, moving to the second, stand by to greet, now doors opening'. Tom was charming, all smiles (beautiful teeth). We went into his bedroom, sat on his bed, and looked at some fabrics that I had with me. Bet you haven't met anyone who has been ON bed with Tom Cruise, not IN bed! He can't sleep if he has any light coming through the curtains, so it has to be pitch black. I suggested 'black out lining,' then if light was still coming in, we could staple the curtains to the wall. He said he never opened the curtains anyway, so that was it. He thanked me and then I was ushered out of the apartment. Pity. I thought I was doing a complete project, but we did get on and I'm hoping he will ask me to do the décor for him when he finds a house here in UK.

I never saw him again as when the curtains were installed, he was at Ascot chatting up lots of women, pity.

Tom Cruise makes their (Ladies') Day

by **DANIEL BINNS** and **ANDREI HARMSWORTH**

GAMBLING can be a risky business. You usually need lots of collateral and you must make all the right moves if you want to see the colour of money.

Not that punters at Glorious Goodwood were paying much attention to the runners and riders after Tom Cruise made a surprise visit to Ladies' Day at the racecourse in West Sussex.

The 52-year-old found himself surrounded by admirers – and 24-year-old model Edie Campbell.

The chemistry between the pair was so strong that William Hill offered odds on them dating in the future, despite him being 28 years older... and 8cm (3in) shorter.

'He seemed very happy with himself when he was presenting the trophy to a supermodel – maybe romance might be on the cards?' said spokesman Jon Ivan-Duke. Cruise also appeared to impress royal show jumper Zara Phillips.

A few good snaps: Tom Cruise poses for a selfie and, below, with model Edie Campbell PICTURES: GETTY

Chapter 13 part 1

Another successful business - no publisher was interested, bad luck for them!

Whilst I was busy with my new career as an interior designer, I was also collecting hundreds of sketches of curtains and blinds. When I went to see a new client, I never knew what the brief would be. It could be just colour schemes or perhaps fabrics for curtains, so I had to go prepared for most events. Curtains and blinds did, generally, feature in most people's plans. As I spent most of the time with a new client waving my arms in the air trying to explain various shapes and headings for curtains, so the best way was to do simple sketches, so they understood what they were having. I could do a working drawing, but nothing fancy, so I asked my talented friend Chrissie to draw my ideas for me. As I said, after a few years, I had so many I thought maybe I should put them together and make a book for other designers; it would be helpful to them, as it was for me. So, Dawson took a bunch of

sketches to his friend Farouk Ayoub at Kall Kwik in Paddington and he printed, laminated and bound them into a book for me. We called the book THE CURTAIN SKETCHBOOK.

That was my first book, the first of hundreds and thousands of them. I decided to see if any publisher would be interested in publishing it. I made an appointment with several of the well- known publishers, like Harper Collins, Quadrille and Ryland Peters and Small. They were all very polite, but none of them could see the enormous untapped market that I had discovered. Wishing me luck, they closed the door firmly behind me. I had been dismissed. That did it for me. I knew the book was a good idea, and the more I thought about it, the more I was convinced it was a 'goer'.

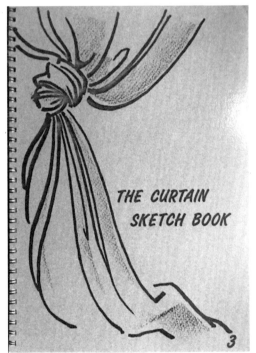

THE CURTAIN SKETCH BOOK

the sketches were only black line

So, I decided to take a stand at a show called IDDI. It was similar to Decorex, where designers show their fabrics, paints, lighting and furniture. It worked out to be rather expensive, but I needed to prove my point to myself, and, more importantly, to others.

Our stand was over the walkway to Wendy Cushing's trimming company. We spread some of the books open on the table in front of us. It wasn't long before we had people pushing to get to see the books. Dawson was on the stand, and he was selling one book every minute. When I joined him to help out, he said quietly, 'This is amazing. We have hit a niche market'. I knew then that we had a real winner. I looked across the corridor, and I saw the other Wendy selling like mad too. We were the only two with busy stands.

We had a set 'spiel'. THE CURTAIN SKETCHBOOK is a tool, really; something to show the clients all the various styles of curtains and blinds that would suit their windows. If the designer had a felt tip pen, they could add frills or buttons here and there. Several people wanted to know why the sketches were only black line drawings. To me it was obvious; you didn't want to put the client off by colouring the sketches; colour can be added later. Then the sketch can be printed for the client to take home to show the family. Another sketch could be sent to the curtain maker with measurements and instructions.

The bestselling point was that there were no words, just sketches, thus no language barriers! That was why in the end The Curtain Sketchbook sold thousands around the world.

Then I met Claire from Potterton Books who also had a stand at the show. She had a good business selling books about interior design at shows around the world. She said she wanted to work with Shoestring Books, the new company name. That was our first wholesale contact but the first of many. After the show at Olympia, we had so many orders, Farouk had to print another 500...big celebrations. We sold the laminated book for £30; the printing and laminating price for the book cost us £12.50, so there was plenty of profit.

A few weeks later, a rep from Christian Fischbacher came to my office trying to sell me a copy of my book in paper. We sued them for £1000, so we were quids in already!

AN ASIDE

Shortly after the show, Claire , the owner of Potterton books, called me and placed an order for 250 books to be shipped to New York…off we go!

ANOTHER ASIDE

I always wanted to be an author and wrote lots of children's books, but I never sent them to a publisher. When I was older, I wrote a silly little 'skit' for the show 'That Was the Week That Was' on TV. At least I got a reply. I think they quite liked it, but I never continued down that path as I was lacking in confidence…now 60 years later I've written my first book, with words!

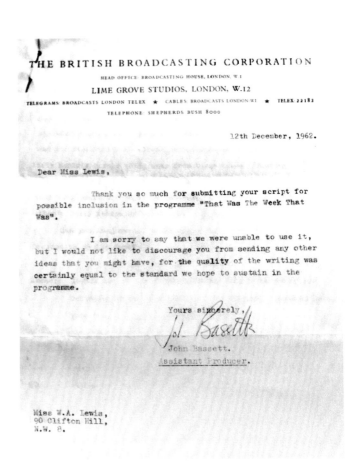

THE BRITISH BROADCASTING CORPORATION

HEAD OFFICE: BROADCASTING HOUSE, LONDON, W.1

LIME GROVE STUDIOS, LONDON, W.12

TELEGRAMS: BROADCASTS LONDON TELEX ★ CABLES: BROADCASTS LONDON W1 ★ TELEX 22183

TELEPHONE: SHEPHERDS BUSH 8000

12th December, 1962.

Dear Miss Lewis,

Thank you so much for submitting your script for possible inclusion in the programme "That Was The Week That Was".

I am sorry to say that we were unable to use it, but I would not like to discourage you from sending any other ideas that you might have, for the quality of the writing was certainly equal to the standard we hope to sustain in the programme.

Yours sincerely,

John Bassett.
Assistant Producer.

Miss W.A. Lewis,
90 Clifton Hill,
N.W. 8.

Chapter 13 part 2

Self publishing on a shoestring...

We didn't expect the business to expand like it did, but it seemed sensible, at the time, to print the laminated book in a paperback version as well. Printed to start with by Farouk, but as the quantities grew, we had to move to a larger setup. As the paperback was much cheaper than the laminated one, sales went through the roof. So now we had 2 Curtain Sketchbooks. I decided that as everyone from interior designers and curtain makers to design colleges were all wanting to buy it, they had to commit to having a box of 20. That didn't deter anyone; they just all bought a box and sold them on to friends.

So, my problem was that we needed to make SKETCHBOOK 2 in bulk, at least 2000 at a time. I started to discontinue the original laminated book as it didn't make sense to have 2 books that were different but the same, if you see what I mean. We made the original for special orders with Farouk only and then found an English printer to handle the larger orders. The stock was held in a barn on the way to Marlborough; a local couple did the shipping as our cottage was already full of boxes. This all worked very well, but I had to write more books as the audience was there, and they needed feeding.

Chrissie, who interpreted all my funny squiggles into beautiful sketches, had now moved from Brighton to Spain, to live with the gypsies. She was margining on madness, my darling friend. She didn't like people very much but adored dogs and cats. When she left for Spain, someone drove her and her animals and her furniture, all from skips, to Villajoyosa, near Alicante. It was a site to remember, very funny and very sad too. She always sat up very erect and as they drove off, I cried my eyes out , for although she was the most annoying person I have ever met, she was also a very dear friend, I know deep down she loved me as I did her. I will always miss her. She died 4 years ago.

I put together another Curtain Sketchbook 3, variations of all the basic designs in the first book. Chrissie worked wonders, she was so creative, but every day shouted at me down the phone from Spain, saying this doesn't work, that's not correct. I just nodded and carried on. Meanwhile, the new book was gathering up speed. We needed more space for sure. As the stock came in, it was shipped out as soon as possible, but never fast enough it seemed. The British printers were very helpful and were always on hand when I got into deep water. Remember, neither of us knew anything about publishing...what the hell is an ISBN number? What is a barcode? How do you handle copyright? We learnt with everyone's help.

Potterton Books, our first wholesale buyer, opened a showroom in Chelsea Harbour Design Centre, and so our orders were doubled. One consistent buyer, part of Colefax and Fowler, opened a shop in Sloane Street; they ordered 60-100 books every week. We used that as our 'flagship,' and people would go there and see how fast they sold and buy the same amount, so it just snowballed.

We were so busy as sales were growing every day. Sadly, the price of the UK printer was too expensive, so we had to move, reluctantly, overseas to Italy. The new printers were wonderful and very helpful. The stock came on time, which was pretty amazing for Italy!

Dawson began to get restless, and we came up with a plan. We had to tackle a different market. America, France, Italy...the world! With no words to translate, there was literally no extra expense.

293

So, we went to the Book Fair and took a stand at IPG, a small stand where young publishers can show their titles. It turned out to be a waste of time as we had no contacts to ask them to come to see the 3 books. We learnt a lesson from that; we needed to do more research before exhibiting at the Book Fair again. Although we did meet a 'rights' lady who took some samples to show her contact. She sold the rights to Russia and Poland. More money!

At the show, I also met a lovely man called Geoff Cowan, who really helped with good advice. His company sold quite a lot to their customers, and he introduced me to an odd character called Pete Randall, an American. He had a book for the American market about curtains, not the same as ours although I had to keep an eye on him, as I never trusted him. In fact, one of his books did have some of my sketches in it. I called him and he just said, 'So!'. Our friendship ended there, but I have to remember that Pete sold huge quantities of my books; he also introduced me to Amir, who lived in Istanbul. He had his own book called 'Home designs", I think. He also sold my books in and around Istanbul. So, we had started to cover little bits of the world, but not enough.

Through my friend Wendy, I was introduced to a company called British Trimmings. They started to order Sketchbook 2 and 3. They, in turn, mentioned them to a company called Wesco, a fabric manufacturer, and they also bought and sold the books. The word soon got around the trade, especially in US. So, I decided to do a visit to some of the new customers and arrange a book signing. What an experience.

I engaged a driver, called Yolanda. I asked her to drive me around to some of the buyers. She was delightful and decided to protect me. So, when I went in to the signings, she 'cased the joint' before letting me out of the car. She amused me with her story about the first night of her honeymoon. Apparently, she was in bed, and her new husband was in another room. All of a sudden, she heard wailing and chanting, and she was terrified, naturally. When he came to bed, she asked what had been going on, and he said he was part of a cult and he needed to keep in touch with the devil!!

Poor Yolanda, she stayed as she was scared to leave; he was so overpowering. I wonder where she is now; sadly, we lost touch.

At the end of my trip, I was known as 'the curtain lady'. The trip had been a huge success.

I never seemed to stop, but without Chrissie I couldn't have done it. Her sketches were wonderful. The hell I had to go through was almost impossible at times, but together through all the shouting we managed it. How, God only knows! When we did fall out, we just picked ourselves up and continued!

One day, thinking back on those early days, when no publisher wanted to publish the book, I decided to get in touch with Anova, which was Collins and Brown before. I had done one book before for lovely Colin Ziegler, and they were only too pleased to see me as they had heard of the incredible sales and now wanted a part of it. I also contacted Quadrille, and they too wanted to do a book with me. I started with them, but Anova offered a contact and £30,000, so I went with the money. Wrong, I found out later.

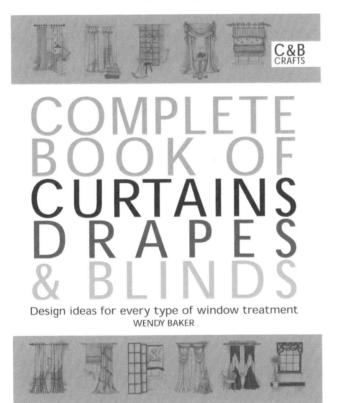

COMPLETE
BOOK OF
CURTAINS
DRAPES
& BLINDS

Design ideas for every type of window treatment
WENDY BAKER

Anova were wonderful to work with, but they didn't understand the success of the books relied on 'Special Sales'. That meant the design schools, the curtain makers, the interior designers, all waiting for a new book from Shoestring. We created a nice book, but they only approached the book trade. I went one day all the way to Crystal Palace, to the Stitches show to do a book signing, the other side of London. When I got there and found the stand, I told them who I was and they looked amazed, 'Why was I here'.

I couldn't believe this was the launch, and they didn't know why I was there. When I told the girls on the stand, they said they did have copy of my book somewhere in a drawer! What a missed opportunity. The show had 30,000 visitors over the 3 days.

As sales were growing at such a speed, I finally, handed all the printing over to China, a lovely company. We still catch up at the book fair, and one day, I will finish my two new books; they will print them for me...one day when I finish those last 3 chapters! We had important shippers ABX bringing everything into

UK. Nice team, Paul was our man and Carol was our woman there, we were a good team.

Then I had a good idea. I approached the Design Schools. KLC was based in Chelsea Harbour, Design Centre. I was there working as an interior designer most days, anyway. They agreed straight away, as Potterton Books had closed, they needed my books. Their students loved them, and the tutors always suggested that they should buy a copy and to use as their 'Bible'.

AN ASIDE

So, now my name, Wendy Baker, and The Curtain Sketchbooks were known virtually everywhere. I had shown that book publishing can make money, but you have to target the right market for your book.

Chapter 13 part 3

Shoestring Books is a big success

Apart from the occasional interior design project, I wasn't that busy and I knew I needed to come up with some more ideas for other Sketchbooks. I wondered each time if I could go through it again with Chrissie, but it all depended on my approach. If I said something like, 'Chrissie, I suppose you haven't got a little spare time to help me with a tiny new Sketchbook?'. Then discuss a fee and then put the phone down, she would leave it for a couple of days and then phone and talk about everything under the sun but never Sketchbooks. So, you just had to wait. The answer was generally somewhat grumpy, 'Alright, I suppose, I can fit it in,' she spoke in her slowest voice.

So, my next step was to write 2 small books, one for blinds and one for accessories. The Curtain Sketchbooks were A4 size so I thought it would be

In this SKETCHBOOK we have tried to show every style of blind imaginable – from ROLLERS to ROMANS and from LONDON to AUSTRIAN blinds – all squeezed into this COMPACT SKETCHBOOK. Although blinds are mainly used as an ALTERNATIVE to curtains they do work very well together and inside are some great ideas...

Inspirational ideas for... TRIMMINGS... ROLLER BLINDS... AUSTRIANS... ROMANS... LONDON... ORIENTAL... LINEN FOLD... FESTOONS... CASCADES... VELUX... DORMERS...LAMBREQUINS... VENETIONS... WOODEN SHUTTERS... PANELS... PORTIERES... and ALTERNATIVE WINDOW COVERINGS...

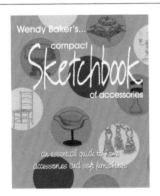

When refurnishing a room the end result can often be spoilt by adding the WRONG ACCESSORIES - so many mistakes are made at this stage...either because there are too many or too few accessories - getting the BALANCE just right is not as easy as it seems. So, in this SKETCHBOOK, we show some room sets with and without accessories - and explain how to group your accessories so as to make more of a statement.

We hope you enjoy some of the ideas and that they prove helpful when placing your accessories - when you manage to create a certain cosiness to a family room or the right kind of elegance to a formal living room by adding the RIGHT ACCESSORY then you are well on the way to a perfect room setting... CUSHIONS... SCREENS... TABLE LINEN... KITCHEN CLUTTER... CHAIRS... LIGHTING...PICTURES... MIRRORS... RUGS... FLOWERS... COLLECTABLES... OUTDOOR ACCESSORIES...

better to do these pocket sized, so they fitted into a designer's handbag or briefcase. 'Good idea,' I said to myself, 'and I will colour some of the sketches, just to be a bit flashy'. They were fun to do, and even Chrissie seemed to be less moody about them. And there were some words too!

Dawson was in charge of paperwork for export and imports. I was happy to leave this to him as it was pretty complicated. He had also approached some of the cloth reps to sell the Sketchbooks when they were visiting their customers in their assigned areas. That wasn't very successful as they were worried that they may get found out. So, we ditched that idea. We also spent quite a bit on advertising, but that didn't work, really. 'Word of mouth' was the best way for us to sell. The books were good, and people wanted them, so why bother with anything else.

Attn Wendy Baker
SHOESTRING BOOK COMPANY
53 Warrington Crescent
London
W9 1EH

14th April 2008

	$	Ave Rate	£
Due for April 2007 Sales	1342.02	1.9877	675.16
Due for May 2007 Sales	498.05	1.9841	251.02
Due for June 2007 Sales	-70.86	1.9850	-35.70
Due for July 2007 Sales	-574.79	2.0308	-283.04
Due for August 2007 Sales	-1272.14	2.0084	-633.41
Due for September 2007 Sales	3482.79	2.0180	1725.86
Due for October 2007 Sales	1082.02	2.0359	531.47
Due for November 2007 Sales	740.11	2.0723	357.14
Due for December 2007 Sales	603.88	2.0507	294.48
Due for January 2008 Sales	-169.88	1.9722	-86.13
Due for February 2008 Sales	676.77	1.9662	344.20
Due for March 2008 Sales	1255.84	2.0007	627.70
Per Statement	7593.83		3768.77

Chargebacks:

Sales Ledger 64929

		$	Ave Rate	£
	Reference:			
Cr Note 15116	Overchg on Inv. 125259	-30.97	2.0308	-15.25
Invoice 133182	Sending Review Copies of 2 Titles	9.01	2.0308	4.44
Invoice 135379	NBN Stock Transfer Fee	91.50	2.0084	45.56
Invoice 138905	NBN Stock Transfer Fee	80.00	2.0359	39.29
Invoice 140932	Storage Charges - Jan to Apr '07	67.96	2.0723	32.79
Invoice 141938	NBN Charges - Various	262.50	2.0507	128.01
Invoice 145666	NBN Stock Transfer Fee	80.00	1.9662	40.69
Invoice 146869	Storage Charges - May to Dec '07	85.04	2.0007	42.51
Invoice 147475	NBN Stock Transfer Fee	40.00	2.0007	19.99
	Total	685.04		338.03

Additional Charges

	$	Ave Rate	£
ACC Fall Catalogue Chg - 2 Books @ $40	120.00	1.9850	60.45
UPS Delivery - July Invoice	70.72	2.0308	34.82
UPS Delivery - September Invoices	50.75	2.0180	25.15

One idea that did work was handing over the overseas sales to a publishing company called ACC, Antique Collectors' Club. At BEA book fair in New York, I met a lovely man called Dan Farrell, what a sweet man. He approached the owner and she agreed. I had to do a presentation to all their sales reps. Boy, did I mess it up. I am hopeless. I stuttered, stumbled and went purple in the face… I was a total disaster. Everyone just looked at me and had no idea what I was trying to tell them. Well, it worked in a way; sales were good but not brilliant. Again, I hadn't got the 'Special Sales' way of selling over to them. One man caught on and went to see all the shops selling curtains and blinds, so bully for him but no-one else followed his lead.

Now we were in big time and needed to control the shipments from China.

Thank goodness for ABX as they handled everything for me.

So now we had colleges, fabric shops, John Lewis and Potterton's doing exhibitions, a German company also doing exhibitions called Westermann, Design Centre was covered with KLC design college and various showrooms like Wendy Cushing, run by lovely Stella, Wendy's number One saleslady. Then I approached a trimmings company in New York when I was there one day with Wendy Cushing. We went on a sales trip but also to have some fun, which believe

STOCK 31-3-08

	UK	ACC U.S.	ACCU.K.	TOTAL	VALUE
CSB 2	36	580	262	878	£ 1141
CSB 3	739	1272	120	2131	£ 2770
W & B	0	149	21	170	£ 221
W & B 2	947	1216	153	2316	£ 3010
* CR CARDS	124	448	0	572	£ 2059
* CR BOOK	14	237	0	251	£ 753
* CRBOOK (SC)	2478	1305	159	1601	£ 3874
BLINDS	557	878	166	1601	£ 3874
ACCESSORIES	3134	578	151	3863	£ 4635
C.F.S.	652	1058	216	1926	£ 3447
					£ 28453
TAKE AWAY CR CARDS, CR HB					2812
					£ 25641

me we had. The company was called Samuel and Son. Another nice man was Sam, the father of the business; he had two sons who joined the company and one son who was in IT, I think. Sam, who had started out in the markets selling trimmings and things has now transformed the company into a well thought of Passementerie company. And he had his own lift!

Every time I went to New York, he would show me off to his friends and take me out for a lovely lunch, such happy memories. I asked Sam if he would like a custom made Curtain Sketchbook. He jumped at it and we set to with a little help from their colourist Dinah. The book sold like hot cakes. They ordered two thousand at a time, and everyone was happy. It was best, once the quantities got so big, to print in China and ship direct to New York.

We also worked on a special book for Edmund Bell, called The Lining Sketchbook. I don't think it was a great success, and I doubt it made them much money, but it was difficult to make a book about linings!

Another bespoke book was for the South African trimmings company Castelano Beltrame and also Blind Fashion.

With the trade companies like Price and Co, Streets and MaCulluch and Wallis buying the books, we soon became well known throughout the UK.

One year I went to Abu Dhabi with Wendy Cushing who had a big stand there selling her Trimmings. In the centre of the stand, she had had shipped out an enormous tassel hanging from the ceiling. It looked great, but I got carried away as I often do. I went up inside it, so you could just see my feet, and pretended it was walking along on its own. Funny, but the whole tassel fell off its giant hook and brought part of the ceiling down in the exhibition hall! Both Wendys ran away until someone fixed it, typical Wendy behaviour!

Whilst Wendy was busy, I didn't seem to have many people wanting my books. On the second day, we were told the day was just for ladies. It was quite amusing as there were women everywhere and you could never really tell if they were looking at your wares or not. I'm afraid I fell into a trap as when two ladies approached the stand, I rushed forwards to explain how the books worked. I did my hard sell; they looked unimpressed, I thought. At that point Wendy came up behind me and whispered, 'You are talking to the ladies' backs!'.

AN ASIDE

Nowadays, if you just say the name Wendy Baker, my name at the time, the reply would be 'The Curtain Sketchbooks'. It seemed that every designer in the world had a copy of one of my books, not bad eh! They would still be selling if the Chinese had not copied them and even turned the sketches into wallpaper! What!

Chapter 13 part 4

A rough time for publishers - Amazon

However well Shoestring Books was doing and however much money we were making, there was never time to pat ourselves on the back or check on the 'opposition'. The publishing business, well 'Self Publishing' I suppose, was not really accepted as proper publishing by those established companies. Now it is different as it seems to me that 'Self Publishing' is becoming very popular. Some of those big publishers are worried about money and orders as all of them have high overheads. I don't think they give big 'upfront' fees anymore; also, they try to encourage new writers to pay themselves to publish their own books, with their guidance, of course. They are desperately hiring young school leavers to set them up on Social Media so that they can get followers...

spoke to an agent just the other day and was amazed that I was not asked how many books I had written but how many followers I had!

So, it seems best to work hard on one title, perfect it and then do a series of 6, or sell the first book to BBC, telling them that you are working on the next story in the series… and pray!

Proper publishers have a rather silly way of selling books. They issue a catalogue each season; then the book shops and book clubs place their orders with the knowledge that anything they don't sell can be returned! We, at Shoestring, never accepted 'returns'; we simply told our customers to only commit to a title they were sure they could sell. We also let them know how lucky they were to be allowed to sell our books…cheeky, but it worked.

We set up a deal with Amazon and the books sold well, but I didn't seem to make any money. I think this was due to the fact that ACC sent all their unused stock to them when we parted company.

Then a new scare, a while ago. Apparently, 'they' say that readers don't want paper books anymore. Then Kindle entered the equation, and I decided I had better try one of the books and see how it went before committing all of the titles. I found a nice guy from Canterbury who setup the Curtain Sketchbook 3 on Amazon website as an e-book. Well, this worked alright for a couple of years, and Amazon paid me every month. They paid me with no reference so It could have been 1000 copies or just one! Then out of the blue, the payments stopped. The e-book is still for sale, but nobody pays me. I have tried to get in touch, but I think it would be easier to get in touch with The Queen!

I have even said, 'I am sending the bailiffs,' and 'You are stealing from me'. So, if you want to buy an e-book or any of my books DO NOT BUY FROM AMAZON! EMAIL ME AND I WILL SEND YOU A COPY …signed.

At that stage, I was still working as an interior designer and thank goodness as I was getting bored. Dawson handled the shipments of books, so I was not needed. I spoke most weeks to Chrissie about possibly doing another book, but I couldn't come up with a plan.

On the next page are a few of my ideas, but none of them made the bookshelves, one day maybe.

Then Wendy Cushing and I went to Paris to a trade show called Maison. It was always exhausting walking the aisles of this show, but I always came away filled with ideas. Not that I didn't have plenty of my own, but it was always very stimulating.

One year, as I thought by then that I was really a fully-fledged publisher, I

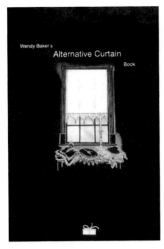

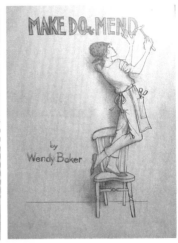

titles in pipeline

decided to go to Frankfurt Book Fair. Very grown-up and very exciting. I heard Bill Clinton talking about his latest book and various other exciting authors. I went with my friend Beth, who had just been very brave and set up her own publishing company, I mean a real one. She asked me to back her, but I was beginning to run short of cash and so declined. She has several titles to her name, and I think she must be making money by now.

At the Book Fair, all the important companies like Random House, Penguin and Ebury had drinks parties at the end of the first day. Shoestring Books didn't have a stand, but I threw a party on one of the trestle tables outside the exit door. I had wine and Frankfurter sausages, yum, and everyone enjoyed themselves. Then Wendy C., Beth and I hit the town. We hit the Frankfurt scene in a big way, not sure we remember much about it!

Chapter 13 part 5

The Chinese copy the Sketchbooks - Happy days in the country

Wendy Cushing works a lot in China and not so long ago went to Beijing for a trade exhibition. There she visited one stand and couldn't believe her eyes; they had printed all the sketches from the Sketchbooks and made wallpaper out of them. The wallpaper was on every wall on the stand! Also, they were selling my books, copies, of course. I thought I could sue them, but, apparently, there is no way to do this as they have no copyright laws in China. One day, the Chinese Embassy said, one day maybe!

no idea what it says!

I asked my Chinese printer if he had had anything to do with this. He said 'NO', and I believe him. So, that is the end of The Curtain Sketchbooks. Why buy a book when you can get the sketches free from PINTEREST and you can have matching wallpaper. Just put in 'Curtains' in Google, and there will be all my sketches! So that's that...

Dawson and I were still enjoying living in Ham, a little village just outside Hungerford. We had made so many friends at that time. Every evening we would cross the Ham green and go to the Hawleys for our usual drinks. It was the same every evening, but they were our really lovely friends, and we had watched their children grow up, so we always felt part of the family. I am still part of the family, but now I am on my own. I still know the Hawleys are not far away, but their lives are busy and I am not driving at the moment, so sadly I rarely see them!

The Old Malthouse and Sue our first visitor

Both Dawson and I always loved throwing parties; well, Dawson generally mocked everything I arranged, but I think he enjoyed himself, even if he growled a lot. We were, by this time, drifting apart in a big way again.. I thought when Sarah had left home, we wouldn't argue so much, but I was wrong. Unfortunately, we never spoke of the situation. I just worked, and he just sat watching TV, something that happens in many households, I think.

Then my poor mother decided she couldn't manage on her own anymore. Sadly, she hated Dawson, so I decided to find a home for 'gentlewomen'. My mother was alright with the idea, mainly as they had a glass of Sherry at 6 every day! Finally, I found a nice place not far away. The day we took her to move into her new home, Dawson got himself into a terrible state. I thought it was because of the situation but later found he had had his first stroke. He had got into the car to bring it around to the front of the house, then put the car into reverse, put his foot down and shot, at great speed, backwards into the lake, empty at the time.

That was the start of a pure nightmare for the next few years to come. Dawson had many TIAs and slowly he changed into a bad-tempered old man. Many of our friends didn't believe there was anything wrong with him, but after various tests and scans, the doctors agreed he had Vascular dementia. As nobody believed me, I had to manage the situation on my own. I spent most of the time pretending Dawson was just joking and didn't mean what he said. I can tell you it was hell, but I stayed. I don't know why, given that he was always making me feel inferior. He was rude to everyone, and especially me. He said I looked like a slug and things like that, so I switched off and worked harder. He said exactly what he felt; he would tell people they were fat or boring. I just carried on in a daze, wishing I could die. I didn't, but inside I was dead. Many of our friends deserted us one by one. I don't blame them as he was hurtful to everyone and had a habit of telling the most disgusting jokes to people he hardly knew. So, bit by bit, we were not asked out and as his driving petrified me, we rarely ventured out.

table all set then the rain came...so we moved it all inside!

Dawson's 60th birthday party..with the Pyramid cake!

We still had some lovely parties at the house at Ham, The Old Malthouse. Our friends from Salisbury were always such fun to be with, and to be honest, they seemed to ignore Dawson's behaviour. Actually, I think they thought I was the difficult one, not Dawson. He seemed to behave when he was with them, but the moment we left, he started again and drove erratically to frighten me. Then the moment I had dreaded for so long. My mother died. I never thought she would die. She was so strong in her mind; her body was a mess, but I think

she just got tired of living in pain, so she just left us. She died in a dreadful hospital in Swindon. She was dying and I was there holding her hand and calling Sarah on my mobile. She was trying to get up the M4, but traffic was bad, so the journey took ages. I kept whispering in my mother's ear, 'Hang on darling, Sarah is coming'. It seemed like several hours before she arrived, but mummy hung on in there, bless her. She did love Sarah so much. The two of them had a wonderful relationship. After all, I was always working to earn money, so I missed a lot of those happy memories... did I make a mess of being a mother, I wonder? Well I did my best in difficult circumstances.

My Mother was buried in Sheen/Richmond. She was buried at an angle, her feet in Sheen and her head in Richmond. She would have hated to be buried in Sheen, but it was a beautiful cemetery. My mother was a terrible snob! Auntie Barbara, Chrissie, Marion, Jane, Melina, and Daisy, her cleaner with her husband, all came. Michael, my stepbrother, was there with his daughter. It was a very simple service. She was at long last at peace with the world, she had had enough. Her life had been tough from the start but in the end, she did have everything she had wished for, except perhaps my wedding.

Chapter 14 part 1

Move to France - grass is always greener

After my mother's death, Dawson brought up the subject of moving to France. He had always wanted to live there since he sold his house in the Dordogne... I always said, 'I can't leave until my mother dies'. Now that had happened, I had no excuse. I didn't mind one way or another. I only ever wanted to be in Italy, my beloved Italy, so as France was closer to Italy than the UK, I agreed.

Of course, looking back it was another wrong move. But at the time, there seemed no reason to stay in Wiltshire. Like everyone that thinks the grass is greener on the other side, we thought only of sunshine on the beach at St Tropez or delicious meals at the Colombe d'Or in St Paul de Vence.

We broke the news to the Hawley's and our friends in Salisbury and told our lovely cleaner called Sue, that we were moving to France. Bill and Bunty threw us a 'leaving' party and for the first time the dream looked as if it was really going to happen.

Bill with his French Onions

The plan was to move, as near as possible, to Valbonne, a village in the hills above Cannes. It was a pretty little town but quite expensive, so we had to go back further; that was the first of many mistakes. We met a lovely lady called Brenda and she took us to see several stone houses, one she liked and thought we should buy, but I knew better, I thought. We finally decided on a fairly large house made of concrete, don't ask me why, but I had a plan. I wanted to have a big house, so we could let it out in the summer for vast amounts of money. That was the plan.

Well the project took two years, cost a lot of money and was not really finished, not the way I wanted it.

looking across the misty
Mimosa in the rain

The day we arrived at the house, Dawson, me and Beatrice, it was raining; it was heavy rain, and we just stood and looked out over the Mimosa and wondered what the hell we had done.

We looked down at the garden, which had been allowed to overgrow, and at the pool, which was now a pool filled with green slim!

We were taken for a ride from day one. A gardener, who was recommended, came and chopped all the weeds away, charged us £1000. There was a pool man, also recommended that charged us £1500 to clear the pool and a lovely electrician who did overcharge a bit, but he made up for it in other ways. He was so helpful to us; I think he understood we were depressed and homesick! I set to with my grand ideas, and we had one builder after another, all overcharging. Finally, we found a company called ACE, and they completed the house for us.

We met a wonderful couple called Ruth and James. James provided us with TV from UK. I think it was a bit illegal, but we didn't care by that time. We just wanted BBC news, and Ruth, his wife was a great cleaner and became a dear friend. Thinking back, we only had them as friends and Brenda, of course, as our village had no little cafes or markets. Our nearest village was Valbonne or

Dawson eating Langoustines in the walking street..such a happy bunny

Grasse, which was horrible. So, we were very lonely, and the winters were very cold, with snow and freezing ice. Well, the sun did shine quite a lot, and we were trying to make the best of a bad job, I kept telling myself. Sometimes we went out to lunch to Cannes, our favourite fish restaurant was there, and to Nice where there were several good places to eat in the walking street. We generally went there after a visit to the lovely market on a Monday.

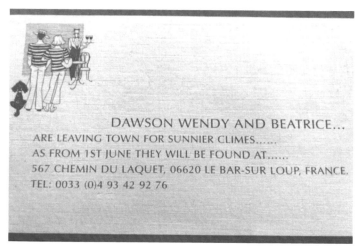

DAWSON WENDY AND BEATRICE...
ARE LEAVING TOWN FOR SUNNIER CLIMES......
AS FROM 1ST JUNE THEY WILL BE FOUND AT......
567 CHEMIN DU LAQUET, 06620 LE BAR-SUR LOUP, FRANCE.
TEL: 0033 (0)4 93 42 92 76

Then we decided to join the Anglo-French club.

Thank goodness we did, or we would never have met our special friends Robert and Caroline McGrail. I can remember when I first HEARD Caroline. I couldn't see her, but her voice bellowed across the room, and I thought she's fun and she was, well is! Our lives changed from then onwards. We saw quite a lot of them although they lived in Mandelieu, down near Cannes, so not exactly next-door neighbours.

Chapter 14 part 2

Renovating a villa in a foreign country - a nightmare

I didn't expect it to be easy. Turning the concrete block we had bought into a stone house, was never going to be easy. I had ideas about cladding the outside walls with old stone, but that was one step too far, I think. It made sense to me but trying to actually do it when I spoke very little French and definitely had no technical words, was a mission too far!

We had only two neighbours, on the left was a Brazilian Coffee magnet; we never met him as he was very ill. On the right were a French couple who disliked us. The only conversation we had was about our trees, which were hanging over their Boule pitch. The trees were Lime and apparently were ruining the pitch. They asked us to cut them down, and we said we would look into it and sort something out when we returned from London. When we returned, we couldn't believe our eyes. The Frenchman had poured petrol over the roots of our trees and they were dead! Difficult to be friends after that. So, we were completely alone, on our hill in Bar Sur Loup, a long way from Kensington, and miles from anywhere.

The tiles behind the range that turned out to be so boring!

Best to get on and renovate the villa. I decided to tackle the kitchen first. I'm still an interior designer and, let's face it, I have designed hundreds of kitchens before, so why would one be difficult? I shed more tears about this kitchen than I ever did with my clients' expensive kitchens.

Everything went wrong. I had it built using blocks which could be cut into all shapes; pity we don't have it here in UK, brilliant stuff. I had a pattern created over the range on the wall behind it from little tiles in rusty colours, and it looked really boring. I can't tell you how exhausting the whole experience was; everything I ordered was delivered in the wrong colour or wrong size. I had a feeling they were just being difficult to spite us! Call Brenda and cry down the phone, yet again!

The next step was the bathroom. I wanted a film star bathroom, try explaining that in French. Poor Brenda, my friend and estate agent, she had to keep coming to our rescue as her French was excellent. I managed the bathroom finally; the bath was in the centre of the room, with a wide rim around it for an ice bucket for Champagne or G&Ts, and the floor was all pebbles, like a beach. It looked stunning. There was a huge walk in shower and a lovely smoky blue Victorian day bed in the corner, very dramatic. When leaving the bathroom into the main bedroom, the view from our bed with the vines around our French doors and the swimming pool was superb, what more can you wish for. In the living room, we had a large log fire and British TV, that was a comfort, and, of course, my Kingcome sofas, which travelled the the world with me. The only thing keeping us going was to drink copious amounts of cheap French Rose wine.

The gardens around the house were enormous, and we had to have a gardener which seemed to cost hundreds of Francs every time. Again, we just paid, we were at their mercy. We had 14 olive trees and we thought it was an idea to go and talk to our local olive mill to see if they could help. They were only too happy to help. They would send 2 men to collect the olives; they just shake the trees into fabric on the ground. Once all the olives were collected, they would be crushed and made into Virgin oil. We would then share the proceeds. Easy. They arrived, collected all the olives, and we never saw them again, nor did we ever get our half share of our Olive oil…surprise!

The winters were so cold there, and the villa was cold too. So, often we decided to go out to a restaurant; we had a favourite in the village of Vence. It was called something like Grandma's, maybe not, but they liked us, and it was always nice to go there. Big log fires and an open fire for cooking over. Simple food, just steaks and jacket potatoes. We always got chatting to people, so it was like being at a family supper. It kept us going during this miserable time.

Sometimes we went down to Cannes for our special fish dishes or Juan Les Pins for a good Pizza followed by a banana ice cream. Near us we had the odd restaurant but nothing fancy and nothing worth leaving our lovely log fire.

Our lovely dog Beatrice, Bee, was the only happy one. Everyone in France loves dogs, and they chat away to them in French, ignoring the owners, of course.

So, Bee was always wagging her tail and rolling over. I wondered if I did that, maybe they would talk to me or rub my tummy, perhaps!

Every Friday, Valbonne, the nearest decent sized village to us, had a wonderful market. General junk but the odd 'find'; it was always busy and so wonderful that the village came to life for 5 hours. We were happy to be part of it.

French apple tart

his speciality tomato and pesto tarts

Dawson's effort was better than anywhere around us.

Afterward, we would have lunch in the square, not very good but the company was welcome.

Unfortunately, there was not many restaurants where the food was good around that area. That's when I came up with the idea of a cookery book called

The Villa

'Teach the French to cook!'. Shock horror, teach the French! But, honestly, we have learnt so much from them that, in some cases, we are better than they are...no publisher would touch it, shame!

AN ASIDE

Years later sitting here, I wonder what went wrong with our adventure. I suppose, it was because nobody came to visit us; they said they would, but life got in the way.

Suzanne and Simon Campbell Jones came down; they were always ready to support people. The Hawleys from Ham came, Bill and Bunty, and part of the Salisbury lot came a couple of times. Wendy C. came too and Mike and Jennie Tweedie. Sarah came once, but we seemed to argue, so that was an unhappy time for me.

Chapter 14 part 3

Adventures - markets - visitors

yellow noise machine that never stopped

Poor Dawson was beginning to get worse and what with the builders banging and drilling 24 hours a day. I think he was about to murder someone, me, I expect. So, a new plan, have some adventures. So, we made a list and went travelling.

I was still grieving for my mother. I seemed to have delayed shock, so going away from our worries was just what I needed. I found a lovely hotel in Lourmarin, not far from Aix. That was our first adventure. We drove to Aix on a Saturday, market day. A fabulous market, expensive, but I always wanted to buy everything. At 2 o'clock the market closed, and the stalls were taken away; then 'our' special restaurant was put together in that place. Wonderful food…and sitting in the middle of the hustle and bustle of a closing market was great.

After our lunch, we went to visit a French friend we had met some time ago. Goodness only knows where we met, I can't remember now. She was going to play the flute at her local church and asked if we wanted to come and hear her. We went and were amazed at the sound of her little flute flying around the enormous church, quite amazing. She played 'Ave Maria'; I have never heard anything so beautiful.

That night we went back to our hotel in Lourmarin and treated ourselves to the Gourmand menu. The first course was good, a green soup, pea I think; then we had an Asparagus mouse with a green sauce, and after that there was a breast of Chicken with sauté potatoes with a GREEN SAUCE on the side. We ate the Chicken and then ran out of the place splitting our sides; how much more green sauce could we eat?

The next day was Sunday, so we had booked at the best restaurant in the area, Bonnieu, run by 2 men who knew how to cook. When we arrived, it was very cold outside, and we were glad to be warm inside by the fire. Our meal took us 3 hours. We could see the snow coming down but didn't realise how deep it was until we tried to open the door to leave. The snow was so deep it was amazing that our car was still visible. We set off slowly and were not sure whether to continue or not. Well, we managed for about 10 miles, but we were sliding dangerously down the road, and there was a sheer drop on the driver's side. All of a sudden, just inside a little village, we shuddered to a halt. My immediate action was to call the AA... stupid woman, Dawson said, he was right. Out of the blue, five young men came rushing along the road and dragged us out of the ditch...we stayed with them and helped them finish a couple of bottles of wine. That seemed to help the car too, and we finally got back to our lovely hotel. Instead of a ghastly drama, it was very pleasurable, and we made some new friends.

When the weather cleared we ventured out to visit Arles. We had never been there before, so we decided to check it out. As luck would have it, we went on the right day. As we sat in the square having a coffee, a parade of Roman soldiers walked past, then various men dressed in loin cloths and twigs and various shrubbery strategically placed on their naked bodies wiggled past us. What the hell it was all about, I have no idea. It happened once a year, so we were lucky as it was very charming.

The Concierge at the hotel told us about a wonderful market in Apt, so off we went. Found a nice restaurant there as well, so we were happy again. It seemed to me that, really, Dawson and I just went from one restaurant to another, and, as long as the food was passable, we were content. Otherwise, the arguments took over, and it was quite a struggle. Very often we would leave the restaurant without paying, I'm amazed I didn't have a heart attack.with all the stress.

One of my favourite markets was the one at St Tropez. We would arrive early and have a coffee by the moored boats, the ones that never went out to sea; the 'posers' boats. Some of them had every luxury, water scooters, hot tubs and a staff of 5-6. They just kept cleaning the boat whilst the owners sat with big sunglasses on, checking out the competition...looked pretty boring to me. Then we would go to the market, generally not buying anything except the odd scarf or new pair of sunglasses, so as to keep up with the latest 'St Trop' fad; fun when you get back to UK to say, 'Oh these, yes I bought them in St Tropez'. Silly really, but we woman like to do that sometimes, suppose it's called showing off.

We often ate at a little place in the market, but, one day, having looked at the menu outside, we went into this very expensive looking café in the harbour. We were put at a table in an alcove; in fact, the waiter had to sort of push the table into the alcove as it was such a squeeze. We ordered some water whilst we looked calmly at the menu. Shock horror, we were so excited about the stuffed Courgettes flowers, and the Calamari with Chili dip that we hadn't noticed the prices. Well, there was no way we were going to pay those prices; so, how to get out from behind our little prison was quite a challenge. I decided that I would find a way to escape; after all, it was my mistake. I stood up letting out a dramatic sigh and said to Dawson loudly, 'I have to have air. I am trapped, let me out now!'. Everyone looked at me. I must say I was a brilliant. The waiter ran to the door clutching a glass of water and threw it open. I staggered out making odd noises, which were really me trying not to giggle. Dawson followed behind ringing his hands in despair. Once outside, we ran back to the car, doubled up with laughter. Whether anyone believed us I have no idea. So, that day we went hungry.

When the summer came, by which time we had almost finished the work on the villa, our phone started to ring. All of a sudden, we were popular, and we started to have visitors. Wonderful for us as we were so bored and lonely by this time.

Simon swimming in his hat naturally!

Suzanne and Simon Campbell Jones were the first to come. They are great company and very good friends. We would do the usual things; go to a couple of markets, go to Nice for lunch and a bit of shopping, sit by the pool and have scrumptious long lunches.

Just picking figs and black cherries in the garden or maybe just opening another bottle of Rose and playing Boule. This was what life was all about,

Nice picture of Sue Hawley, me and Dawson in St Paul de Vence before lunch.

friends, food and fun!

Bill and Bunty came down one year, and we had a great time. Bill always playing the clown, Dawson and Bill got on so well as they both told brilliant jokes, but as Dawson got worse, even Bill was keeping clear. This upset Dawson, of course; he didn't understand

how angry he was all the time. He used to go skiing with the 'boys' too, but they gave up on him and that was difficult for Dawson to understand as he loved his holiday with them. Poor Dawson, it upset me and him, but I understood, least I think I did!

Bill and Bunty were great fun always and we have happy happy memories of the 2 or 3 sunny holidays we had with them.

Our dear friends from Ham, the Hawleys, came a couple of times at the beginning when we were just trying to cope with the whole drama of the move. We were OK as long as we had a Cuba Libre or a Harvey Wallbanger in our hands by George Hawley who was in charge of the bar.

Bill and Bunty outside Colombe d'Or

A lot of drinking I think!

Bunty, Sarah. Jimmy and me... guess where!

with our friends the Campbell Jones at the Colombo D'Or

us and the Hawley's at the Colombe d'Or...of course

glorious Sunflowers in the South of France

Chapter 14 part 4

Starting work on a new book - Amazon

Life in France was decidedly better after we met the McGrail's, Caroline and Bob. They were game for most things and although they didn't have much money, they were great hosts and were always fun to be with. Often, we would grab a lunch in the square in Valbonne after the market on a Friday. During the summer, we would join them for lunch at the beach restaurant near their house in Mandelieu, called Le Sweet. Sea Bass and Rose, we always had the same, utterly delicious. Days on the beach at Le Sweet and lunches at the Colombe d'Or in St Paul de Vence will always be amongst my most favourite memories during the six years we spent in the South of France.

One of the funniest things happened to the four of us one day when we were going to the beach for the day. Parking was always a big drama, but this time we were lucky, or so we thought. Bob turned off the engine and we all started to open the car doors, when, like a bolt from the sky, a woman landed on the bonnet; like a pancake. Her legs wide open and her arms spread-eagled! She looked crazed, and she was shouting and spitting at the same time. The four of us just sat ridged, not daring to move. She continued for another few minutes, tearing off the windscreen wipers and scratching at the paintwork. Finally, she climbed off the bonnet and went back to, we presume, her terrified husband, who was perhaps waiting to park! We still laugh about it years later!

As I still had my mother's flat in Chiswick, I stayed there whenever I popped back to London. I popped back and forth quite often to see friends and to check on stock of the books and for a break from Dawson's bad behaviour. I would go out most days with my old friends like Jerry Mason, a photographer friend from many years ago. There were always people to see and check up on and it saved the day, rather than being with builders every day seemingly getting nowhere. I managed to collect 170,000 air miles too.

Every time I went back to France and Dawson and Beatrice came to meet me from Nice airport, I noticed a change in Dawson's behaviour. He was short tempered with the dog and with me, and I felt mean having left him alone for another week. So, I vowed I would get on and write two more books in France, instead of England, so as not to leave him alone. Also, the building works were so slow, and I couldn't really leave them too long on their own. I remember one day the builder said to me that he needed extra money for the walls.

I was furious as all he did was a day's work and then ask for more money. So, shouting at the top of my voice, across the valley of Mimosa I screamed, 'ma cheque book et dans ma poche!'. I slapped my back pocket and walked away; I think the builder was so shocked he never asked again!

Sales for the Curtain Sketchbook 2 and 3 were still strong, but I had a feeling that the public wanted something new. So, I put my thinking cap on and within a few days came up with an idea. I would do a how to make curtains and blinds book, and the title would be The Curtain Recipe Book. I set to, full of enthusiasm; this was going to be easy. I planned the outline of the book within a week but realised that the book would have to be for the complete novice, and maybe even for schools. It was far too simple for interior designers and obviously also curtain makers. I could always do a more complicated one with 'swags and tails' later if this was successful.

Then I also realised that although I did know roughly how to make curtains, I wasn't actually capable of teaching someone to make them from scratch.

As an interior designer, I designed the curtains, but my curtain makers, James Interiors, made them in the workroom. So, Chrissie had to come on board. She could make curtains, so I needed her once again. I dreaded asking her, but to my surprise she liked the idea and with loads of enthusiasm we started work. I had designed all the styles and all Chrissie had to do was draw everything in her usual wonderful style and check my instructions. This time, I asked her if she would like to come to France to work with me, and she was delighted.

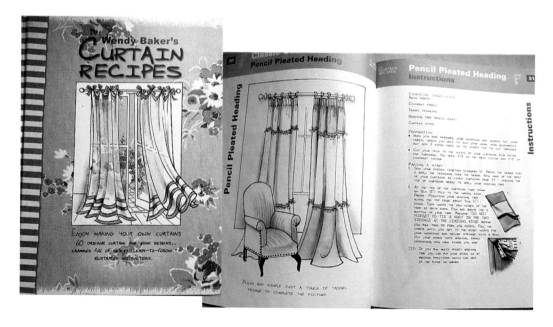

Meanwhile, I wanted a 'cute' cover, so as Cath Kidston was all the rage at the time, I asked her if I could use one of her prints; she agreed but charged me £250 for the honour.

Then I had a good idea and also designed a box of Recipe cards, which could be taken out of the box to the sewing machine, a gimmick that everyone loved.

Sometime later, Chrissie said, 'We didn't even go out to the village!'. I didn't realise I just made her work hard, then drove her to the airport back to Spain. What am I like?

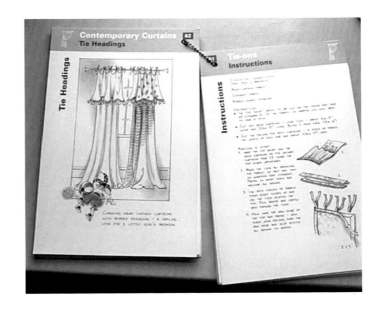

The first order was from Cath Kidston, she bought 100. Then another 20 a few weeks later, which I didn't actually have in stock. So, I had to make them especially for her. About 6 weeks later, her assistant called and said, 'We don't want them. Actually, I don't think we ordered them!'. I sent her a LATE PAYMENT letter and finally she paid, but she was not a happy bunny. What a strange way to do business.

Our next order was for 30,000 from Dunelm Mills! I couldn't believe it, so I called to check with the buyer expecting her to say 300 or even 3000 but no, she wanted 30,000! Actually, they never ordered anymore, and I have a feeling they were not a success. Why, I don't know. Maybe I didn't market them properly as now I can see I should have targeted schools and sewing classes at colleges.

AN ASIDE

Thinking about the sales of these books now, I think I should try marketing them again. They will sell, I am sure. I just have to find the right market, and that's the same with anything you design. You can't just design something and expect it to sell itself. Yes, I will have another go!

Chapter 14 part 5

Sailing in the Virgin Islands - Goodbye Jean

We went to have lunch one day with Caroline and Bob, and they were buzzing with news. It was going to be Bob's 70th birthday in a few weeks' time, and Caroline and four of their friends had arranged a sailing holiday to the Virgin Isles. Bob and Caroline were beside themselves with excitement. That was all they ever wanted to do in life and as this was most probably going to be the last trip in their lives, they planned to do the 'works'. I was quite jealous, really, having never been on a yacht, let alone sailed to the Virgin Isles.

A few days later, Caroline called to say one of the members of the crew had just been diagnosed with cancer and had decided to cancel their trip. Understandable, of course, but I hadn't been expecting the next part of the conversation. 'We have had a meeting with the others going on the trip, and we all decided that we would like to ask you to join us!' My immediate answer was, 'Thank you, but no'. The thought of Dawson upsetting everyone was more than I could face. By now I was exhausted with his constant shouting and being in a confined space would be disastrous for sure.

I got on with cooking the supper, but whilst I was chopping up the garlic, I started to say to myself, 'When is anyone going to ask you to join them on a yacht sailing to the Virgin Islands again?'. NEVER, so I picked up the phone to Caroline and said 'YES!'.

I don't know if it was the most wonderful holiday I have ever had or not. I think parts of it were, but other parts were not. Not just Dawson being difficult. He was, partly because he slipped and hurt his Coexist, and partly because he was just bloody minded. We had a slight clash with the other couple. She didn't like to sleep with the air conditioning on, so we all sweated all night. The cabins were very small, so some nights I would go up on deck to cool down. Her husband was generally up there for the same reason, but she didn't like that. So, I stopped it; therefore, neither of us got much sleep. We had a kitty for the shopping and we three women would go ashore to stock up. To Caroline and me that meant copious amounts of Rose as well as basic food, but to the other woman, it meant bananas. She ate only bananas, so that's what we bought Rose and Bananas and then there was, of course, an argument about the difference in the price. I gave up, and poor Caroline was left to sort it out.

It didn't help that Caroline and I got on really well and laughed a lot, and I realised that the situation was becoming tense.

Caroline was a real ships mate. She helped Bob on board, she cooked a fry up every morning and produced a meal most evenings, and she kept the peace. I think without her, we would have all shot each other.

I loved sailing, the wind in my hair, the seagulls crying above us. We waved to other boats and when we moored in the bay, there would be 'an ice cream boat' coming alongside to sell us lollies or coconut ice cream.

We went to many lovely little towns, all painted with vibrant colours, and the locals selling their goods on the Quay.

The big night was Bob's 70th birthday. We went to St Peter's Island and had a wonderful meal. We were all dressed up in our best gear as we had been told to do, but the Americans were dressed in shorts and had caps on with fans on the top. Typical American behaviour, can't take them anywhere!

One day the clouds started to gather and as it was getting quite dark, Bob suggested we go and moor the yacht in the Marina to sleep. We had to go through customs first, of course. The young man, in a shiny new Customs uniform, was at the dock. We handed all our passports in, and we were just laughing and chatting to each other when he said, 'Only Robert McGrail and his wife are welcome to step ashore. The rest of you must leave within five minutes!'. Bob started to object saying these are my guests, but the young man pumped himself up and said, 'You and your wife have American passports, but your friends don't, so leave now!'.

By this time, the sea was very rough, and the waves were beginning to lap over the deck. It was now dark and breezy. Bob said, 'Don't be ridiculous. We can't set sail in this. It's too dangerous'. The Customs man just looked straight ahead and said, 'If you get into trouble, call the Coast Guards!'.

So, we had to set sail. Luckily, Bob was a good navigator, and we managed to get to the next island in one piece, what a fright.

Shows what a uniform can do for some people!

Shortly after we got home, poor Beatrice (our special French speaking Cocker Spaniel) was not well. The vet diagnosed her with Pancreatitis. She had eaten some pork chops out of the food bin which might have caused the problem, but for three weeks it was touch and go. The vet was wonderful and every evening she let us come to the surgery and give Bee a cuddle. All ended well and finally we had the all clear; our baby had survived.

Life went back into its set pattern of shopping, cooking, eating and swimming. We went to a few Anglo-French dinner parties and met a few new people but nothing exciting. Well I say that but there was one lovely couple who were actually American. He used to work for Campbells Soups and seemed to have a hell of a lot of money. He bought his wife a theatre in Antibes called The Red Pear Theatre. She produced plays and had all her actor friends coming over to appear in them. Fabulous idea. I don't think they made money, but it was amazing to be part of the whole experience. We would buy tickets and see the play; then they would ask people they liked to come home with them where supper would be waiting. We were in favour and went for supper a couple of times. First time an actor friend of mine Edward De Sousa was in the play, our daughters went to school together, so it was nice to catch up. The next time I sat next to Art Garfunkel, of Simon and Garfunkel fame, and we got on like a house on fire, a lovely evening. I heard much later that the theatre had to close as it was not making money. Very sad, but happy memories for us.

It was 3am in the morning when the phone rang. It was Jean calling from New Zealand. She was crying, she was dying. I tried to take it all in, but I couldn't make sense of what she was saying. Apparently, she had had a lump in one of her breasts and not bothered to go to the doctor. Marjorie, her sister, finally persuaded her to go to have a check-up. It was breast cancer, and it was too late to save her. She was going to die, and she needed me there. I sat up properly in bed and without turning on the light, I got out of bed. To my horror, my feet were totally submerged in water!

Apparently, the rain had been building up in the hills and finally it burst forth heading for our house, like a river. As our bedroom was on the ground floor, the water found its way in and flooded our bedroom and bathroom. Whilst Dawson called Brenda for help, I phoned to book a flight to New Zealand. It cost me £3000 Business class, but I didn't care. I knew I had to be with Jean.

The taxi came to take me to Nice airport, and, as I looked back at the house, there were 3 men chucking boxes over the driveway; all my china, all my precious things just being flung out of the way of the torrent of water…I had to go, I had to be with her.

The journey, if you have ever done it, was long, very long. Thank goodness I had flown Business class, so it was bearable. Sammy, my goddaughter, was there to meet me. We hugged and drove into Auckland.

Jean was overjoyed to see me. I had got to her in time. She was looking thin and a bit of a funny colour, but she was alive. They had recently had to take one breast off and Jean being Jean wanted the other one off too, so she was even! She even had a proposal from a male friend of hers to come over and make love to her for old time's sake! Men!

Sammy had arranged a house where we could all stay as there were several people coming to say 'goodbye' to her. That was a drama in itself. The agent had double booked the house, so when we arrived, there was someone else living there. With much shouting and cross phone calls, we moved in. It was like a squat, but we couldn't complain as poor Sammy was beside herself with worry. Still, she was strong, like Jean, and coped as well as can be expected. Marj, Jean's sister, arrived a few days later; in fact, people were coming out of the woodwork. Somehow, we all got fed, and we all had somewhere to stay; even if it was grim, it was a bed.

Jean wanted to go around to say 'goodbye' to everyone, so Sammy drove us around. We had a 'goodbye' tea party for all her art class pals then we went to see the 'Flynns', the group called Crowded House. Jean was very edgy most of the time. I was exhausted, but Jean wanted to keep going. We had lunch in Auckland with a dear friend of ours, Tony with the beard, and I left them to say 'goodbye'.

A few days later, we packed up Jeans little flat and all moved to Arrowtown on South Island. A pretty little mining town. Sammy lived there, so thankfully things calmed down a bit.

I didn't take in much of the scenery as we were all on edge. I had hoped to talk to Jean, but there was always someone hanging around, so we didn't talk. A couple of weeks later, Sammy said she had booked Jean and me into the Hilton in Auckland. Thank goodness, some time to ourselves. The room was amazing. We looked out to sea and, at the time, there was an important yacht race on. The yachts went under our room, quite extraordinary. We had an Oyster supper and met up with some people. As I was talking, too much I suppose, Jean said loudly, 'Don't talk to them. I'm the one that is dying'.

So, I realised she was scared, but we never talked about it.

We went back to Arrowtown, and I knew my time had come to leave. I had been there for 3 weeks, and Marjorie and Sammy could be with her. I was not really being any help at all. So, Sammy cooked some supper and said she and her husband David were going out. That way, Jean and I had time to say 'goodbye'. Jean didn't know this was the last night we would be together. We put the video Cabaret on and danced around the room; then we played our favourite songs from Barbra Streisand, then watched a new singer called Robbie Williams …and she said, 'Watch out for this guy. I think he will go far'. And, of course, she was right; he did.

We cuddled and cried, we cuddled and laughed, we drank too much and then fell asleep.

Early the next morning, Sammy and I crept out of the house so as not to wake Jean.

We drove to the airport in silence. Dropped my bag at the desk and then there was lots of commotion behind me. Jean and her sister were there! 'There's no way you are leaving me without a final kiss, kid!'. Well, that was all I needed for floods of tears to cascade out of my eyes. Most people at the airport joined in too, so I had a good send off.

AN ASIDE

I flew to Sydney for two days before my flight back to UK. I stayed at the 'W' hotel on Woolamarroo but stayed in my room. I didn't want to face the world. At one point, I wanted a bath, but the bath was so huge that I kept slipping down almost drowning. Beside the bath was a phone with a notice. WHATEVER WHENEVER. It's 'W's motto. So, I phoned down to ask reception to send up a young man as ballast! They fell about laughing but they didn't send anyone!

ANOTHER ASIDE

About three years later Sammy called from New Zealand and said she was bringing Jean's ashes home. She asked for Sarah, Marjorie and me to meet at The Sun in Barnes in a couple of weeks' time.

We all met, had a glass of Rose and toasted Jean. Sammy had put a little of Jean's ashes in 4 Tupperware boxes for us. We all chose a place to scatter her ashes. Sarah came up with the idea to go to the Brook and drop the ashes over the bridge like Poo sticks. Jean would have liked that. I took mine to my flat in London and to the beautiful Norland Square gardens and sprinkled them around my swing chair. So, at last we have a special space together.

Chapter 15 part 1

Warrington Crescent - Nail bar

When I returned from being with Jean, we decided to go home to the UK. We put the house on the market, and it took some time to sell. The estate agent had said he could get about a million pounds, easily; then changed his mind and dropped the price to £700,000. We didn't care in the end as we were ready to clear out of France. The latest horror was that the Tunisians, living in Grasse, were coming down to the villages like Bar sur Loup and putting gas into the air conditioning to drug the inhabitants, so they could rob them. That was the bitter end; we were off.

We planned to go to stay in Chiswick at my mother's old flat to look for a property. Then perhaps we would sell her flat or rent it out. We were lucky as almost the first property we saw was the one. It was just a large room in a wonderful road in Little Venice. The big bay window overlooked the most beautiful garden square, iron steps down to the garden for Bee. All it needed was my expertise to turn it into a flat for the 3 of us.

Everything went very smoothly; the builders were excellent. Of course, it cost more than expected, but that is always the case.

We hadn't been there long before the elderly lady living below moved, and her flat went on the market. We thought it would be sensible to buy her flat too, but we hesitated and didn't buy it. Bad move as we could have had a large maisonette in a fabulous street. The people who moved in were unpleasant, and, before long, they asked us if we would sell our flat to them. They said, 'name your price'....so I did and asked £800,000. Not a bad profit when we bought it for £245,000! They then turned it into a maisonette, and it was valued at £2.5 million! Damn!

Dawson and I had decided to go back to live in the country as we had our friends, the Hawleys, and the 'Salisbury lot' there. Really, I didn't have the energy to make new friends after the France headache.

So again, we found something that was perfect for us. Only problem was that the agent, Knight Frank and Cutlery, hadn't managed to persuade the lady of the house to sell. Her husband wanted to move, but she was hanging on. I understood; she had lived there for 20 years and brought her children up in the cottage. I decided I wanted it, so I offered another £100,000. They said yes, but then I came to my senses and lowered the offer by £75,000 over the asking price. They accepted.

before

We had a lot of work to do on the cottage, Bridge Cottage, Little Bedwyn, but the couple didn't want to be rushed. So, we agreed to a delayed completion date of three months.

after

Beatrice loved it especially in the snow as you can see!

Meanwhile, I had a new project to start on. One morning I had a call from a young girl, saying that she had heard I was an amazing interior Designer, and she thought I would be perfect for this particular project.

She asked me to meet her at the premises, which were in Formosa Street, just around the corner from the flat in Warrington Crescent. As that was convenient, I agreed. She, or was it her dreadful stepfather, had bought a whole building and wanted to open a nail bar on the ground floor and basement. What she needed from me was an image, one that she could use when she opens lots of nail bars around the country. Her name was Tilly and that was to be the name over the door. I spent some time talking to her to see what made her happy. Also, I needed a budget. She had grand ideas but not a very big budget; that's usual with my clients. There was something odd about Tilly, and when I met her stepfather, Stuart, I knew what it was. She was completely under his thumb, and he was extremely unpleasant. Basically, he treated everyone with contempt, which is difficult if you want the best out of your crew. That meant I had to work harder to make up for his rudeness.

I came up with a couple of ideas, and she liked the 'farm one' - lots of stripped and washed pine. A big desk in the middle of the shop with high stools all around it, and a giant clock hanging from the ceiling. There was a coffee machine and you could have as much as you could drink. There were bails of straw dotted about upstairs and downstairs. I had created some private cubicles for any of her famous celebrates, which Tilly continually mentioned. As my builders were renovating the flat at Warrington Crescent, I was a bit stuck. I asked a friend if she knew any builders. Her husband was Moroccan, and there are a lot of Moroccans in London who were not, I found, very good builders; but at the time I didn't know that. Tilly wanted the whole job done over Christmas, and as they don't celebrate Christmas, it worked out well. To start with, everyone worked hard, but then everything went wrong, all at the same time. The electrician was chatting to Stuart and was asked if he was a qualified electrician; the Moroccan said, 'No, I'm nearly finished the course!'. Well, that did it. As the building was being used as commercial premises, the electrician had to be qualified; you can't have an apprentice working on the job. The builder said, 'Don't worry. We can get a qualified electrician to issue a certificate'. Of course, that doesn't work. So, we were reported to the council, and they sent an inspector around. They insisted that the job had to be done all over again PLUS the upstairs floors which hadn't actually been done by my team. I paid a new electrician £2000 and had to deduct it from the builder. I felt sorry for them, but I tried to explain to them that I had asked and was told that the man was qualified. So, the lie cost them £2000, and they were not happy.

Everything seemed to be on time, and it began to look like my drawings, quite rewarding, normally. But in this case, the stepfather was creeping around looking for trouble. He started to criticise everything, so there was a terrible atmosphere. I decided to get the team to speed up and they did. The only thing to be done was the floor, which had to be painted with floor paint. I got the paint, told them that they must sweep and wash the floor before the paint, then left.

About 4 hours later, Tilly was on the phone crying. The stepfather was swearing in the background. I put the phone down and rushed up the road. The builders had been told to leave the premises; they were cowering in the doorway when I arrived. 'What the hell has happened?' I shouted. The builders were terrified, and I told them to leave until I had sorted out the problem. The damn builders had decided they wanted to get out as soon as possible; so, thinking no one was watching them, they painted all the furniture and the floors without sweeping them first. They hadn't even rubbed down the metal furniture! You could see the lumps of dirt on the floor. What made them think they could get away with it, I don't know! Anyway, Stuart wouldn't pay them and had arranged for new painters to start the next day. I argued with Stuart saying that the outstanding money had to be paid, but he was adamant that he was going to deduct £4000 for the painting, saying that the new painters were charging that so he would deduct it from my invoice. I didn't have a leg to stand on.

I went the next morning to clear up the builders' mess and to collect the cheque from Stuart. When I arrived, there was a terrible atmosphere; obviously Stuart and Tilly had told the new painters what a dreadful set of builders I had. They whispered and had smirks on their faces, uttering things like, 'These stupid interior designers. They have no idea what they are doing. It gives the trade a bad name!'. I was close to tears, but I hadn't got a leg to stand on, so I fled the premises. Looking back at the shop, I was proud of the final design, but nobody had a nice word to say to me...really unfair, but I was to blame for the builders' bad work.

Trying to explain to the head builder why they had £2000 deducted for electrics and £4000 for the bad painting was very very difficult as his English wasn't that good and he couldn't understand why there was a deduction. He had completed the project, he said, and he wanted to be paid...I mentioned the standard was not good enough...but I had to just walk away. Now, I am known as a bad payer, which I am defiantly not, but hey walk on!

Unfortunately, the builders were recommended by my dear friend Wendy's husband, so it was difficult, but our friendship is strong. We are really good friends. She is a strong woman like me and talented like me; called Wendy too!...she is one of the kindest people I know, and I hope we will be friends forever...even if she talks nonstop 'POM POM talk! When we sold Warrington Crescent, we had three months to wait before we could move into our new house by the canal, so we rented a little cottage in Lechlade, tiny but we were quite happy there for a change! Also, we had such a lovely house to go to... happy days ahead...maybe!

Chapter 15 part 2

Bridge Cottage my dream project

We had all our furniture, some from France and some from Warrington, in various storage places. I had thrown or given away a lot of our furniture. It never suits the next house, I find, but there are always pieces I won't part with, like the big Mahogany chest of drawers, the Bergere 3-piece suite and, of course, the 2 Kingcome sofas. They get dragged from house to house. The covers are remade, the colour of the paint is changed, but they are still mine, and I will never part with them.

The day we moved into the cottage, Sue Hawley came over to check it out, and she approved. We had fish and chips and went to bed early as moving, even if we were frequent movers, was always exhausting. Everything looks better in the morning. Tonight, I was thinking we had too much furniture. I'd misjudged the room sizes.

Chrissie drew us arriving on a barge, Me Dawson and Bee

The morning came and I was right, we had found paradise. The ducks were quacking at the back door. I looked out of the window, and there was a Kingfisher sitting on the end of the little pier.

The cottage consisted of 3 bedrooms and 2 bathrooms upstairs. Downstairs was going to be opened up to make a living room, leading to a conservatory which ran beside the pretty canal. The kitchen was small, but we intended to lose the dining room and make one enormous kitchen, utility area, a loo and a flower room. Wonderful. Then we had an annex which we intended to do up and let. Great plan, I kept saying to myself. Let's hope this time it works. The builders moved in and we tried to live around them. The dust was the worst part, but what the hell. You have to suffer a bit of dust and banging if you want to live in paradise!

It was hard work trying to turn a run down, out of date cottage into our dream place to live. Dawson and Beatrice were bored already. Dawson complained continuously, and Bee took to her bed. As usual, I was on my own, but I was confident that my plan would work. I worked like mad choosing the beams for conversion of the little barn, trying to make the cottage cosy and a home, not a designer's dream but a 'mother hen' trying to make her depleted family a happy home.

Whilst the builders were breaking down walls and rebuilding them in different places to enlarge the ground floor, I decided that it would be an idea to get to know the villagers. The best way to do that was to volunteer to help with the flowers at the church. So, I found a number for the Parish church and offered my services. They were very grateful and said that my name would be added to the rota for church flowers, and I would be working with three other ladies from the congregation. I had a call a few days later to say could I help out this Saturday as one lady had been taken ill. Of course, I agreed. It was suggested that I bring the greenery as the flowers were already at the church.

Off I went on that Saturday morning, a bit nervous as I had no idea what one actually had to do. But I took some secateurs and some ferns for the display. When I arrived, I went into the church and said 'hello' to the two ladies already working on the flowers. They took one look at me and downed tools and left without a word. I just stood in the empty church not knowing what I had done. Then I realised that one of the women was the person we had bought the canal house from. She made our lives a misery as she obviously couldn't forgive us for buying her cottage. Every fair, every local pub, in the only local shop, she had told them what we had done. Nobody spoke to us. It was a nasty thing to do, but it was no good trying to change their minds; they didn't want to hear our side of the story. How sad. I was so angry and there was no way I was going to walk into that church again. I thought church goers were better than that. At the end of the garden, we had raspberry and strawberry nets and various beds ready to plant vegetables, so Dawson was put to work there. At least, it stopped him kicking the builders' tools across the room!

Bridge cottage

BRIDGE COTTAGE
Little Bedwyn, Wiltshire

spent too much money!

Bit by bit the cottage was transformed. When it came to the painting upstairs, one of the bedrooms had measurements up the wall, and I realised that it was the measurements of the three children who had lived there, so we left them uncovered. Why, I don't know as the mother had been so rude to me, but I just thought they were too special to cover up.

Dawson and Jerry on his birthday

the little quay and the even smaller boat ready for Jerry's surprise.

We decided to have a party once the cottage was finished, and as it was Jerry's 80th birthday, we would have one for him. Bill and Bunty had a little rowing boat that they didn't want anymore, so we asked if we could give it to Jerry. Jerry was a photographer, but he was originally a sailor, and loved the water. So, we hoped this little boat would make him happy.

Once again, we seem to have no friends around us, other than the Hawleys. Most of our friends were spread apart, so it was an effort to go visiting them, and they rarely came to visit us. So, we had to make the effort.

We let the little annex easily, and one tenant was special; her name was Caroline and she was taking a course locally, to become a therapist. We asked her to supper occasionally but didn't want to become friends particularly. One day Dawson and I had a terrible argument. Dawson kicked the bedroom door so hard, in one of his violent fits, the door stuck, and there was no way we could get out. The only thing we could think to do was to call Caroline, thank goodness for mobile phones. We explained what had happened; well, we made up a slightly less violent version. I explained where there was a long ladder and we also needed a screwdriver a saw and hammer! Bless her, the next thing we saw was Caroline, in one of the builders' hard hats, climbing up the ladder clutching the tools. We fell about laughing. Dawson set to and managed to cut the door away from the damaged frame. Never a dull moment.

Caroline was on a grant from the Wiltshire county council and so didn't have much money. One of her interfering boyfriends got in touch with the council and asked if she had to pay council tax as she was a student.

That was it. The next day, a council worker knocked on the door and asked to see the little annex. He brought with him papers relating to the main cottage and the annex. Apparently, the previous owners never registered the annex, so they hadn't paid tax for years. A few days later, we got a fine and a £3000 backdated bill. In future, we would have to pay £1000 more a year. It was disastrous as I was not earning much money and the plan worked on paper but with the extra bill, we had to think of something to do to earn more money. I had a couple of smallish projects in London. A flat in Shepherd's Market for Brenda, our friend from France, and one for my crazy therapist in Surbiton. Neither contract would make me much money, and the one in Surbiton nearly drove me mad...another story, another time. Dawson continued to kick the dog; the builders had gone, so there was only TV to watch 24/7, very loudly! Life wasn't exactly what I had envisaged.

Chapter 15 part 3

My dog Beatrice - car crash - Richard Branson

My poor Beatrice, Bee, was blind now and deaf. She was not in pain and slept most of the day. Every morning, I took her for a walk up the canal path, past the lock, and then for another half a mile. It was a routine walk. One particular morning, we did a quickie, just to the lock and back as I had to get on the M4 to go to a contractors' meeting in London. I called out to Dawson to keep the canal gate closed and left.

I had lunch with Jerry at Carluccio's in Putney, as usual, after the meeting and then returned down the M4 to home.

As I drove into the driveway, I looked for Bee. She always came to meet me when I came back from London. She was not there, strange. So, I went to look in her bed, not there. I asked Dawson where she was, and he didn't know and went back to the TV. I found the back gate open! Dawson, as usual had left the bloody back gate open.

I called Sarah to come and help me look for her. So, half an hour later the two of us split up and walked both ways along the canal. She was nowhere to be found.

a right off... of course!

Then Sarah came over to me and put her arms around me. She had found my Bee. She had drowned in the lock, there was about 4' of water in it, and nobody heard her squealing, so she drowned. She must have thought she would go for another walk as we did in the morning. She was blind, and we think when she turned to come back, she must have misjudged how near she was to the lock.

Sarah was wonderful.

She wrapped Bee up in her favourite blanket, and we went to find a basket for her. She was buried in Sarah's garden in a Fortnum and Mason's picnic basket.

I must say, I couldn't get myself up and running afterwards. My life seemed to be filled with nothing. I had lost my little Bee. So, a few days later, I decided to go and see Sarah and to put flowers on Bee's grave. I drove along the A338 towards the M4, and, as I drove, I looked down to check Bee, to see if she was OK, the car hit the high curb and spun across the road, missing cars coming the other way. My Mini crashed into a wall and the trees in front of the wall came through the windscreen. The airbag nearly knocked me out, and for a moment I was stunned. I looked down at my feet and saw that the engine was not there. It looked to me like the gap was in fact fire, so I managed to get the window open and climbed out rolling down the slight decline. That's all I remember. The ambulance was there, the Hawleys, Dawson and Sarah were all there for me.

I got away with virtually no injuries, except I had painful arms and shoulders as I had hung on to the steering wheel when I hit the trees. The hospital sent me home. Sarah put me to bed with a hot water bottle and a cup of tea, and I cried myself to sleep.

The Police came to interview me the next day. They seemed to think I had tried to kill myself, not true. They asked me for my driving licence and explained that it was out of date as I was now 70 and it had to be renewed every 3 years. They could see how upset I was and decided not to charge me.

I couldn't go near the canal; I could hear Bee squealing, in my imagination. My bedroom was just beside the lock, so it was more than I could bear. Dawson didn't feel any sympathy for me. He just said I was cruel to keep her alive anyway, as she was blind, and went back to TV channel swapping.

I decided to sell the house and go and live nearer to Sarah in Cirencester. Not one of the neighbours came to say how sorry they were; it was as if we didn't exist. I only had Sarah, really, and I felt I wanted to be nearer to her.

Frank Knight and Cutlery loved the cottage, and I put it with them to sell.

A friend of Richard Branson's, Robert Devereaux, finally bought it for his son who was at Marlborough. Robert, who I think was involved with SOHO HOUSE at the time, wanted the look I had created as it was similar to the SOHO HOUSE LOOK. So, he insisted that he wanted to buy everything, including furniture and lighting. When I said, 'NO,' he said, 'Then I won't buy it!' So, because I didn't care anymore, I said 'OK'. Except my 3-piece Bergere and the Kingcomes. I also added that I would not sell the French wheelbarrow which he really coveted. Why I wanted the wheelbarrow I do not know, but it became a matter of principle. Robert insisted he had to move his son in on the day we moved out. He was going to Africa the next day to protect white Rhinos or something. It was a nightmare, and it ended up with us leaving many of my most precious paintings behind on the towpath. We never recovered them. Robert was married to Richard Branson's sister, and then they split up and when Robert left, Richard never forgave him. I think it was something like that.

AN ASIDE

I remembered when I first met Richard Branson. I had been asked to have lunch with a group of influential businesswomen, and Richard Branson had been asked to attend the luncheon at The Royal Lancaster Hotel to see if anything we had to put forward was of any use to Virgin. Richard introduced me to his father who was delightful, and we chatted away until luncheon was served. I sat down beside his father and a couple of seats away from Richard, who then joined in our conversation. I was about to speak to Richard about a venture that he might be interested in when a loud clatter and lots of gasps later an entire roast turkey meal landed on my head then slid down my body! The waiter screamed, so did I as they rushed me into the kitchen to try to clean me up. Half an hour later, when I went back to the table, Richard had left. He had a meeting to go to, so I never put my scheme to him. Pity, it was a good idea if I remember!

ANOTHER ASIDE

Actually, the first time I really met Richard Branson was in an alleyway shop in Notting Hill Gate where he was selling copies of records or videos, I think...

Chapter 15 part 4

I could go on, but I won't!

The cottage was sold. We moved into a rented lake house just outside Cirencester, whilst we were deciding what to do next. We bought another dog, a Cocker Spaniel, of course, called Harriet, or Harry for short. I just wanted to keep the name alive, as I was no longer using it as my design name. Harriet was, and is, one of the loves of my life. She looks after me and we love each other.

Then Sarah found us a lovely cottage for us to rent on Cecily Hill, in the centre of Cirencester, which was supposed to be a temporary move until we found a house to buy, but 7 years later here I am, alone, with my wonderful dog Harriet. Dawson died eighteen months ago, Did I let him down in the end? ...Yes, I suppose I did, but I think I deserve a medal for years and years of hell. I say that but, I stayed, we did have some amazing times too and those are the ones I'm trying to remember now...I'm happy on 'the hill,' I have a few really nice friends around me, and a new 'best' friend called Norma!

I also have a tiny flat in Holland Park which I love. It's for my London life for I am, if nothing else, a Londoner. Well, 58% is Greater London and the remainder is 5% Irish and 37% Northern European, in other words I'm a VIKING! I think, maybe, that's enough from me. You may have been bored to death, for which I am sorry, or maybe you enjoyed my little memoir. Anyway, as far as I am concerned, I've done it. Of course, there was a lot I missed out, events that were not necessary to mention, or perhaps would have hurt some people, so best left unsaid.

The parts untold I will write in another short memoir just for me to put it in words, then I will burn it!

So, now I can look back and realise that all I did, all that working my guts out, trying to prove I was something special didn't get me anywhere. I've ended up with some money, a lovely daughter, lovely dog and some amazing friends...I didn't marry, maybe Mr Right didn't come to find me, or maybe I didn't think a piece of paper would make a difference to my life. My mother would have been happy, I know, but I think I have done enough to get my mother's approval! I tried to become what she wanted, and I almost did achieve that, but I am a rebel and I intend to go out as a SPINSTER...as Wendy Darling.

Chapter 15 part 5

Memories

My Family

1

2

3

4

5

6

My Daughter

1

2

3

4

5

6

7

8

My Animals

1

Simon

4

2

3

5

6

12

7

9

8

10

11

1

2

3

4

5

6

7

8

9

10

11

12

13

14

15

16

347

Photographs Index

My Family

My Daughter

My Animals

My Friends

Some of my favourite pictures

am I free at last?

THE VERY LAST ASIDE

Is getting old when you start to open boxes on the top shelves of the wardrobe or the ones shoved under the bed, long forgotten, those boxes you have lugged from home to home but unmarked and rarely opened, just ignored?

You know one day you need to open them although they are full of memories and general rubbish. But they can never be thrown away as they hold your past. Love letters, funny ones, sad ones and those very serious ones: 'Darling I love you so much I can hardly breathe when you are not at my side' or 'Without your hand in mine I can't see my way forward' or maybe 'I will love you until I die…and even 'just hearing your voice and kissing your yearning lips is all I live for. 'SHIT' is all I think as I read those love letters! Where are those guys now? Did they die of love for me when I left or are they just old like me and I am just a distant memory?

What amazes me is that I have had such a full and exciting life and I worked so hard to achieve what I thought was important but I never gave myself time to 'stand and stare.' I didn't see an end, I didn't notice that time was flying past and now all I can say is 'where the hell has my life gone?'

Could I have played it differently? I'm sure I could have planned it better, but life just happens, and when things are thrown at you react accordingly to suit that moment and making a plan doesn't work. Perhaps in hindsight you can mentally correct things but then it's too late. Boy did I have things thrown at me, I ducked some of them but as I have not lived before I acted accordingly… later down the line you may stop and look back briefly to take stock and maybe pass judgement on your actions. Perhaps I broke a few hearts. I messed up some lives I'm sure. Did I play my cards right, even if sometimes I had a duff hand, or am I just a fucked up kid who's now just old…who knows, it's too late now but that's life isn't it?!

Thank you to......

my friends who have had to listen to my constant talk about this memoir

Chrissie Carriere, my best friend, for her funny fabulous sketches

Vince for his patience with my scribbles and odd instructions.

and to my dog, Harriet, for standing by me and trusting me!

WAITING FOR PERMISSION...

Page 66   Cliveden - *permission granted by Alamy*
Page 67   John Profumo - *permission granted by Alamy*
Page 68   Stephen Ward - *permission granted by Alamy*
Page 84   Wendy in Jennifer's Diary
Page 89   Avedon
Page 95   Vogue cover
Page 149   Dolphin Square - *permission granted by Alamy*
Page 165   Julie Christie
Page 166   Fanny Craddock - *permission granted by Topfoto*
Page 172   Sketch of Coco Chanel
Page 175   YSL logo
Page 200   Cosmo - Pepsi Cola
Page 202   Joan Collins
Page 205   Sketches by Veronica Papworth
Page 207   Sketch by Veronica Papworth
Page 219   Wendy by John French - *permission granted by V & A*
Page 222   Record cover by Simon and Garfunkel
Page 227   Vogue - Helmut Newton
                 Queen – my Cire collection
Page 228/229   EVA - 19 magazine - Petticoat - The Guardian - Queen - Courtelle
Page 230   Queen - Cecil Beaton
Page 269   Sunday Times Magazine - Mafia murder
Page 288   Tom Cruise at Ascot - *permission granted by Alamy*

Layout by Vince Danks, who can be contacted at: info@vincentdanks.com

contact details:

shoestring book company
info@shoestringbooks.co.uk
www.wendybakerinteriors.co.uk
mob. 07778 769904

Wendy's other books
for Shoestring Books

The Curtain Sketchbook 3

ISBN: 978-09549758-4-5
Price: £17.95 paperback | €25.99 | US $29.95
Pages: 168
Author: Wendy Baker

Order from Shoestring Book Co.
info@shoestringbooks.co.uk

STOCK

Fashion Designers' Notebooks

ISBN: 978-0-9549758-9-0
Price: To be confirmed
Pages: 168
Author: Wendy Darling

Coming September 2020

NEXT TITLE

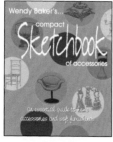

Compact Sketchbook of Accessories

ISBN: 978-095329399--5
Price: £12.99 paperback | €18.95 | US $18.95
Pages: 168
Author: Wendy Baker

Order from Shoestring Book Co.
info@shoestringbooks.co.uk

STOCK

Compact Sketchbook of Blinds

ISBN: 978-09532939-8-8
Price: £14.99 paperback | €21.95 | US $26.95
Pages: 288
Author: Wendy Baker

Order from Shoestring Book Co.
info@shoestringbooks.co.uk

STOCK